The Curriculum Beyond School

std an - pp 101-2

stage pp 103 ff

heterogeneity pp 111-2

markets & modules p 126

modules (ft) p 114

Studies in Teaching and Learning
General Editor
Denis Lawton, B.A., Ph.D.
Professor of Education and Director
University of London Institute of Education

In the series:

The Curriculum
Beyond School

Geoffrey Squires

HODDER AND STOUGHTON
LONDON   SYDNEY   AUCKLAND   TORONTO

For M.P.F.C.

ISBN 0 340 39701 2

First published 1987

Copyright © 1987 Geoffrey Squires

Typeset by Graphicraft Ltd, Hong Kong
Printed and bound in Great Britain for
Hodder and Stoughton Educational,
a divison of Hodder and Stoughton Ltd,
Mill Road, Dunton Green, Sevenoaks, Kent by
Page Bros (Norwich) Ltd, Norwich

Contents

Studies in Teaching and Learning

The purpose of this series of short books on education is to make available readable, up-to-date views on educational issues and controversies. Its aim will be to provide teachers and students (and perhaps parents and governors) with a series of books which will introduce those educational topics which any intelligent and professional educationist ought to be familiar with. One of the criticisms levelled against 'teacher-education' is that there is so little agreement about what ground should be covered in courses at various levels; one assumption behind this series of texts is that there is a common core of knowledge and skills that all teachers need to be aware of, and the series is designed to map out this territory.

Although the major intention of the series is to provide general coverage, each volume will consist of more than a review of the relevant literature; the individual authors will be encouraged to give their own personal interpretation of the field and the way it is developing.

Abbreviations

ACACE	Advisory Council for Adult and Continuing Education
ALBSU	Adult Literacy and Basic Skills Unit
BTEC	Business/Technician Education Council
CATE	Council for the Accreditation of Teacher Education
CEE	Certificate of Extended Education
CGLI	City and Guilds of London Institute
CNAA	Council for National Academic Awards
CPVE	Certificate of Pre-Vocational Education
CRAC	Careers Research and Advisory Centre
DES	Department of Education and Science
FESC	Further Education Staff College
FEU	Further Education Unit
HNC/D	Higher National Certificate/Diploma
IMS	Institute of Manpower Studies
IT	Information Technology
LEA	Local Education Authority
MSC	Manpower Services Commission
NAB	National Advisory Body
NAFE	Non-Advanced Further Education
NEDO	National Economic Development Office
NIA (C) E	National Institute for Adult (Continuing) Education
NIESR	National Institute for Economic and Social Research
OECD	Organisation for Economic Co-operation and Development
ONC/D	Ordinary National Certificate/Diploma
OU	Open University
PEVE	Post Experience Vocational Education
RSA	Royal Society of Arts
SED	Scottish Education Department
SRHE	Society for Research into Higher Education
SSRC	Social Science Research Council

TVEI	Technical and Vocational Education Initiative
UCACE	Universities Council for Adult and Continuing Education
UGC	University Grants Committee
UNESCO	United Nations Educational, Scientific, and Cultural Organisation
WEA	Workers' Educational Association
YTS	Youth Training Scheme

Introduction

This book represents an attempt to look at post-school education as a whole, in terms of the curriculum, of what is taught. There are good reasons for not undertaking such a task. Chief among them is the enormous range and diversity of provision. Compared with the schools there are, in post-school education, more kinds of institution, more ways of attending them, more subjects to be studied, more ways of studying them, and more types of assessment leading to a veritable multitude of qualifications. The organisational and financial structures which support all this are correspondingly complex and diverse. It is little wonder that when post-school education is referred to as a system, the word is often used in inverted commas. Moreover, no one person can expect to have direct experience of all the parts of that system. My own work has been in adult and higher education, so what I know about the 16–19 field is at second hand; and I owe a particular debt of gratitude to colleagues and students in that sector for what I hope I have learned from them.

There are, however, good reasons also for undertaking this task, particularly at the moment. A great deal of change is going on in all areas of post-school education and training, and indeed some of these changes challenge the familiar demarcations between sectors – further, higher, adult – which we use. The sectors themselves also seem less coherent or unified than they used to be: witness the distinction that is now made between 'traditional FE' and the 'new FE', or between 'adult education' and 'continuing education'. It is difficult to think of post-school education as a whole, but it is becoming increasingly difficult to think of it simply as a collection of parts: and that dilemma provides both the rationale for, and problem of, this book. My main aim has been to work out some kind of framework for thinking about what is taught (sometimes self-taught) after the end of schooling, and I hope that even where readers may disagree with the particular conclusions that I sometimes draw about curriculum policy, they may still find the analytic framework useful.

The book divides into two halves. The first three chapters are primarily conceptual. Chapter 1 explores what we mean by curriculum, and the ways in which the concept has evolved in the field of curriculum studies, going beyond the traditional notion of the syllabus in several ways.

In Chapters 2 and 3, it is argued that whereas the curriculum in school is typically general in aim and scope, in post-school education it is typically specific: post-school courses usually have a particular emphasis or purpose. Like most very broad distinctions, this one is not entirely accurate, but it opens up a way of classifying and analysing the apparently chaotic abundance of what goes on in further, higher and adult education, and indeed beyond them, in less formal settings. The main dimensions of general education, it is suggested, constitute in a much looser way the main orientations of post-school education, and provide a means of mapping it, so that we can locate familiar labels such as 'professional', 'vocational', 'liberal' and 'recreational' within the total picture.

The second half of the book is devoted to the three main sectors of post-school education: 16–19 (here called the 'consecutive phase'), higher education, and adult education. The analysis of the curriculum in each case refers back to the framework established in the early chapters, but it also develops certain themes which seem particularly relevant to the sector concerned. Thus in 16–19 education, the concept of 'transition' is important; in higher education the concept of 'discipline'; and in adult education the notion of 'non-formal education'. But it is a measure of the increasing interrelatedness of the various sectors that many of these themes illuminate the whole of post-school education, criss-crossing the institutional and curricular boundaries in a way that suggests deeper affinities and concerns. At the end of each chapter, some implications of the analysis are explored, and there is a brief concluding chapter which raises some more general points.

I have said already that the book is intended primarily to do an analytic and conceptual job, but the fact that it is also in some parts a critique of policy – the two cannot be totally separated – perhaps reflects the fact that it grew out of a number of studies I have made for the OECD and other policy-oriented bodies over the last ten years. This fact also explains the occasional references to other countries, although I would in no way claim that it is a comparative work. In the hope that I would find readers among those who teach and study in post-school education and training, as distinct from specialists in curriculum studies or educational policy, I have tried to write as non-technically as possible about concepts and problems which, like all those in education, uneasily bestride common sense and special expertise. I have therefore consigned much of the specialist detail to the notes at the end of each chapter. The sheer scope of the study means that some topics have a few paragraphs devoted to them when they should have (as they sometimes do elsewhere) a sizeable literature; but I hope that these disadvantages can be traded off against the advantages of taking, for once, the wider view.

My debts, both academic and practical, to friends, colleagues, and students are numerous, and I hope those people will understand if I simply acknowledge my gratitude to them in a general but sincere way. Besides, one is not always aware of what one has learned, and from whom.

Acknowledgments

The author and publishers would like to thank Academic Press, Florida for permission to reproduce the diagram on p. 179 from P. B. Baltes *et al.*, 1980 'Life-span Developmental Psychology', *Annual Review of Psychology* and Routledge and Kegan Paul for permission to use the extract on p. 41 from D. Hargreaves, 1982, *The Challenge for the Comprehensive School* and the extract on pp. 187–8 from R. Paterson, 1979, *Values, Education and the Adult.*

1 The Nature of the Curriculum

What is taught?

What is taught? What ought to be taught? Taylor and Richards, in their *Introduction to Curriculum Studies* (1985) identify these two questions as the fundamental concerns of curriculum studies. The curriculum, they say,

> is at the heart of the educational enterprise. It is the means through which education is transacted. Without a curriculum education has no vehicle, nothing through which to transmit its messages, to convey its meanings, to exemplify its values. It is because of the crucial role which the curriculum plays in educational activities that it is worthy of study. (page 2)

A recent American report referred to the curriculum rather more bluntly as 'the stuff of education'.

Interest in the curriculum is as old as formal education itself. The 'great educators' from Plato to Dewey have been concerned with what is taught and what should be taught. However, the use of the term 'curriculum' to refer to these questions is rather more recent. Hamilton (1981) gives the earliest known educational use of the word (it originally meant a course in the sense of 'race-course' in Latin) as occurred at the Universities of Glasgow and Leyden in the late sixteenth century. But Marsden (1979) dates the emergence of curriculum as a field of educational studies from the last decades of the nineteenth century in the United States.[1] The growing interest in the purpose and content of school curricula in that period resulted in a number of important publications in the years following World War I.

Much of the writing on the curriculum in the inter-war years in the United States was, however, administrative and managerial in emphasis. Pinar and Grumet (1981) argue that curriculum was primarily an administrative category in those decades, rather than an intellectual or academic one. It was something for which some-body (usually a 'superintendent') had a designated responsibility in American school systems, a fact later reflected in the name of the relevant professional body, the Association for Supervision and Curriculum Development.[2] Some revaluation of the work that went on in those years is now taking place, but it was in the decades following World War II that the analytic and systematic study of the curriculum really took off. A number of seminal American works by Tyler (1949), Herrick and Tyler (1950), Smith *et al.* (1950), Bruner (1960), Taba (1962), and Broudy *et al.* (1964) laid the foundations for a subsequent upsurge of interest first in the United States, and slightly later in this country. British work in the field emerged much more strongly in the 1960s and 1970s. The UK *Journal of Curriculum Studies* was established in 1968, and by 1984 Richards could point to a greatly increased British contribution to the second edition of his annotated bibliography of the field (Richards, 1984).

There are two main reasons why the study of the curriculum developed so rapidly in the last 30 years, one financial and one academic. A great deal of money was invested in changing school curricula in both the United States and the United Kingdom during this period. Major curriculum projects sought to reform or even transform the study of mathematics, the natural sciences, and, eventually, a wide range of subjects and fields, particularly at the secondary school level. In the United States, these projects were on a regional or even national scale, and drew in academic specialists in a number of fields who might not otherwise have become directly involved in the school curriculum. In the United Kingdom, the Nuffield Foundation and then the Schools Council played the leading roles in school curriculum development. The approach to development and innovation differed from that in the United States, with less reliance on 'experts', but again these projects drew in a wide range of people who might not otherwise have concerned themselves with curricular matters. Now, at the time of writing, this kind of funding for school curriculum development is much scarcer in both countries.

A second reason for the development of the curriculum as a field of study was the growing impact on it of a range of academic disciplines. In the past, questions about what was or should be taught seemed to be largely the preserve of philosophers. The managerial and administrative emphasis in the inter-war years has already been mentioned. Increasingly, however, psychologists, sociologists, historians, and economists have brought their frames of reference to bear. Many different types of question are now asked about curricula from many different perspectives.

It is clear that the curriculum has become a much more complex and extensive field of study than it used to be, but it is not clear how far it has developed into a coherent 'discipline' based on unifying theory. Indeed, Schwab (1969) declared that the theoretical endeavour was fruitless, and called for a rigorous analysis of practice as a basis for future development. The debate about the nature of curriculum theory, the nature of practice, the relationship between them, and the role of foundation or constituent disciplines, has been going on ever since.[3] Perhaps for this reason, it is not easy or even useful to attempt to define the term 'curriculum' tightly, since the definitions that are given tend to reflect the particular perspectives and emphases of those who construct them: they encapsulate a particular approach. In the vernacular of the common room the word 'curriculum' is used, if at all, to refer to courses of study, or sets of courses (in the United States, programmes). But in the literature on the curriculum, the term keeps shifting, evolving. It connotes as well as denotes, and perhaps the best way to tease out some of its meanings and connotations is to contrast it with the more traditional and, in some quarters, familiar concept of the syllabus.

The typical syllabus consists of an unadorned list of headings. Some of these will have subheadings, and there may be an implicit order in the list. These headings and subheadings are to be 'covered'. There may be some indication of how long should be spent on each (such as Weeks 1–5 ...) and some reference to how they will be examined. Some headings will refer to topics or subjects; others may simply refer to a text (*Hamlet* or *Pride and Prejudice*). There may be some indications about options and alternatives, or about special requirements for practical or field work.

It is easy to caricature this kind of document, which often looks as if it has been worked out on the back of an envelope, and no doubt sometimes is. It is important to remember that teachers and lecturers do not simply read a syllabus; they interpret it, drawing on complex knowledge about the context they are working in, and sometimes showing considerable subtlety in attending to oblique signals and cues about their environment. Nevertheless, the modern concept of the curriculum goes beyond that of the syllabus in a number of ways.

First, the curriculum is concerned with aims or outcomes, as well as content. This is not the bland statement that it might seem, however, for reasons to do with the way curriculum studies has developed historically. It is possible, and indeed quite common, for education to go on without any explicit statements about aims. Education is an activity: it is something that teachers and students do, and can become involved and immersed in. It is not surprising that sometimes this activity seems self-justifying or self-evident, and that even when the participants have some sense of progress or development, that this does automatically issue in clear, or explicit goals. Hence it has been quite possible for formal education to take place for hundreds of years without explicit goal-statements, as is the case with the traditional syllabus.

The challenge to this apparent aimlessness has come from three quarters. First, the advent of rational planning models, particularly in the management field (such as management by objectives), has at various times in this century influenced curriculum planning – for example, in the influence of Taylor's 'scientific management' on Bobbitt in the 1920s (Patty, 1938), in the 1950s with the growth of systems analysis, and in the 1980s in the name of public accountability. Second, behavioural psychologists have insisted strongly that learning outcomes should be observable, and must be stated in terms of changes in behaviour, rather than 'internal' notions such as understanding, knowledge, or appreciation. This insistence was at its strongest in the 1950s and 1960s, and became embodied in the concept of programmed learning and the idea that teaching could itself be a technology, as distinct from making use of technology. Third, much of the early work on curriculum development in fact derived from work on assessment and evaluation, and was hence very much concerned with measuring what had been learned. That question quickly refers one back to the question of what should have been learned, and thus to the matter of aims and objectives.[4]

A lively and sometimes acrimonious debate has gone on in curriculum circles for many years now as to the desirability or otherwise of spelling out aims in general or specific form, or indeed any form (see MacDonald-Ross, 1975). The 'objectives movement' never had as much impact in the United Kingdom as it did in the United States, probably because behaviourism never dominated educational psychology here to the same extent. Powerful counter-attacks were mounted in the United States by Eisner (1967) and in this country by Stenhouse (1975). And perhaps the English distaste for philosophising about aims also attenuated the influence of the objectives movement to some extent, at least in the school sector. It is worth noting, however, the influence of this aspect of curriculum theory on developments in further education in the 1970s and 1980s, particularly under the auspices of the Business and Technician Education Councils (now B/TEC), and even to some degree in higher education in the validation procedures of the Council for National Academic Awards (CNAA).

The pendulum seems to have swung back to some extent against the idea of specifying objectives. The difficulties of doing so in the more open-ended humanities subjects, the problems of achieving consensus, the dangers of pre-specified rigidity, the fragmentation of understanding that can follow from long lists of specific objectives have become more apparent with time. However, like many movements or fashions in education, the objectives movement has meant that things will never quite be the same again, that a certain residue has been left in curriculum theory. At a minimum, questions about what one is trying to achieve can prod teachers and lecturers into thinking their courses through more than they might otherwise do. Where more than one lecturer is involved in teaching a course, such questions also help to draw out aspects of the collaboration between them into open discussion. Explicit statements about aims and outcomes can also make it easier for students to know what is expected of them, and reduce their dependence on oblique cues and signals. And where such outcomes can be stated in a precise and unambiguous way – as, for example, in some training contexts – it seems only rational to do so.

The issues related to aims and objectives, however, remain complex and cannot be discussed in any detail here. Education is generally regarded as being a purposive activity, but it does not automatically follow from this that its purposes can always be stated clearly or unambiguously, or that its ends can be sharply distinguished from its means – the *sine qua non* of rational planning. Questions about the longer-term and indirect (that is, transfer) aims of education are particularly difficult both to formulate and investigate. Some emphasis on the spelling out of aims, however, represents a step forward in curriculum planning in that it directs lecturers' and students' attention not only to what the curriculum is, but what it does.

The second way in which the concept of a curriculum goes beyond that of the traditional syllabus depends on a distinction between content and process. The syllabus is a list of content to be covered, but it does not usually say what is meant by 'covered'. If a geography syllabus includes the heading 'The Humber Estuary', does it mean that the student has to learn the names of the rivers that flow into it and the towns that lie around it, or to analyse why the rivers flow where they do and the towns grew up where they are, or to conceptualise what is meant by estuarial development, or to be able to construct models of tidal flow? Teachers have always known that students may process content in various ways, from the simple learning of facts, through the more complex handling of concepts and relationships, to the sophisticated analysis, modelling, and solving of problems. However, it was largely the work of Bloom *et al.* (1956), Krathwohl *et al.* (1964), and Gagne (1969) which spelled out this dimension of the curriculum in taxonomies of processes which went from simple to complex. In the case of Gagne, it was a reaction against the notion that all learning was essentially the same, and an attempt to distinguish between different types of learning in a way that would to some extent reconcile conflicting schools of learning theory. With Bloom and his colleagues, the point of departure was the need to assess educational achievements more precisely, and the result was a taxonomy of educational objectives. Despite these differences in intention and nomenclature, the general result in both cases was to provide a framework which allowed a much more systematic unpacking of terms like 'coverage', 'understanding', and 'learning' than had been possible before.

Both writers have attracted considerable criticism since their works first appeared.[5] Some of this has been directed at the taxonomies themselves, and some at the crude use to which they have sometimes been put. Bloom has been criticised for attempting to divide cognitive learning (to do with knowledge and understanding) and affective learning (to do with attitudes and values) into two distinct domains. It has also been argued that some of the terms he uses are not content-free, in that their meaning varies from subject to subject: in other words, process cannot be completely divorced from content. There are also criticisms of the order of ascent in Bloom's taxonomy, particularly in the middle levels of the cognitive domain, where he employs concepts such as interpretation, application, and analysis. Gagne has subsequently modified his scheme, particularly at the top end, suggesting some uncertainty about the classification of higher or more complex forms of learning. And it has proved very difficult to devise any corresponding taxonomy for psychomotor skills.[6]

Nevertheless, the process–content distinction has become firmly embedded in curricular thinking. The general effect has been to make lecturers much more aware of what students do with content, or, to put it another way, of the incompleteness, even impossibility, of talking simply in content terms. It was not that the traditional syllabus ignored the process dimension; it was left implicit and had to be inferred from the context of the course. People knew (or it was assumed they knew) that 'The Humber Estuary' meant one thing in the primary school and another in the university. However, the content–process distinction has helped to clarify the familiar but complex notions of 'level' and 'difficulty'. Everyone knows that O and A levels are different and that the second are in some way more difficult than the first; and that undergraduate work is at another level again. To some extent, level and difficulty are a matter of knowing more: there are more texts to read, more experiments to be done, more skills to be mastered. But level and difficulty are also and more crucially a matter of process; of how one engages with content. Examiners who criticise an answer for being 'merely descriptive, lacking penetration' are saying something about process, and it is this kind of shift which helps to explain why some students can do well at a particular level yet fail at a higher one. The concept of process complicates the notion of progression from one level to another, which has been an important theme in recent thinking in vocational education, because it implies that one moves sideways, as well as up.

There are two general problems with the content–process distinction. The first and more tractable one is that the emphasis on the process dimension has led in some cases to the unquestioned assumption that more complex processes are always better. This has led to a shift of emphasis in some school curricula, away from facts towards concepts and problem-solving. Although, in terms of process, the latter two are 'higher', it does not always mean they are more appropriate. That decision depends on an analysis both of the internal structure of the subject or field, and of the aims of the course. The relationship between 'facts' and 'strategies' may differ from one subject to another; the language of process tends to assume that all kinds of content have the same gradient from 'lower' to 'higher' processes.[7] Moreover, a lot depends on what the student is going to do with her studies. Some of the reforms of secondary school curricula seem to have been oriented much more towards progression to higher education with its emphasis on conceptualisation and analysis than to non-advanced further education, where the capacity to perform the simpler operations may be important.

The other, more difficult problem arises from the very nature of the distinction. Bloom attempted to provide a standard language for talking about process; this implies that all subjects, all kinds of content, all disciplines and fields, are somehow the same. Yet one of the interesting features of subjects is that they have to some extent their own subcultures, and their own languages. The way that historians talk about their discipline is not quite the same as the way physicists or economists or mathematicians talk about theirs.

Even if the same words are used (such as 'theory' or 'analysis' or 'application') they do not necessarily mean quite the same thing in each case. Yet the fact that people in different subjects and fields do communicate and co-operate in the common enterprise of education suggests that all forms of organised knowledge have some things in common. The problem is to find a language of process which allows people in different fields to discuss levels and processes, while doing justice to the special characteristics of their own subject-matter.

The third main way in which the concept of the curriculum goes beyond that of the traditional syllabus is that it is concerned not merely with the course on paper, but the course in action. The syllabus is, as it were, the script for the play; and in the past it was often assumed that putting the play on was a straightforward matter. The concept of the curriculum, by contrast, recognises that the syllabus is always embodied and embedded in particular actors and particular settings. This implies, to begin with, that the way things are taught and learned – the *how* of education – permeates *what* is taught and learned. Method is also a kind of content; and indeed adults often seem to remember how they were taught at school when they have forgotten what. The emphasis on the curriculum-in-action also points to the impact that assessment can have on the curriculum; far from being something tacked on at the end (as it may be in the minds of teachers), it may condition students' perceptions and priorities right through the course. But the curriculum-in-action also points towards the institutional and social frame of the syllabus: the rooms, the relationships, the timetables, the regulations, the ethos or milieu of the course. The institution is also a kind of content; and the norms and patterns that are associated with it can come to constitute a 'hidden curriculum'. When Snyder's (1971) book of that title first appeared, the phrase referred mainly to cues that students learned (or did not learn) to pick up about what to do and what not to do on their course, in order to cope, survive, succeed, or play the system. Since then, the 'hidden curriculum' has come to mean many other things as well, and Meighan (1981), ten years later, devotes a whole section of his book to it. There are implications that the 'real' curriculum of education is not simply hidden but disguised, with the formal or official curriculum merely a pretext or vehicle for more important intentions and functions. Some sociologists of education have explored the ways in which the hidden curriculum of educational institutions may mirror, and socialise students into, the pattern of social and economic relationships that exists in the wider society. The 'hidden' or 'informal' curriculum also points to the importance of role models and social learning in education. The teacher also is a kind of content.

There are three problems with the concept of the hidden curriculum. The first is that, like many fruitful concepts, it has become rather overloaded with its own fruit (Cornbleth, 1984), and it has become difficult to know now what it excludes. Secondly, it is often assumed that the hidden curriculum is in fact effective (Raffe, 1983). There are prima facie reasons for believing that it may affect students: it is covert (thus bypassing conscious defences), repetitive in its daily and weekly patterns, and often attended by powerful institutional sanctions in the form of rewards and penalties, and social pressures from either authority figures or peer groups. However, a good deal of educational research has demonstrated the relative ineffectiveness of the formal curriculum in teaching what it aims to teach, so it would be unwise to assume that the hidden curriculum 'works' any better. Tactical adjustments on the part of students do not necessarily mean that there is a longer-term effect on them; they may simply be adapting while they have to. There are indeed some signs that the initial rather sweeping assertions about the reproductive nature of teaching (Bourdieu and Passeron, 1977) and the hegemony of the curriculum (Apple, 1979, 1981) are now being qualified in the light of newer empirical work which investigates how the hidden curriculum actually operates (Hammersley and Hargreaves, 1983).

The third problem with the notion of the hidden curriculum is that it underestimates the significance of the formal curriculum. After all, in order for there to be a hidden curriculum at all, there has to be a formal curriculum in the first place; and it is unlikely that the two exist in entirely separate worlds. A bridge between them is provided by the concept of disciplinary cultures (Becher, 1981). Disciplines and subjects carry messages which are not exactly the official 'content' of the discipline, but are nevertheless part of it. In this respect, subjects or disciplines can be thought of as subcultures or micro-cultures within the larger cultures of education or training, and, like all subcultures, they attempt to socialise the student into certain attitudes and values, certain ways of thinking and looking at the world.

Despite these objections and reservations, the emphasis on the curriculum-in-action and the concepts that it has spawned is a distinct advance on the traditional syllabus-on-paper. It is no longer possible in curriculum thinking to treat the syllabus as a transparent, disembodied, decontextualised entity which in some mysterious way gets transmitted from teacher to student: a perfect meeting of minds in a perfect vacuum. In this respect, as in the two previous cases of the content – process distinction and the analysis of aims and outcomes, the way of thinking about what is taught seems to have been changed irreversibly.

In recent decades, the old narrow conception of the curriculum as content or subject-matter has thus become broadened to include questions about purposes and effects, about processes and levels, and about the grounding of what is taught in particular educational circumstances. The problem now is to know where to stop, because if the curriculum is thought of as the totality of the student's learning experience (a common contemporary view), it becomes difficult to draw boundaries around it at all. Such a view logically embraces not only the learning experiences organised by the institution, but any external factors which have a bearing on them as well. The tendency to speak of teaching and learning rather than teaching suggests that the emphasis has also shifted from the intentional element in teaching, to the experiential element in learning.[8] Concepts which are too broad are as useless as ones which are too narrow, and terms like 'totality' and 'experience' are much more difficult to employ than they appear to be. It will be assumed here that the notion of the curriculum is centred on, though not confined to, the intentional and planned activity of teaching, and thus with the two questions cited at the beginning of this chapter. There are other possible perspectives, but they are not the ones of this book.

What ought to be taught?

Nothing that has been said so far points to any particular kind of curriculum. An analysis of aims, of content-process relationships, and of the curriculum-in-action could lead equally to a highly subject-centred curriculum or to a student-centred one, a tightly pre-specified curriculum or a loose, open-ended one. Indeed, such an analysis could even lead to what one might call a non-curriculum or anti-curriculum, in which most of the 'normal features' of formal courses were either absent or inverted. The answers to the question: What ought to be taught? come from outside the curriculum itself.

It is not easy however to say where they come from. Organised knowledge in the form of academic disciplines or subjects may provide a frame of reference for thinking about what should be taught. For example, the concept of culture (in the descriptive, social anthropological sense, rather than the normative literary one) has been an important point of reference in thinking about the secondary school curriculum, from the work of Smith (1950) and the 'Illinois school' in the United States to the approaches of Reynolds and Skilbeck (1976) and Lawton (1983a and b) in this country. The frame of reference there is fairly clearly that of sociology and social anthropology. By contrast, epistemology – the analysis of the nature and forms of knowledge – has provided a quite different frame of reference for some philosophers of education, such as Phenix (1964) and Hirst (1974). Psychological notions of human development provide a framework for Rogers (1969) and Maslow (1973). In a loose sense, then, one can say that organised disciplines often provide the 'source' of aims for the curriculum.

However, the problem is that the same frame of reference can lead different theorists to quite different views on the curriculum. The analysis of culture, for example, which in Lawton and Skilbeck and the Illinois school leads to an essentially common and fairly egalitarian curriculum, leads Bantock (1980) to propose different curricula for different social classes. The notion of liberal education, involving certain key forms of knowledge, can be viewed as something appropriate to an elite or, since it is intrinsically good, good for everybody. Analysis of the nature and forms of knowledge can lead to disciplinary or interdisciplinary conclusions.

One way of explaining the different conclusions drawn from similar frames of reference is to introduce the concept of educational ideologies. Scrimshaw (1983), for example, defines an educational ideology as a 'system of beliefs that gives general direction to the educational policies and activities of those who hold these beliefs' (page 6). These are beliefs about human nature, society, knowledge, and education, and they may be consciously or unconsciously held. Scrimshaw uses this approach to distinguish between five main contemporary ideologies:

progressivism, which stresses the needs, aspirations, and development of either individuals or communities;

instrumentalism, stressing utility and relevance to the existing social and economic order, which may itself be static or changing;

reconstructionism, which emphasises the role of education in bringing about social change;

classical humanism, which stresses the inheritance of knowledge and culture, especially for an elite;

liberal humanism, which aspires to give access to the best in the cultural inheritance to everyone.

One might add to this list radical or revolutionary ideologies which see education as a means of transforming society. Although this list is formulated mainly in relation to the schools, it will no doubt strike chords with many in post-school education. The 'progressive' student-centred mood of higher education in the 1960s has now largely given way to various forms of instrumentalism. In vocational education, instrumentalism is itself challenged by the unpredictability of the labour market. And in adult education, progressivism, reconstructionism, and liberal humanism have coexisted, often uneasily, for many years.

Although Scrimshaw's analysis helps one to classify curriculum policies, it does not entirely solve the problem of how to analyse what ought to be taught. The various ideologies cannot be taken in isolation from one another; they need to be compared and contrasted, and that is not possible unless there is a common frame of reference for analysing them all. To say that they simply involve beliefs precludes any rational analysis of them. But any analysis of them soon refers one back to the frames of reference of organised knowledge; is one talking in sociological or historical or philosophical or psychological terms? And if so, why should any one of these frames of reference have priority over the others? The very use of the concept 'ideology' gives an implicit priority to a particular intellectual tradition.

It is perhaps easy to see now why the issue of what ought to be taught is often referred to as 'curriculum theory' and why that is both an appropriate and problematic label. These normative questions quickly lead one to abstract and fundamental questions, so in that sense they are 'theoretical'; but no one theory of curriculum purposes or justifications exists which commands widespread assent, so there is no unifying or underlying theory in that sense. There are also two important differences between compulsory and post-compulsory education in this regard. Since compulsory education is compulsory the question of what ought to be taught takes on a particular urgency; but since most post-compulsory education is, at least in formal terms, voluntary, adults have some freedom to accept or reject the values and assumptions embodied in what is provided. Secondly, the 'ought' questions become even more crucial in so far as one thinks there should be a core curriculum for all children; the core curriculum becomes a cockpit for competing ideologies. Because post-school education is to some extent subdivided into specific forms and types, curricular pluralism can allow people to duck some of these issues. One can provide both instrumental and progressive forms of education in different sectors, different institutions or courses, and the conflicts and challenges are thereby avoided. This is only partly the case: 'ought' questions loom large within major sectors and types of curriculum (for example, within the undergraduate curriculum, and within non-advanced further education and training). And, as will be pointed out in Chapter 6, even 'voting with one's feet' does not really solve the problem. But enough has been said to suggest why the question of what ought to be taught has generated more and sharper debate in the school sector than it seems to have done, so far, in post-school education.

There is another aspect of 'ought' questions, however, which is often taken for granted in both compulsory and post-compulsory education. This is the belief that the effects of the curriculum are not confined to the course or institution, but go well beyond it, to the student's life and work. Indeed, all the ideologies listed above share the unstated assumption that the effects of education reach beyond education itself, and impinge on individual lives, the community, the social and economic order, the culture, and so on. That assumption is so obvious and familiar that it may seem at first sight rather odd to question it; but that assumption in turn involves other assumptions about the extent to which learning which occurs in one context (the classroom, the course, the college) affects or is transferred to other contexts, and something must be said here about this fundamental issue in the psychology of learning.   *transfer*

There are both conceptual and methodological problems in the research on transfer of learning. Transfer takes place when something which is learned in one situation affects (usually facilitates, though it may inhibit) performance in a dissimilar situation. But how dissimilar? Even the most standardised tasks and situations are rarely exactly the same from one instance to the next. In that minimal sense, nearly all performance involves transfer of learning. However, the term 'transfer' is usually reserved for situations which are substantially dissimilar, though what counts as 'substantial' in this case is open to debate. Driving the same car down two different streets would not usually be considered to involve significant transfer; driving two different cars down the same street probably would. Likewise, typing different letters on the same typewriter would not usually count, whereas typing the same letters on two different machines would. Why? The criteria are to some extent arbitrary, but we tend not to invoke the concept of transfer where operations are easily routinisable, which they are when one goes on using the same car or same typewriter.

The methodological problems in research on transfer of learning are considerable, since one has not only to evaluate the person's performance in the transfer situation, but also to assess the contribution that learning in the initial situation has made to it. If a person picks up a new language quickly, how do we assess the relative contribution (supposing there is any) of (1) having learned another language already, (2) having a 'good ear', or (3) being socially skilled and confident? These connections may look tenuous enough; even more indirect are the assumptions of some teachers that their course makes students think logically, or be precise, or respond flexibly when faced with new problems and phenomena.

The research on general transfer of learning has gone through several historical phases. The late nineteenth-century faculty psychology (which believed that Latin made one think logically, and so on) gave way to behaviourist scepticism in the early twentieth century, with the research of Thorndike, who believed that 'the intellectual value of studies should be determined largely by the special information, habits, interests, attitudes and ideals which they demonstrably produce' (Thorndike, 1924). More recently, with the resurgence of cognitive/information-processing models, transfer seems to be back in favour; indeed, it has become so intrinsic to information-processing models that it is seen as an essential element in all cognition (Simon, 1979a and b). Ironically, the greater stress now laid on transfer in vocational training (see Hayes, 1983) comes when it has almost disappeared from the psychological literature in the form in which it was originally conceptualised. Differences in expectations about transfer reflect different models of mind. Behavioural psychology emphasises the mind's capacity to recognise, discriminate, and generalise. The degree of similarity/dissimilarity between two phenomena or situations is therefore crucial, and transfer is thus largely a function of the extent to which similarities of content or process exist; in other words, transfer depends largely on the situation, not the person. Cognitive psychology sees the mind as a developer of strategies, schemas, structures, and programmes. These are continually tested out on the world, and modified. What is crucial for transfer is the extent to which the mind has a strategy to develop strategies – in other words, to seek deliberately instances where something learned in situation X can be used in situation Y. Thus transfer of learning is largely a function of the person rather than the situation; not only the person's cognitive processes, but also what might be called the cognitive disposition.

This is to polarise and oversimplify the two positions, but the implications for the curriculum differ markedly. Cognitive psychology tends to support indirect 'training the mind' arguments; behavioural psychology points towards a direct, 'relevant' curriculum. What both schools of thought tend to ignore is the affective *affective* aspect of transfer. Transfer involves risk-taking, going out on a *aspect* limb, since by definition one has recourse to something which is not normally or conventionally associated with the situation. This aspect of transfer becomes clearer if one considers creativity as an extreme form of transfer, in which the connection between situation X and situation Y needs an imaginative leap. If we wish to encourage transfer of learning, then perhaps we need, in addition to the usual ploys (practice in varying situations, conceptualisation of transfer, solid initial learning, and so on) to make sure that there is a curricular environment in which risk-taking is encouraged, rather than being suppressed by sarcasm, haste, or rigid convergence.

Current information-processing models of learning and cognition thus seem more optimistic about the possibilities of transfer than was the case with the older behavioural ones. In practice, teachers and lecturers in the United Kingdom seem to have been largely oblivious of the theoretical debate, and there has always been a widespread assumption that education should develop the 'general powers of the mind' (to quote Robbins) and students could be 'taught to think'. Indeed, the prevalence of such assumptions has made the relationship between education and employment rather more flexible than it would have been otherwise (and is in some countries) and counteracts some of the rigidities caused by early specialisation. But there is still room for scepticism about the transfer effects of the curriculum, particularly in post-school education, where those effects may be 'mediated' through a number of other factors. For many post-school students, education is only one among a number of things they are involved in: work, family life, personal relationships, leisure interests, social activities. Even if they are full-time students (which is the exception rather than the rule), their perception of the curriculum is mediated through an already complex and often sophisticated frame of reference; mature students, in particular, can be highly selective in what they take from a course, filtering it through an established set of priorities, assumptions, habits, and beliefs; indeed, the problems of learning for adults are sometimes outweighed by the problems of unlearning. This means that the notion of 'educational ideologies' has to be firmly placed in a mediating, modifying context; and that discussions about what ought to be taught have to be accompanied by some awareness of the possible discrepancies between intention and effect.

Curriculum change

So far, this chapter has addressed the two basic questions about the curriculum posed by Taylor and Richards: what is taught? and what ought to be taught? There are two other subsidiary but important questions which need to be raised, however briefly. The first is how the curriculum changes or is changed. Several terms are typically used in the literature. Curriculum design is sometimes used to refer to the conscious and systematic planning of a course or set of courses. The use of the word 'design' often signals that either the planning process is a fairly 'mechanistic' one (identification of aims leading to specification of objectives leading to selection of content and methods and so on), or that the course is of a kind where outcomes can be clearly and unambiguously targeted (for example in some kinds of training) or both. In fact, within the field of curriculum planning a long-term struggle has been going on between those who believe in rational, systematic (or 'scientific') approaches to planning and those who favour a 'softer' approach.[9] The latter is often indicated by the use of the term 'development' rather than 'design', suggesting a more incremental or evolutionary process, negotiation between different perspectives rather than the use of planning algorithms, and a degree of flexibility or openness about the end result. Some people reject even the word 'development' as being too directive, and favour a participatory process in which the practitioners (i.e. the teachers and students) play the key roles. The term 'curriculum innovation' usually refers to the process whereby curriculum changes spread, or do not spread, through the relevant part of the system. Here again, there are differences between those who favour centralised, diffusionist approaches, and those who favour decentralised models, such as networks, local initiatives, and 'workshops'. The two sections on curriculum design and curriculum development in Richards' (1984) bibliography provide a good overview of the literature.

This literature is, however, largely based on compulsory education, in the United Kingdom, United States, and, to a lesser extent, other countries such as Canada and Australia, and two points must be made here in relation to post-school education. First, there is relatively little emphasis on what one might call 'curriculum evolution', yet this may be an important aspect of the curriculum in some sectors of post-school education. In higher education, the relatively close links between research and teaching mean that developments in the former can lead to changes in courses which are not thought of as, or labelled, curriculum development, because they are regarded as part of the 'normal' processes of teaching. Indeed, the characteristic vagueness of many curricula in universities in particular may be partly (if sometimes speciously) justified in terms of allowing for the continual, rolling changes emanating from research. In vocational education likewise, changes in the workplace (new technologies, new work practices, new forms of organisation) can trickle across into vocational courses in a way that does not seem dramatic enough to label curriculum development, but cumulatively over a period of time can change a course out of all recognition. In adult education, in so far as courses respond to the market demands of adult students, they may be continually changing, both in terms of content and ethos. In all three cases, one must not overstate the case: higher education courses can be moribund, further education ones hidebound, and adult education courses tutor-bound. Examination and syllabus regulations may also act as a brake, particularly in the vocational and professional sectors. Nevertheless, the proximity of external stimuli to curriculum change in post-school education is perhaps greater in some cases than it is in the schools, so that the balance between curriculum evolution and curriculum development is somewhat different.

The second point has to do with models of innovation, on which a great deal has been written in the school context, partly because of the failure of some planned curriculum projects to influence the system at large. Models of innovation, diffusion, and change depend upon a prior analysis of the locus and nature of control within the system. It is possible to identify different loci or sources of power and influence within the educational system (teachers, students, local government, professional bodies, publishers, and so on) and also to analyse the nature of their influence (whether it takes financial, legislative, administrative, normative, or operational forms, for example). Teachers (and students) usually have a good deal of operational control over what goes on in the classroom; professional bodies can influence curriculum objectives, as they do, for example, in medicine, pharmacy, social work, and law. This kind of analysis is complex and can only be alluded to here; it raises questions about shifts over time in the pattern and nature of controls, and also about the extent to which such patterns are really pluralistic or hegemonic.[10]

The point to be made here is that the locus and nature of controls that pertain to the schools may not be the same as those that operate in post-school education, and furthermore that the pattern may differ from one sector or type of post-school education to another. For example, the relatively centralised control of vocational courses, by bodies such as the Business and Technician Education Council (B/TEC) and the City and Guilds of London Institute (CGLI), or the highly centralised controls operated by the Manpower Services Commission (MSC) are unlike anything in the schools, and unlike one another. There is nothing in the school system which resembles the market-led sectors of adult and continuing education. And the operational control of lecturers and students over their courses and classroom behaviour varies from one part of post-school education to another: lecturers in higher education often have a good deal of freedom to decide what and how they shall teach, whereas in non-advanced further education, they are often more constrained. The implications of this are that while a good deal can be learned from the work on curriculum innovation in the schools, the point of departure for such thinking in post-school education has to be a careful analysis of the sources and types of controls that exist in each sector or even subsector. It will not be easy to generalise about which innovation strategies work best, except in so far as education or teaching can be said to have common characteristics across all sectors and forms of post-school education.

Curriculum evaluation

While curriculum evaluation is usually seen as an integral part of curriculum studies – and indeed has a common parentage in the work of Tyler and Bloom – it is usually given a separate chapter heading in books on the curriculum and has to some extent developed into a distinct sub-specialism in recent years. Curriculum evaluation goes beyond the traditional assessment of the student, to ask how well the teachers and the course did. The students' achievements are of course part of this wider analysis and judgement, but curriculum evaluation raises questions which are less familiar and perhaps less comfortable. Did the course achieve what it set out to do? Was what it set out to do worthwhile anyway? Do people even know what it set out to do? And even if it did 'succeed', might not things have been done more quickly or at less cost? And what did the course do that it did *not* set out to do? What unintended or side effects did it have? And so on.

The main controversies in curriculum evaluation have been about what kinds of questions to ask and how to find out the answers to them. Some models take the course aims for granted and begin from there; others question the questions. Some rely heavily on quantitative data (marks, questionnaire responses, drop-out rates), while others go for the 'softer' techniques of interviewing and participant observation. There is disagreement also over the role and responsibilities of the evaluator: should he describe or judge? Should he provide an external statement or draw the participants into the process of evaluating themselves? Should he report only to those who asked or commissioned him to do the job? Who is accountable, for what and to whom? The texts by Jenkins (1976) and Hamilton (1976), though now nearly ten years old, still provide succinct introductions to the field and its problems.[11]

Some of what was said in the previous section about the differences between curriculum change in the school and post-school sectors applies also to evaluation. The questions one asks and the way one asks them are to some extent contingent upon the kind of sector or institution one is working in; likewise the concept of accountability. The notion of validation, for example, is a familiar one in polytechnics and colleges which have their courses validated by the Council for National Academic Awards (CNAA), but apart from some professional courses, it is alien in the universities. External examiner systems operate in some countries and not others; and some external examiners interpret their role much more widely than others, and feel they can comment on the course as well as on the students' performance. It can even be argued that the need for evaluation is largely a function of the compulsory nature of schooling: where students or sponsors can choose to give or withhold their custom, the educational market-place does the evaluating. The imperfections of that market weaken that argument, but the challenge forces one to relate evaluation to notions of control, quality, demand, and accountability.

There is one aspect of curriculum evaluation which, while it certainly affects the schools, is even more important in post-school education. Most evaluation is of short-term effects – that is, during, at the end of, or soon after, a course. Such evaluations are relatively easy to carry out in logistical if not methodological terms, and their findings can be fed back quickly into the system. There has also been some work on long-term evaluation – for example, by Hyman and others (Hyman, 1975, 1979) – to try to measure the effects of education ten, twenty, and more years after. The problems of disentangling the 'contribution' of education from all the other factors involved in people's lives and careers make this kind of research very difficult to carry out. What is largely lacking, and very much needed, is medium-term evaluations, between one and (say) five years after the course. Many curricula in post-school education are justified precisely in terms of such medium-term effects: they are said to provide a 'foundation' for the first few years in an occupation or profession; or to allow a choice of occupations through a transferable 'training of the mind'; or to enable people in mid-life and mid-career to reorientate themselves; or to develop leadership, confidence, analytic capability, social skills, problem-solving abilities, and skills that people can 'own' and 'take with them'. Such are the claims, but they need to be checked, and much more systematically than they typically are.

Problems and directions

The purpose of this chapter has been to establish the terms of the analysis in the rest of the book, to say what it is we are talking about. The curriculum, it has been argued, is a matter of what is taught and what should be taught. That involves, among other things, questions about aims, processes, contexts, and justifications. It also raises related questions about innovation and evaluation. The treatment has necessarily been brief, and readers who wish to pursue these matters in more depth can follow up the references cited, or make use of Richards' (1984) bibliography. It is hoped that it has been made clear that curriculum matters are deserving of study and care, like any other field; they cannot be simply taken for granted, or justified in terms of what is 'natural' or 'normal'. It may be useful in this final section to attempt a brief overview of where the field of curriculum studies has got to, the problems that still exercise it, and the directions it now seems to be taking.

There is no doubt that the systematic study of the curriculum has now become an established part of the study of education generally. Courses on the curriculum are now common in teacher education, and the number of publications and research studies in the field continues to grow apace. Despite these signs that curriculum studies have finally arrived and are unlikely to disappear again, there is some doubt and unease among those working in the field, a mood captured in a Social Science Research Council (SSRC) seminar on the subject held in the early 1980s (SSRC, 1981). Other writers have indicated a need to re-think the field (Reid, 1978; Lawn and Barton, 1981) or even referred to a 'crisis' in the curriculum (Cuff and Payne, 1985). As with the growth of curriculum studies in the 1950s and 1960s, there seem to be both practical and academic reasons for this unease. The pattern of curriculum development in the school sector has changed. There are few large-scale development projects of the kind associated in this country with the Nuffield Foundation and Schools Council, and indeed a good deal of retrospective criticism of the impact that such projects made, or did not make. Instead, changes in the secondary curriculum are being increasingly initiated by the Department of Education and Science (DES) itself, in the form of guidelines for core curricula and standards to be reached in various subjects. This is still curriculum development, but of a style and from a direction which are unlike those of previous decades.

There are also, however, academic reasons for unease. The relationship between theory and practice in curriculum studies is still unresolved. In one way, this is hardly surprising; the nature of theory, the nature of practice and the links between them is one of the oldest, if not the oldest, of all educational issues. To accuse curriculum studies of not having developed unifying theory is to ignore the problems of doing so in all the human or social sciences. To the extent that curriculum studies draws on several disciplines which are themselves problematic in that respect, the problem is compounded; there is a confluence of uncertainties.

Unease has also arisen from the experience of the major curriculum projects of previous decades. In a changed educational climate, reflecting a wider conservatism, there is now some doubt about the aims and directions of some such projects. Was the 'new maths' really such a good thing? Did integrated studies lead to a decline or confusion in standards? Do the schools not have a responsibility to transmit as well as contest contemporary culture? Some curriculum 'theory' now seems very much part of the general optimistic, student-centred, progressive rhetoric of the 1960s. However, curiously, along with these criticisms goes the charge that such curriculum development did not in fact bring about much change at all, merely scratching the surface of school norms and values. Too much emphasis was placed on teaching materials, it is argued, too little on teachers and school structures. There is a much greater realisation of the degree of operational control that teachers and students have over what goes on in the classroom, and their capacity to ignore, find ways round, or modify 'innovations' which they do not like. So the field of curriculum studies is afflicted by doubts about the theory of what it is doing, the direction in which it is going, and the impact of what it has done.

Nevertheless, the field continues to develop, and two trends in particular – towards the 'micro' and the 'macro' – have been evident in recent years. The first concentrates on detailed studies of what goes on in the classroom or teaching-learning situation in terms of dialogue, conversation, social interaction, and the construction and exchange of meanings (Edwards and Furlong, 1978; Payne and Cuff, 1982). In other cases, there is a more phenomenological emphasis on how teaching and learning are experienced by those involved (Pinar and Grumet, 1981). Such studies give a much more detailed and subtle account of what happens in education than the conventional concepts of content and method usually allow.[12]

At the other end of the spectrum, there is an increasing concern with the 'macro', with the curriculum as a reflection of wider social and economic relations, which stems partly from the work of Young and others in the 1970s (Young, 1971). The emphasis in this has been on the curriculum as a vehicle for various forms of socialisation and selection, which serve to legitimate authority, conformity, and inequality in society at large. Whereas much of this work has been concerned with the schools, there is growing interest in the 16–19 sector in this connection (Grignon, 1971; Willis, 1977; Gleeson and Mardle, 1980).

It is not possible to explore here either of these developments in any detail, interesting though they are. Both tend to lead away from what might be called the middle ground of curriculum studies and the two questions with which we began. Our concern in this book is with the overt, intended curriculum, and it is worth pointing out that if *that* did not exist, there would be no basis for classroom interaction, and no pretext for socialisation or selection. But the curriculum is much more than a basis or vehicle for something else: the choices made in planning and teaching it are significant choices. At the very least, they involve what economists call 'opportunity costs': the time, effort and money spent learning one thing cannot be devoted to learning something else. But, beyond that, curriculum decisions have personal, social and economic consequences which need to be carefully and systematically explored. It will be the task of the chapters that follow in this book to do so in relation to post-school education.

NOTES

General Notes
Post-school education refers, strictly speaking, to education over the age of 18 in the United Kingdom (though the term 'school' is used of some

post-18 institutions in arts education) and *post-compulsory education* refers to 16+. My concern in this book is with education beyond the end of compulsory schooling, and I have tended to interchange the two terms, partly to avoid repetition, and partly because I think current changes in 16–19 provision (such as tertiary and sixth-form colleges) will lead to their eventual alignment.

I have also interchanged the terms 'subject and 'discipline', since the difference seems to me one of usage rather than definition: 'subject' is used more in the schools, 'discipline' in higher education. Likewise, where 'integrated' tends to be used in the school context, the preferred word in higher education is usually 'interdisciplinary'.

1 The history of the study of the curriculum is not, of course, the same as the study of the history of the curriculum, and this chapter is only concerned with the first, and the concomitant shifts in the concept of curriculum. Historical accounts of curricula in post-school education are still rather thin on the ground, but can be found sometimes in the literature on specific disciplines (such as the history of History) and on particular institutions or types of institutions (for instance, the City and Guilds of London Institute, the universities).

2 The managerial emphasis must not be over-stated. Bobbitt may have had a rather narrow 'scientific' view of curriculum planning, but not of curriculum aims: his first major book includes, as well as a chapter on occupational efficiency, chapters on education for citizenship, leisure, and social intercommunication. He was also well aware of the value of out-of-school learning (Bobbitt, 1918). For a general account see Cremin (1971). The Association for Supervision and Curriculum Development (ASCD) adopted that title only in 1946, but it evolved from earlier associations concerned with the supervision and direction of instruction, which merged with the Society for Curriculum Study. The prevailing emphasis seems to have been practical and applied, leading to charges that curriculum studies was later hijacked by academic theorists – yet another case perhaps of 'academic drift' (see Chapter 5 below).

3 Recent issues of both *Curriculum Enquiry* and the *Journal of Further and Higher Education* have contained papers on the theory – practice problem. The topic is discussed at more length in Chapter 5 below.

4 For a useful collection of publications on the subject, see C. Richards (1984, pp. 32–6).

5 Bloom's Foreword to the first handbook justifies the taxonomy on several grounds. My view is that its main value lies in the attempt to specify levels of processes, rather than in the general emphasis on making goals explicit, which was not peculiar to Bloom and his colleagues. Bloom did not use the term 'process' to refer to this,

but others have, and it still seems to me the best available term,
especially as a verb: to process content or information. The wide
resistance to Bloom in this country does not seem to me to be
altogether praiseworthy, and I tend to ascribe it partly to an
aversion to explicitness in some aspects of English life, a characteristic perhaps of a subtle and complex culture, but one which makes
it difficult to confront major change.

6 No taxonomy of psychomotor or perceptual-motor skills has yet
achieved the kind of currency of Bloom's and Krathwohl's cognitive and affective domains. Such a taxonomy would surely have to
be multidimensional, since skills can become more sophisticated or
difficult or 'higher' in any or all of three ways (at least): increasing
precision (decreasing tolerances); increasing speed; and increasing
complexity of components or sub-operations.

7 The concept of gradient here relates to thresholds of competence.
When a foreman says he cannot yet let an apprentice loose on a
particular machine, or an adult education tutor asserts that anyone
can start reading a Hardy novel straight away, or an economist
insists on certain prerequisites for his course, or a biologist assures
his students that they will see the point of something in a few
weeks' time, implicit statements about thresholds and gradients
are involved. The issue is further complicated by Bruner's (1960)
notion of a 'spiral' curriculum involving different modes of
understanding (enactive, iconic, symbolic). The development of
understanding of a subject may in some cases be a gradual,
evolutionary affair; in other cases, there may be periods where,
because of the structure of the subject, that development is
discontinuous; and in others again, perhaps where 'experience' is
felt to be valuable, there is more immediate access to all aspects of
it. A medical professor once said to me: 'Students come up here to
look over my shoulder, but they're not really tall enough till the
third year.' The whole topic seems to me an extraordinarily
complex one, and points to the need for more work on the internal
structures or logics of different subjects. I have simply tried to
raise the issue here.

8 It is now *de rigueur* to speak of teaching and learning rather than
teaching. This seems sometimes little more than a ritual nod in the
direction of students, but it may also reflect the influence on
education of subjectivist theories of knowledge in the last twenty
years ('multiple realities') and also a move beyond the simplistic
communication models of teaching (sender, message, receiver)
which were fashionable in the 1950s and 1960s. It must also be said
that curriculum evaluation studies have sometimes demonstrated
the difference of perspective to a surprising and alarming degree.
Here I shall use teaching, rather than the longer alternative, to
include these ambiguities.

9 The conflict between hard and soft models, or 'scientific' and 'deliberative' ones, tends to ignore the possibility that the answer may be a contingent one – i.e., it all depends what kind of course/subject/institution/context one is talking about. The task then becomes to identify the relevant contingencies which would allow one to make the appropriate choice among different development strategies. For an attempt to develop a contingent model of teaching, see Squires (1983).

10 The sources of influence and control are relatively easy to pinpoint, the means or types of control much less so. We know that teachers usually have a good deal of 'operational' control over curricula, but exactly how is it exercised? Central government obviously has legislative and financial levers at its disposal, but does it operate in different ways, and through 'secondary' sources as well? What about opinion formation? How does the 'operating climate' of policy become established? The use of the term 'hegemony' here does not imply adherence to a central conspiracy theory, merely a check on too easy assumptions about 'pluralism' in educational policy-making.

11 There is no doubt that the concept and methodology of evaluation have become much more sophisticated over the years. Nevertheless, I detect something of the same pendulum motion in this field as in curriculum development; initial 'hard' or 'scientific' models countered by softer 'illuminative' models which have recently themselves come in for criticism from those concerned with 'accountability'. Changes in the external social and economic climate cannot but affect such trends.

12 It is difficult to summarise here what has become a very rich and complex aspect of curriculum studies. Investigation of the 'micro' stems from a number of sources: interest in social interaction in the classroom; in the construction of meanings; in conversation *per se*; and the frames of reference likewise include social interactionism, ethnomethodology, and certain forms of linguistics. Such studies tend to treat as problematic everything that curriculum theory has previously taken for granted. For example, one assumes that in a seminar, everyone is there; but the 'lived experience' of the student may be that the presence of different people is perceived with different intensity at different times; to the point where one may be oblivious of certain people, or of the setting, or of time passing. One does not even always have a sense of oneself. It is not clear if and how such insights can intervene in the grosser processes of curriculum planning and teaching; but they are surely interesting.

2 General Education

General and specific education

The key to understanding the curriculum beyond school is the distinction between general and specific education.[1] This is not an absolute distinction: there are degrees of generality and degrees of specificity, and much depends on the context of discussion. Nevertheless, it is useful to distinguish on the one hand between curricula which are described and justified in broad terms, and those which have a more particular orientation, purpose, or scope.

This distinction can be used to contrast compulsory with post-compulsory education. Whereas compulsory education is typically general in scope and intent, post-compulsory education is typically specific. Again, the contrast is not absolute. The current debate about the advantages and disadvantages of a common core curriculum in the schools is a sign that agreement on the generality of compulsory education is far from complete. There may be a good deal of consensus that the first six or seven years of schooling should provide a general platform for development, but beyond that the issues become much more contentious. Whereas some current trends, such as the emphasis on criterion-referenced assessment in certain key subjects, point towards a common core with common standards, others, such as the Technical and Vocational Education Initiative (TVEI), open up the possibility of a more differentiated curriculum, and even a more stratified school system, recalling the older tripartite model. Conversely, one finds some discussion of general education in post-compulsory education, not only in the 'general studies' element in non-advanced further education, but in the newer emphasis on generic skills in vocational preparation. And there has long been a concern with general education in higher education, especially in the United States (Squires, 1976a; Gaff, 1983).

Even with these exceptions, however, the distinction between 'general' compulsory education and 'specific' post-compulsory education is useful. The generality of the first is evident not only in the way in which schools are described and justified, but even sometimes in the labels used: the General Certificate of Education (GCE, soon to become GCSE); the foreign terms which mean 'grounding' or 'basic'; and words such as 'comprehensive'. Likewise, the specificity of post-compulsory education is apparent from its labels, and in particular the plethora of qualifications that exists. That specificity is also evident in more subtle ways – for example, in the lack of communication between different sectors and types of institution. Lecturers in one kind of institution may know little of, and care less about, what goes on in another kind; indeed the very idea that one can consider post-compulsory education *as a whole* is largely alien both to official policy and private discourse.

It might seem, on the basis of what has just been said, that compulsory and post-compulsory education are therefore quite dissimilar; that the schools do one thing, and that post-school institutions do many others, and that there is no connection. But it will be argued that there is a relationship, as well as a distinction, between the general and the specific: that the curriculum beyond school can be seen as an unpacking or breaking-out of the aspects of a general education in school; that the configuration loosens, but that the elements are the same. The model used to analyse general education in the schools will also serve to analyse the curriculum beyond school; the dimensions of the first become the orientations of the second. Hence the analysis of the curriculum beyond school has to begin with the school.

This chapter therefore draws largely on writing about aspects of general education in the schools, but it must be made clear right away that this is only a means to an end here, not an end in itself. The aim is not to develop a common curriculum for schools; that difficult task lies beyond the scope of this book or the competence of the author, and has already been addressed by many others.[2] Rather, the purpose of this chapter is to explore what may be meant by a general education, in relation to the schools, so that a basis can be laid for the analysis of the specific curricula which are the business of the rest of this book.

What follows leans heavily on the work of three writers on the school curriculum, chosen here because they seem to articulate key dimensions of general education. The treatment of their ideas is by no means complete, nor is there any attempt to review the many other contributors to the debate. The perspective is largely one of hindsight: if the schools provide some sort of general basis, foundation, or platform for post-school education, what kind of a basis is it? There are of course different ways of looking at what the schools do, but they are not the concern here. Two brief points should be made. First, although it is difficult both to arrive at an adequate model of general education, and to translate it into an effective curriculum, it is nevertheless an idea which seems hard to do without. Both individualism and collectivism in different ways point towards some notion of generality, in terms of roundedness, balance, individuation, the whole man, the common weal, the community, the general good; in the end, the 'human'. The image of oneness, of unity, is perhaps never entirely absent. Moreover, the justification of compulsion in education is linked to the notion of generality, in that if children's development is believed to be an entirely individual and unique affair it becomes difficult to say why it should not, in some cases or some respects, take place outside formal education. The collective nature of schooling partly implies some common or general purpose, which is similar to some extent for everyone. One may not think this a very good argument, but it helps to explain why compulsory education has to concern itself with general rationales.

Second, the term 'basic' is also sometimes used of compulsory education. It is typically applied to the earlier years (i.e., primary or elementary education), but it has also been used by international bodies such as UNESCO and the OECD to refer to the whole of the compulsory sector. It will be implied here that what can be said about the concept of general education can also be applied to basic education, writ small; that the ideas and dimensions which can constitute generality also exist, though in a less developed and differentiated form, in concepts of basic education. This points to a more complex approach to basic education than is implied either by the slogan 'back to basics' as applied to schools, or by some approaches to basic education for 16–19-year-olds, or older adults. In particular, it will be suggested in Chapter 3 that basic education for adults is not just a matter of knowledge and skills; that it has to do with social and personal development as well.

The next three sections look at three approaches to general education: in terms of organised knowledge; in terms of the culture; and in terms of types of abilities. Although an exclusive emphasis on any one of these can lead to curricula that differ markedly from one another, it will be suggested at the end that they are not logically incompatible, merely different ways of slicing the same cake. In practice, knowledge-referenced models of general education tend to underpin the traditional grammar school, or its equivalent in other countries, whereas culture-referenced models underlie the 'modern' secondary school. The third dimension – abilities – tends to be less salient in secondary curricula than in some kinds of primary education.

General education in terms of knowledge

It is useful to distinguish broadly between common-sense knowledge and organised knowledge.[3] In our everyday lives we come to know many things about the world, about other people, places, tools, machines, and so on. This is the stock of knowledge which we acquire and which we need to perform the transactions and operations of everyday living. Where such knowledge is commonly held, rather than being peculiar to one individual, we tend to speak of 'common knowledge' and the rather more normative 'common sense'. This kind of knowledge is picked up in and through the normal processes of everyday living – work, family life, leisure pursuits, the media – and although it may also be acquired in the education system, it is not the kind of knowledge which education is, in principle, concerned with. Indeed, it would seem on the face of it odd to isolate people from normal social processes, as education does, in order to teach them about those processes.

Education is primarily concerned with organised knowledge. That is not to say that it is anti-common sense, but rather that it is typically concerned with bodies of knowledge; configurations of facts, concepts, models, theories, and procedures which are called 'subjects' or 'disciplines' and which bear familiar labels such as 'biology', 'economics', 'law', or 'electronics'. The distinction between common-sense knowledge and organised knowledge is not absolute: organised knowledge can build on or derive from common-sense knowledge, and conversely, organised knowledge can modify common-sense knowledge.

One distinguishing feature of organised knowledge is that it attempts to be progressive, whereas common-sense knowledge tends to rest on adequacy. People do say, of course, 'I wish I knew then what I know now', and one can certainly speak of knowing more, or being wiser, or thinking more deeply, in a common-sense way. But as long as things are going reasonably well, there is no great stimulus for common-sense knowledge to develop. By contrast, in organised knowledge there is a institutionalised restlessness, a drive to accummulate or improve or understand which seems to be intrinsic to the process of study and research. People are

constantly questioning assumptions, testing hypotheses, collec-
ting information, examining procedures, formulating models and
theories; it is always a case of 'work in progress', and any sense of
culmination is temporary, a respite rather than rest. Of course, this
is a rather idealised picture of organised knowledge. The knowledge
professions have their share of time-servers and their periods of
stagnation. Indeed, Kuhn[4] has suggested that the progress of
science alternates between long stretches of fairly routine work and
periodic upheavals. Moreover, the face of organised knowledge that
is presented to the student is more often the face of certainty than
uncertainty, of a body of knowledge rather than a process of
enquiry. The right balance between these two has been a major issue
in secondary-school curriculum development ever since the major
American school curriculum reform projects of the 1950s mentioned
in the last chapter.

There are three main rationales for conceptualising a general
curriculum in terms of organised knowledge. The first and most
obvious is that it allows students to proceed to further levels or types
of education by providing the necessary foundation or grounding.
This rationale is institutionalised in entrance requirements for
further or higher education which may specify O- and A-level passes
in particular subjects, although some subjects (in particular O-level
English and Mathematics) are also treated as general-purpose
passes, admitting students to a wide range of courses.

The assumption that studies in secondary education are an
essential prerequisite for success in further and higher education has
been dented by the substantial numbers of adults who, in recent
years, have got their degrees or other higher qualifications without
the normal entrance requirements (Hore and West, 1980; Squires,
1983). Higher and further education institutions now typically have
'exception clauses' in their entry regulations for unqualified adults,
and use them, on a case-by-case basis, to admit such non-traditional
students. On reflection, the success of some such students is not
surprising, since prior knowledge is only one among several factors
(such as motivation, relevant experience, or effective study) which
can affect educational achievement.

The 'prerequisite' argument for a general curriculum has also
been dented by the low correlations between secondary-school
achievement and performance in higher education (Choppin, 1973;
Goacher, 1984). Again, this is not wholly surprising. Secondary-
school examinations are not designed to be predictive; the mode of
study in higher education is always different, and the subjects
sometimes so; and three or four years is a long time in a student's

life, in which a good deal may change in terms of motivation, orientation, and maturity.

However, the combined effect of successful adult achievement and the research on admission to post-school education must be to weaken the now-or-never argument that 'if you don't lay a foundation at school you won't be able to pick it up later'. Both the recent research on adult learning, which modifies or contests the notion of irreversible and general decline in abilities (see Chapter 6), and the opening up of access to education for adults in everything from apprenticeships to higher education suggest that one will be able to pick some of it up later. The main doubts and exceptions relate to certain kinds of perceptual-motor skills.

The second argument for conceiving of a general education in terms of knowledge is that organised knowledge embodies all our modes of understanding and relating to the world, and hence to miss out on any of these is to give a person a partial, incomplete education. This is a 'deprivation' or 'incompleteness' argument rather than a now-or-never one. It is held that to deprive people of any of the ways in which mankind has come to apprehend or know the world is both intrinsically wrong, because it is less than fully human, and may also foreclose certain opportunities for that person's development. If one has never been exposed to, say, the natural sciences, not only will one miss out on one of mankind's main modes of understanding the world, but one will never be able to bring science into one's life (whether in one's job, leisure interests, political stance, or general view of the world) and, worse still, one may never know what has been missed.

A rigorous basis for designing a general, knowledge-referenced curriculum has been provided by Hirst (1969, 1974) and Phenix (1964) in their analyses of 'forms of knowledge' and 'realms of meaning' respectively. There are significant differences in their approaches, but both attempt to identify a smallish number of distinct types of knowledge or understanding into which the rather larger number of subjects can be grouped. The essential element in planning a general curriculum thus becomes the inclusion of each type of knowledge rather than each faculty grouping, or discipline. Hirst (1969) identifies his forms of knowledge in the following way:

the development of mind has been marked by the progressive differentiation in human consciousness of some seven or eight distinguishable cognitive structures, each of which involves the making of a distinctive form of reasoned judgement and is, therefore, a unique expression of man's rationality. This is to say that all knowledge and understanding is logically locatable within a number of domains, within, I suggest, mathematics, the physical sciences, the human sciences and history, literature and the fine arts, morals, religion and philosophy. These would seem to me to be the logically distinct areas, though this division might well be disputed. It is not, of course, that these forms of knowledge are totally separate from each other. That is not what I am saying. Manifestly there are overlaps in the concepts used in the different forms, and there are overlaps in the patterns of valid reasoning. But in respect of the distinctive rational judgements concerned, each structure involves elements which are irreducible to any of the others, singly or in combination. (page 151)

Several points can be made about this argument. Firstly, while the idea of deprivation is easy enough to understand, its opposite is less easy to conceptualise. 'Completeness', 'roundedness', 'wholeness', or 'balance' imply agreement on what constitutes the full scope of human mind, and this is itself problematic. Secondly, as Hirst (1974) himself recognises, there are problems in talking about literature and the fine arts as forms of knowledge. The problem also arises with physical education. If one excludes, say, music and physical education from the general curriculum, is one excluding forms of knowledge, or understanding, or being? Even a phrase like 'physical well-being' raises the question, and the difficulties of talking *about* music in any except technical terms are well known. If education is about knowledge, and music is part of the curriculum, what kind of knowledge is it?

A further point can be made about the 'deprivation' argument. The difficulty of justifying curricula on intrinsic grounds (that is, 'inherently good', 'worthwhile in itself', 'for its own sake') should not lead one into believing that instrumental or extrinsic arguments are any simpler. Instrumentalism, in the form of vocationalism, is on the increase in educational policy-making at the moment, and instrumental arguments are increasingly used to justify a much more specific or practical curriculum not only in post-compulsory education, but at the 14+ stage in the schools. But instrumental arguments always contain several steps, and in the end tend to disappear into intrinsic arguments. We need more information technology in the curriculum (is there no transfer of learning from other subjects?); because we need more information technologists (is there no learning-on-the-job, no substitutability among trained manpower?); because they will increase our productivity in the Information Technology (IT) sector (is skill level the only factor in productivity?); because that will boost the economy generally (is IT necessarily an important sector?); because that will lead to a higher standard of living (automatically? for everyone?); because that will make us happier (will it?); because happiness is good in itself.

In addition to the 'now-or-never' and 'deprivation' arguments for a knowledge-referenced curriculum there is a third argument, which relates to the concept of disciplinary cultures introduced in Chapter 1. This is the argument that a disciplined exposure to organised knowledge affects the way people think, not only about the knowledge, but generally; that it affects the way people view the world. The argument has taken on different forms and emphases at different times, and these can only be referred to briefly here (see Lauwerys, 1967; Lauglo, 1983). What they all have in common, however, is the assumption that both the process and the effect of involvement with organised knowledge transcends particular disciplines and transfers beyond the curriculum. These assumptions are or were present in the Humboldtian notion of *Einheit von Wissenschaft* (unity of knowledge/science) which originally, but not for long, underpinned the curriculum of the German gymnasium. There was, it was argued, an essential similarity in the procedures and methodology of all forms of knowledge, which could be applied both to nature and man. These procedures lay at the heart not only of organised knowledge, but also of culture, society – indeed, man's whole existence. The German term *Allgemeine Bildung* does not translate exactly as 'general education'; it connotes a culture, a way of thinking and a mode of being as well.

In French education, the comparable argument stresses above all lucidity, rationality, and clarity, to the point of transparency. Perhaps this is partly why mathematics seems to be the paradigmatic discipline in the French curriculum; it is pure rationality, unsullied by the empirical. Excellence in mathematics opens many doors in the French system, and the status of subjects in French education seems to fall off partly to the extent that they depart from the model of mathematics. Even in 'unclear' subjects like literature, the drive towards classification, and the fascination with structure are still evident.

In England, the disciplinary culture argument has become embodied in the concept of a 'liberal education'. This concept has changed over time, and some of its historical shifts will be discussed in the next chapter. A liberal education has, at various times, been seen as the education appropriate to a particular class, the education appropriate for particular occupations (notably the civil service), as an education in certain subjects, and as an education through certain subjects. These shifts are too subtle to document here, but it is important to stress the essential element in all of them – namely, that a liberal education has to do with liberation, of both individuals and societies. At first sight, the relating of 'liberal' to 'liberation' is surprising. But the root notion in a liberal education is that of freedom from ignorance and illusion. Put like this, it sounds distinctly old-fashioned; it is not so much that we no longer believe in knowledge, but that we no longer believe in ignorance. However, if it is argued that a liberal education can liberate people from unexamined assumptions, unjustified prejudices, parochial perspectives, faulty reasoning, unscientific theories, inadequate models, poor methodology, and the general tendency to take things for granted, then many people would applaud it. The particular philosophical views that allowed people to distinguish happily between illusion and reality may have lost general support, but bodies of knowledge still have their criteria for judging standards and progress. The above 'forms of ignorance' merely constitute a cross-section of such criteria.

In each of the three versions of the disciplinary culture argument described here the emphasis is on education through knowledge as well as in knowledge. The relationship between process and content varies, however. The German version implies the full range of important subjects which can and did lead quickly to an overloaded curriculum and a rather mechanistic approach to covering each subject. The French version also implies some breadth, but singles out certain subjects – mathematics, philosophy – as being particularly significant or effective in inculcating the desired attitudes and values. In England, the emphasis on a wide range of subjects has always been weaker, and the key role played by certain subjects, notably classics, has now given way to the view that almost any subject, taught in the right way and the right spirit, can provide a liberal education. Thus the English version has been less demanding in terms of range of content, but more demanding in terms of the teaching process. In all three cases, however, the assumption has been that the effect of such an education would spread well beyond a person's current and subsequent studies, to permeate her work, attitudes, and, in the English version, character.

Each of the three main rationales for a knowledge-referenced approach to general education – the now or never argument, the deprivation argument and the disciplinary culture argument – can issue in either a collection of subjects or an integrated approach. It is important to recognise that Hirst's and Phenix's analyses provide not a prescription for a curriculum, but for how to go about planning one; and to remember that integrated foundation courses as well as collections of subjects can, and do, provide access to higher studies.

There are, however, both practical and theoretical problems with attempts to use knowledge as the guiding curriculum principle, as Kelly (1977) has noted. At the practical level, the growth of knowledge, and the difficulty of knowing what to leave out, can lead to overloaded curricula. The long-term, deferred nature of both the deprivation and disciplinary culture arguments means that pupils may not see the point of some subjects. The pre-academic nature of some curricula is not necessarily appropriate for students who do not go on to higher education. The main practical challenge to this knowledge-referenced approach therefore has been contained in terms like 'relevance', 'needs', and 'interests'.

The main theoretical challenge has come from the sociology of knowledge, which has turned the spotlight on how knowledge is socially produced, disseminated or withheld, and controlled; indeed, going further, how knowledge is socially constructed. Griffin (1983) for example, picks up Hirst's emphasis on 'public criteria' for knowledge, translates 'public' to 'social', and then asks: which part of society? which social group? Thus arguments based on 'essential disciplines', 'forms of knowledge', and 'rationality', 'knowledge' and 'objectivity' are treated sociologically by asking: who defined them as such? what social function did that definition fulfil? The attention is turned from questions about the nature of knowledge with which philosophers are typically concerned, to questions about the nurture of knowledge, which are the domain of sociology. This leads us on naturally to the second main model of general education, in terms of society or culture.

General education in terms of culture

The word 'culture' is used in two different ways in English. In literature and the arts, it usually refers to an appreciation of the best artefacts of civilisation, and an understanding of the thought that lies in and around them. In this sense, some people are cultured and others are not, although this rather stark view has more recently been expressed in terms of 'high' culture and 'popular' culture. In anthropology and sociology, culture refers to the way of life of a group of people. It is impossible not to have culture in this sense, or to be acculturated, although the distinction may be drawn between a main or dominant culture and subcultures, which deviate from it to varying degrees.

The distinction between the two senses of 'culture' is not as clear-cut as it may seem. One may argue that an appreciation of the cultural artefacts – the drama, sculpture, music, painting, and so on – involves an understanding of, or is even only a means to understanding, the way of life. Certainly, understanding the way of life must include some appreciation of the artefacts. But there is a real problem in relating the two senses, which reflects the general problem of relating man's artefacts to his way of life. This is a problem both of connection and criteria. Do certain ways of life necessarily produce certain artefacts? And do we use the same, or different criteria, in evaluating the way of life and the artefacts? Do 'good' societies produce 'good' art? Do violent or stable societies produce better art/science/technology/ideas? And when we say that a society, or a painting, or a theory, is a good one, are we invoking the same criteria in each case, or different ones? And where do these criteria come from?

The issues are crudely stated, but unavoidable in any discussion of 'culture' as a guiding principle for a generic curriculum. Culture in the first sense – appreciation of the best that has been thought and said – has underpinned the 'classical' or 'liberal' curriculum for a long time, and continues to do so. Although this may result in a curriculum very similiar to the one based on 'forms of knowledge', the nature of the justification is subtly different. Acquaintance with the best provides the student with paradigms, exemplars, and models which he can attempt to imitate and live up to. It is a form of social learning (Bandura, 1971), except that reference groups rather than actual groups are involved. Good teaching, in this context, means making the people, events and artefacts of culture as immediate and real – indeed, more so than – the people, events, and artefacts around one. The student is apprenticed to his imagination.

Culture in this sense is weaker as a guiding principle in education than it used to be, partly because it is now seen to be in some respects the culture of a particular class, and partly because of intrinsic doubts about its value and power to civilise behaviour. Nevertheless, there is in the United Kingdom a powerful tradition of the 'education of the sensibility' and in the United States a continuing belief in the humanities, not simply as a group of subjects, but as an induction into Western culture.

Culture in the second sense – the way of life of a group – has also been widely invoked as a guiding principle for the curriculum. The idea that compulsory education should prepare children for, and equip them to live in their particular society has influenced curricula in many countries, but is perhaps most powerful in the United

States and the Soviet Union, where, in different ways, pragmatist philosophy and praxist ideology have each oriented the curriculum towards what the child *will actually do* after leaving school. Thus the curriculum may include driver education, work experience, and community projects, all of which point to a particular way of life. This kind of thinking has influenced curriculum planning in all industrialised countries, and indeed it is impossible to understand the non-formal education of traditional societies without it. Initiation, *rites de passage*, role-typing, transmission of knowledge and skills are all concepts which help one to understand the relationship between education and culture in this second sense.

One of the most systematic attempts to analyse general education in terms of culture (that is, as way of life) has been that of Lawton (1983a and b) who argues that all cultures can be divided into eight structures or subsystems:

(1) social structure/social system;
(2) economic system;
(3) communication system;
(4) rationality system;
(5) technology system;
(6) morality system;
(7) belief system;
(8) aesthetic system.

These subsystems interact with each other, and some may appear more important or fundamental than others. Conflicts and contradictions may be evident, as may regional or other variations. Nevertheless, Lawton suggests, a curriculum may be derived from an analysis of these eight subsystems; it would not cover each subsystem, but rather select from it in such a way as to acquaint the student with its essential elements.

Lawton's list stands in roughly the same relationship to the actual curriculum as do Hirst's forms of knowledge; it provides a prescription for planning, rather than a list of subjects. Indeed, as he makes clear later, some subsystems correspond quite closely to some conventional secondary-school subjects, while others necessitate the addition of new subjects or topics, and others again (such as rationality, morality, and belief) tend to cut across several subjects.

One can argue over the detail of Lawton's analysis as applied to the United Kingdom, but the exercise is interesting in that it identifies gaps and mismatches when one looks at the existing curriculum pattern in the light of cultural analysis. Lawton points out that political and social education are commonly lacking, that economics is usually only an option, that technology has low status, and that the arts are often seen as peripheral. It is clear that if one took this approach to planning general education, one would arrive at a curriculum which was both substantially different from a curriculum planned in terms of organised knowledge, and different from the existing pattern in schools in the United Kingdom. There are, however, theoretical difficulties in applying this method of curriculum planning, not least in being able to stand outside the culture in order to analyse it. If the analysis depends heavily on who does the analysing, and from what social or ideological stance, there is not much chance that it will either be 'objective' or command general assent. The problem is the familiar one of the 'point of view', and the apparently 'neutral' or 'descriptive' frameworks of social anthropology have increasingly been recognised as problematic in this respect.

There is also a moral problem. If crime is widespread in the society, it is arguably part of the social, economic, and morality subsystems. Should the curriculum, then, include some instruction in mugging, burglary, or fraud, on the grounds that they are a 'normal' part of the way of life, and that students would be disadvantaged if they did not know something about them? In fact, Lawton's 'objective' cultural analysis also has normative elements which seem to derive from assumptions and values outside that analysis:

> Another difficulty which has gradually emerged is the fact that law and morality are increasingly seen as separate issues. One danger in that situation is an aspect of what Durkheim referred to as 'anomie' – not knowing what the rules of society really are; a second and connected danger, is the retreat to moral relativism – the suggestion that morality is simply a matter of taste, or that one rule or rule-system is as good as any other. (page 47)

It was suggested earlier that culture in the first sense is clearly value-laden and culture in the second sense, if not value-free, was at least descriptive rather than normative in its intent. However, it may be that the very conceptions of culture and society that have developed within sociology and anthropology contain certain values within them: a preference for societies that are 'integrated wholes' rather than mere aggregates, for a strong rather than weak sense of community, for the organic as against the merely contractual. The influence of Durkheim, for example, is clear and overt in Hargreaves (1982), who goes back to him to provide inspiration for a more community-oriented curriculum.

There is a second and more subtle way in which the social anthropological concept of culture is problematic in relation to the curriculum. Culture sounds as if it is an all-embracing concept, as if it refers to the totality or whole or sum of a group's way of life. Nothing, one assumes, could be more general, more inclusive; there should be no danger of anything being omitted, or excluded in the formulation of curriculum aims. If culture is the totality of a way of life, then it should provide, *par excellence*, the general principle which is being sought.

However, from the outside, it is clear that cultures exclude and preclude as well as include. They delimit the possibilities of thought, belief, and behaviour; they channel attention and energy in particular directions. Each culture constitutes a space, and a boundary to that space: a boundary patrolled not only by the overt forces of social control but by the intimate limitations of language itself. Just as one can make a much wider range of sounds than one eventually learns to use in one's mother tongue (a process of elimination of 'useless' sounds), so the possibilities of consciousness are much greater and more open than the consciousness one eventually comes to think of as normal or complete. Part of the fascination of art is perhaps that it makes one see or hear or think afresh, by going beyond the usual, culture-limited perceptions and ideas, and opening up the possibilities of consciousness to one again and again. Whether this is a simply a greater openness, or an apprehension of a different order of reality is not the issue here: the point is that culture – and even language and thought – appears as a limitation, perhaps necessary, in this light.

A curriculum that moves only within the culture is thus going to be a restricted and restrictive curriculum. It will not go beyond, or transcend; it will not make one come new to the world as the arts do, and in a different way, the sciences do. Both of these are constantly engaged in redefining what is meant by 'the world' or 'life' or 'existence'; they move back and forward across the boundary that divides the familiar from the strange, the known from the unknown, the taken-for-granted from the problematic.

How one conceptualises culture will therefore affect one's concept of general education. If culture is thought of as a totality and a system, then a general curriculum will be one which covers or samples the various subsystems that go to make up the totality. Stress may be laid on interrelating the parts of the curriculum, so that the student can see how it, and the culture, constitute a whole.

If culture is thought of as a limited space within a potentially limitless or at least unknown consciousness, then the curriculum would need to both mirror the culture and transcend it: to teach about the space, and to teach that it is a space. The third possibility – that of teaching only how to go beyond the cultural space – is rarely found in Western education, but is characteristic of mystic and esoteric traditions.

All this may seem a long way from driver education, health education, and civics. The culture-referenced curriculum of the twentieth century was in part due to the efforts of great educational reformers such as Dewey to move the curriculum away from academic subjects, and make it more relevant, problem-centred and nearer the 'needs' or realities of everyday life. That movement was also reinforced by some of the early behavioural psychologists, who discounted much transfer of learning, and said that if anything was to be taught it should be taught directly, and not 'through' Latin, literature, or anything else. At the time, it must have seemed like a liberation of the curriculum. It is only with the passage of time that the limitations inherent in this approach have become as evident as its advantages.

General education in terms of ability

So far, two ways of conceptualising a general education, in terms of knowledge, and in terms of culture, have been discussed. In the first case, the various categories of organised knowledge (subjects/ disciplines, integrated fields of study, themes, topics, forms of knowledge) provide the framework for thinking about the curriculum. In the second case, it is the culture (some would say society) and its various aspects or subsystems which provides the conceptual framework.

There is, however, a third way of thinking about general education, and that is in terms of ability or abilities. In the educational and psychological literature, ability often connotes intelligence, as measured by intelligence tests, or achievement in terms of the school curriculum. Here it will be used in the wider, more popular, and less exact sense, of anything that a person is able to do. Several years ago there was an advertisement for the army which bore the slogan: 'If you have it in you, we'll bring it out!' It is this very broad sense of actualising potential that is intended here, a sense that covers everything from quite specific aptitudes to that generalised change sometimes called 'growth' or 'development'.

It is common enough to hear general education described in these terms, both in the schools and in post-school education. Many lecturers in higher education would argue that they are concerned with the whole person; and even in vocational education, which is supposedly narrower, concern for the student as an individual has always been a characteristic of the thoughtful lecturer or job supervisor. Some forms of adult education are quite consciously person-centred or growth-centred rather than subject-centred, an emphasis which leads teachers to see themselves as tutors or facilitators rather than lecturers.

Hargreaves (1982), however, points to a discrepancy between what schoolteachers often say (and believe) about abilities, and what schools do, through their curriculum-assessment-value system:

> Other abilities and skills, apart from the intellectual cognitive ones, were not, even in the most conventional of grammar schools, totally ignored. Schools have always recognized that at least four other types – the aesthetic-artistic, the affective-emotional, the physical-manual, and the personal-social – have an important place in education. It is by no means uncommon to hear teachers and headteachers extolling their importance, or to read books on the curriculum and its objectives making a very similar plea. *In practice*, however, they tend to be given a secondary importance. They can never be removed from the curriculum, for the distinction between these five types of ability and skills is only analytic, and it would be impossible to teach, say, English language and literature without paying attention to the aesthetic-artistic, the affective-emotional and the personal-social. Yet those school subjects in which these have a particularly strong if not primary significance, such as art, craft, music, woodwork, drama and physical education (to mention just traditional curriculum fare), tend to appear on the timetable in the lowly status of one-period-a-week subjects and, as pupils become older, to become *optional* subjects. They are not, in short, subjects which are seen as essential and thus compulsory to young people. The hidden-curriculum message is clear: the only knowledge and skills which *really* count in school, especially for the older adolescent, are primarily intellectual-cognitive in content. (pages 51–2)

There are two issues here. First, are the five types of ability which Hargreaves identifies really distinguishable? Secondly, even if they are, should an equal emphasis be placed on each of them?

Hargreaves' categories are based on experience and analysis rather than systematic research. (For a similar French list, see Prost, 1983.) Nevertheless, the issue involved – the nature and structure of ability – has been a central concern of educational psychology ever since the growth of intelligence testing at the beginning of the century. Psychological thought has been pulled in two opposing directions on the issue. On the one side, there has been a tendency towards a unitary conception of ability as something very fundamental and generalised which underlies and permeates all manifestations of human intelligence, skill, and aptitude. This came to be labelled 'intelligence' or simply 'g', meaning general intelligence, and referred to what was described (sometimes) as general mental efficiency. The conceptualisation of 'g', which always has to be inferred from batteries of tests, has changed over the years. In the earlier research, it was often described in terms of 'reasoning'; more recently, it has been described in terms of 'processing'. The contrary tendency has been towards a pluralistic conception of human abilities, in which 'general' intelligence tends to disappear into a number of forms of more specific ability. This tendency was evident in, for example, Spearman's two-factor theory, Thurstone's notion of primary mental abilities, and Guilford's 'structure of intellect' which postulated 120 mental factors, along three dimensions (operations, contents, and products). An intermediate position, between the unitary and pluralist views, was suggested by Cattell (1971) who argued that a generalised intelligence could nevertheless be invested in particular directions or types of activity, only some of which would normally be associated with education. Gustafsson (1984) has provided useful summaries of these various models, and has advanced a unifying one of his own.[5]

The issues involved in the structure of abilities are complex and cannot be explored in detail here. The problem is partly conceptual (what do we mean by intelligence or ability, what does it include or exclude?) and partly methodological (what kinds of tests do we use to measure it, how do we analyse the data from such tests?). Hargreaves has suggested that schools claim to develop non-cognitive abilities as well as cognitive ones, but a lot depends on what one means by 'cognitive'. In its broad sense, cognitive can refer to any processing of information, and it is difficult to think of any activity which does not involve this. On the other hand, defined more narrowly (cf. Hargreaves' 'cognitive-intellectual') the term is closer to what in ordinary language might be called 'intellectual', 'cerebral', or 'academic'.

Nor do current trends in psychology resolve the problem. The 'cognitive revolution' has led to a great increase in the scope and detail of studies of cognitive processing which is, from this point of view anyway, a great advance on the 'assembly' models of behaviourism. However, as Michael Eysenck (1984) notes, the cognitive revolution shows a distressing tendency to go in all directions at once, so it becomes increasingly difficult to say what it is, or what it is not. In the last decade, there has nevertheless been a great deal of psychological research into central or general processes, and their likely components (Sternberg, 1982). Computing has influenced both the language and models of cognitive psychology (Simon, 1979a and b) and there has been a good deal of interest in what are called central strategies or executive strategies (Baron, 1978, 1985). The net result has been a reinforcement of generic models of intelligence and ability, although in much more componential detail than before. There have, however, been counter-vailing trends. The great mass of research on cognitive styles (Messick, 1978; Squires, 1981a) has investigated differences between people in the way they process information and approach problems. There is some ambiguity as to whether one is talking about relatively fixed 'styles', or flexible 'strategies' which the person can deploy at will, but the net effect has been to push the notion of ability in a more pluralistic direction. Writers on the subject tend to say that the opposing poles of each style (for example, convergent/divergent, serialist/holist, field-dependent/field-independent) may each be appropriate or valuable in particular circumstances: a case not so much of better and worse, as different. The main trends in cognitive psychology have also come under fire. Claxton (1980) has questioned the assumed generality of cognitive processes, and Allport in the same volume has argued that cognitive mechanisms may to some extent be content-specific, and 'called' by certain perceptual cues. Fredericksen et al. (1984) have argued that much more attention needs to be paid to 'social intelligence' in any taxonomy of cognitive abilities, and Sternberg's latest writing (1985a, 1985b) reaches out to include practical and tacit forms of intelligence. The extreme case has been put by Gardner (1983), who argues that there are at least six distinct kinds of intelligence: linguistic; musical; logic-mathematical; spatial; bodily-kinaesthetic; and personal.

One of the most interesting recent contributions to the generic/specific debate on ability has been that of Fodor (1983) in his *Modularity of Mind*. Fodor argues that the mind processes information in both generic and specific ways. The inputs of visual, auditory, linguistic, and other data are analysed by systems which are specifically dedicated to those kinds of information; such processes are, he believes, domain-specific, modular, autonomous, hard-wired, and encapsulated. By contrast, the central processes of mind serve the 'fixation of perceptual belief'. They handle the tasks of general problem-formulation and problem-solving, with a potentially unlimited frame of reference. Far from being modular and limited in their scope, they can take account of, or relate, any kind of information that is at hand. It is impossible to do justice to Fodor's tightly-argued thesis in the space available here, or indeed to the complexities of the overall debate about the structure of ability/abilities. Though the kinds of psychological arguments for the specific nature of some cognitive processing do not automatically translate into something like Hargreaves' five types of ability, they may in the longer term move educational thinking in that direction.

The educational and social arguments in favour of distinguishing between different types, as distinct from levels, of ability have already been clearly spelled out by Cross (1976), drawing on the work of Taylor (1968) and McClelland (1973).[6] A single measure of ability, normally distributed, ensures that 50 per cent of the population will automatically be 'below average' – in other words, will see themselves as relative failures. Two unrelated measures of ability increase the chance of being above average on one measure to 75 per cent, three unrelated measures to 87.5 per cent, and so on. It is unlikely that the kinds of ability being measured are totally unrelated; one of the problems that arises with the 'specific' view of abilities is how such abilities become organised or related in the whole that is the student. However, as Cross argues, the answer to the problem of the inequality of educational achievements lies not in trying to fudge failure, or in criterion-referenced tests, which simply shift the grounds of comparison, but in pluralising the criteria of success. Most people will be relatively good at something; and any experience of relative success at school is more likely to predispose them to continue learning and studying throughout their lives. It is the peculiar narrowness of the criteria used by the school system which defines so many pupils as relative failures; not only that, such criteria are much narrower than the broad range of types of ability and competence needed in the world of work and in adult life. In particular, Cross argues, the school system undervalues manipulative and practical skills, and virtually ignores the interpersonal skills which are a key element in many jobs in the service sector, not to mention private and social life. And Eisner (1982) has argued powerfully for the importance of the aesthetic-artistic not as a frill or luxury, but in terms of how we orient ourselves to our world.

It has been necessary to spell out the arguments about the structure of ability/abilities here at some length, because this is the least familiar of the three dimensions or bases for general education. Clearly, there is much more that could be said on the subject, but there is room here only to make three final points. First, even if distinct types of ability exist, it does not necessarily follow that they can be systematically developed through teaching; indeed, the word 'gift' implies that they cannot. If Fodor is correct in his assumption that some forms of input analysis are both highly specific and 'hard-wired', then the extent to which, say, a sense of pitch, or perception of line, or feel for tactile consistency, can be altered or developed, may be limited. Such doubts probably centre most on the artistic and bodily-kinaesthetic domains. On the other hand, if teachers and students are constantly told that violinists, painters, or potters are born not made, it is hardly surprising that inability tends to be attributed to some inherent deficit, rather than educational and other circumstances; and indeed there are plenty of examples, not least in adult education, where people have been enabled to develop talents which they were quite convinced they never had.

Second, even if a certain type of ability exists, it does not follow that it should be developed, or given the same emphasis as other abilities. The main doubts in this case centre not on the arts, but on interpersonal abilities or skills. As Cross notes, there is a good deal of resistance to the idea of teaching people to relate to other people, even though this is now a normal and apparently effective part of many kinds of occupational training.[7] There is some evidence even that abilities that are usually thought of as 'given', such as empathy, can be systematically developed and applied (Natale, 1972; Portal, 1983). There is a continuing interest in personal and social education in the schools (Pring, 1984). Nevertheless, there is the feeling that this kind of thing is intrusive, manipulative, and unnatural. It must be pointed out here that just as such abilities and skills can be used for good or ill (social skills training can be applied to counselling, nursing, indoctrinating, or interrogating), so can rationality and reasoning. There is nothing in cognitive development that guarantees beneficent application or use; recent history provides many examples of planning and problem-solving applied to destruction and death.

The last point to be made about the structure of abilities will arise again in later chapters. The rhetoric of compulsory education has often gone beyond what Hargreaves described as five different kinds of ability, to a more general commitment to 'development' or 'developing potential', in personal, moral, or spiritual terms. 'Character' was and still is to some extent a central concept; the muscular Christianity of the Victorian public school indeed often seemed to place moral and spiritual development above cognitive development. In a more secular and less consensual age, such emphases have perhaps weakened in the schools, but paradoxically the

literature on adult education now shows a central concern with
'development' in these broader senses. The basis for such thinking
is not Victorian Christianity and notions of character, leadership,
and teamwork, but twentieth-century writing, often American, on
'human potential', 'humanistic psychology', and 'life-span development'. This literature will be discussed in more detail in Chapter 6.
Here, however, some problems must be noted. There is a good
deal of disagreement about the description of stages in such
development; what follows what, and when. There is even more
disagreement about the normative aspects of such schemes. Why is
X better or 'higher' than Y? Is 'potential' potential for evil as well as
good? How far do notions about development reflect the values of
particular cultures, particular social classes, men or women, at
particular times? The analysis of the structure of abilities in this
section has been couched largely in descriptive terms; such abilities
exist or do not exist, are distinct or less distinct – likewise the
analysis of forms of knowledge, and subsystems of the culture.
Indeed, the whole concept of general education has been
approached descriptively; there is nothing about generality *per se*
which is necessarily *good*. However, people who write about general
education typically do so because they believe it is not only general,
but good; that the forms of knowledge comprise human rationality
which is intrinsically desirable; that an analysis of culture will lead
to a better society; that the development of abilities will lead to
fuller lives. Because the aim here has been to produce a descriptive,
analytic framework, the discussion in this section has been in terms
of abilities rather than development or potential. But that does not
quite solve the problem; for values impinge on facts in subtle as well
as obvious ways. The point made in Chapter 1, that even our
descriptive concepts are not 'free-floating', means that even in the
present largely analytic exercise, a certain normative element is
unavoidable.

The dimensions of general education

What is a general education? In what way or ways may a general
education be general? In attempting to answer these questions, this
chapter has explored three kinds of reply. An education may be
called general if it introduces people to the complete range of forms
of knowledge. Hirst, it will be recalled, suggested seven or eight
distinct domains: mathematics, the physical sciences, the human
sciences and history, literature and the fine arts, morals, religion,

and philosophy. Together, these comprise our main means of understanding the world; they constitute what we usually call 'mind'; and they form the necessary basis for progression to higher levels of study. Lawton, by contrast, took as his starting-point not the concept of knowledge but that of culture, and identified eight structures or subsystems of any culture for which students must be equipped: social; economic; communication; rationality; technology; morality; belief; and aesthetic. To omit any of these would be to disadvantage the student and give him a partial or limited induction to his social world. Hargreaves identified five types of ability or skill that schools often claim (if speciously) to develop: cognitive-intellectual; aesthetic-artistic; affective-emotional; physical-manual) and personal-social. A general education, on this basis, is one which gives an adequate emphasis to each of these, rather than stressing one at the expense, or to the exclusion, of others. It should be noted that this third approach is not an individualistic one, to be contrasted with the societal frame of reference of the second. It is not a question of the familiar, if misleading, antithesis between individual and society, but of a quite different dimension and mode of analysis. Abilities, after all, are both 'social' and 'individual'.

Several points can be made in conclusion. First, the purpose of this analysis has not been to devise a blueprint of a common core school curriculum.[8] Thus there has been no discussion of how these frameworks might be used either singly or together to plan such a curriculum, or to what extent they are embodied in current curriculum patterns in secondary education. All that will be said here is that in so far as schools see general education as a desirable thing, there are strong arguments for planning in terms of all three, rather than one or two, of the above dimensions. A common curriculum planned entirely in terms of forms of knowledge may ill-equip students to live as adults in their society, and define out certain important types of ability and talent. A curriculum planned entirely in cultural terms may fail to provide an adequate foundation for the study of organised knowledge at higher levels, and likewise be narrowly cognitive. One that concentrates on the development of abilities may end up doing so without reference to bodies of knowledge, and in a social vacuum.

The argument goes further, however. Whichever basis is used for planning a general education – knowledge, culture, or abilities – these three aspects are always present. One cannot have a curriculum which is somehow concept-free, contextless, or mindless. All forms of knowledge are culturally located and involve cognitive processes; all cultural subsystems are conceptualised and involve

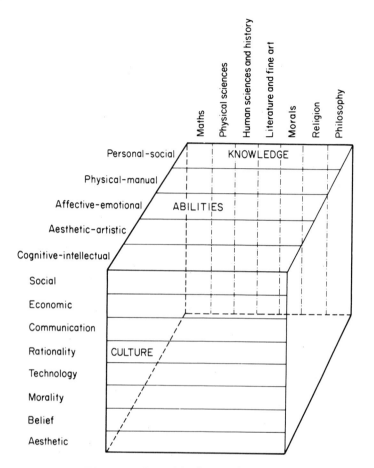

Figure 1   A model of general education

cognitive processes; and all cognitive processes have some content and cultural context. It therefore seems more useful to think of these three models or approaches as three dimensions of a general education (see Figure 1). Some dimensions may be ignored or undervalued in the planning, but that does not mean they are not there: they simply have not been thought through.

A three-dimensional model of this kind only provides a general framework for thinking about general education, not a detailed guide to planning. It is not meant to imply that all the elements in the model should automatically receive equal emphasis; nor does it indicate how such aims and emphases should be translated into the curriculum-in-action.

It also shelves the more abstract arguments about whether knowledge is a social construct or society a mental construct. However, it seems potentially useful as a framework for analysing existing examples of general education, and in particular highlighting gaps in them; and, more to the point here, it provides a basis for bringing some kind of order to the manifold forms of the curriculum beyond school.

NOTES

1 I am indebted here to a paper by W. Mitter (1984) on the relationship between general and vocational education, which argues that the latter is only one of several forms of special education. However, since special education in English connotes education of the handicapped, I have used the term 'specific' instead, and occasionally its opposite, 'generic', instead of 'general'. On the Continent, general education tends to connote academic models of general education.

2 Crittenden (1982) provides a useful account of the arguments for and against, and a summary of various proposals for core curricula. For a critical view, see Tripp and Watt (1984); and for two American perspectives, see Warren (1982) and Boyer (1983).

3 The concept of common-sense knowledge or everyday knowledge owes a good deal to Berger and Luckmann (1971), who in turn drew on the work of Alfred Schutz and ultimately the later work of Husserl. See also the work of Garfinkel (1967) and other ethnomethodologists.

4 See Kuhn (1962), and also Lakatos and Musgrave (1970) for some of the subsequent debate.

5 There is also a useful analysis of this issue in terms of the number and structure of factors in Sternberg (1985a), who seems to suggest that the answer one comes up with is partly a function of what one is looking for, and that both unitary and pluralistic views have some justification. This would throw the argument back to curricular and educational criteria rather than purely psychological ones.

6 The opposing view, that standard cognitive measures are central to the measurement and prediction of all abilities, is represented by Ghiselli (1966) and Kline (1975). As noted earlier, it depends what one means by cognitive; but I am attracted to Fodor's model because it seems to accommodate both generic processes and specific abilities. In concrete terms, even if one has a very good sense of pitch or rhythm or movement, one still needs to be able to analyse problems, learn from feedback, consider related phenomena, and so on, to develop them.

7   Part of the problem with 'social abilities' lies in conceptualising them. What are they? It seems to me that many jobs involving such abilities (and the training for them) involve a combination of projection (coming across) and empathy (putting yourself in someone's place). Comedians clearly need the first, counsellors the second; but I would suggest that many jobs need a bit of both. However, it is interesting, first, that alternative emphases seem possible in some occupations (hard sell versus soft sell in sales work, different 'methods' in acting); and second, that some people may naturally take to one better than the other (the charismatic lecturer versus the sensitive tutor).

8   It should be noted that the design of core curricula in schools is affected by the extent to which certain tasks are seen to be the responsibility of the school rather than of the family, community, church, youth organisations, etc.; and the age at which the core curriculum gives way, or at least gives room, to more specific curricula. Another important question has to do with the level of achievement expected of children across the core. I would be in favour of the argument for, and recent moves towards, criterion-referenced measurement here (see Popham, 1978), since the underlying purpose of assessment at this stage should, I think, be to register competency rather than to select. However, I would suggest that two levels of achievement (basic and general) are appropriate, following Cross's (1976) argument that we can reasonably expect nearly everyone to be good at a few things and adequate at everything else. The aims and curricula at the two levels might therefore be rather different; in physical education, for example, the basic level might be much closer to what is done in adult keep fit and associated classes than to what goes on in PE in many schools currently, with all its emphasis on competitive performance. As regards the scope of the core, I would suggest that one could do justice to the three dimensions of the model with about nine fields of study: language; mathematics and computing; humanities; social studies; natural science; craft and technology; human relations; physical and health education; and creative arts. I would also argue the need for relatively unrestricted individual learning projects, of the kind described by Tough (see Chapter 6). From the point of view of post-school education, failure is probably more serious than irrelevance. Irrelevance can be attributed to the teacher or the system and shrugged off; failure, I suspect, is often attributed partly to oneself (see Hargreaves, 1982, p. 63) and can create profound resistance to continuing education. It seems to me that attribution theory (see Eiser, 1978) has a good deal to offer in the analysis of these problems.

3 Specific Education

The curriculum beyond school

It was noted in the Introduction that education beyond school is extraordinarily diverse – so diverse, indeed, that it is difficult to conceive of it as a whole, let alone speak of a system. To begin with, it is usual to refer to various 'sectors', such as further education (often subdivided into non-advanced and advanced), higher education, adult education and industrial training, although the boundaries between these are to some extent unclear or arbitrary. Then within each sector, one can identify different types of institution or agency: within higher education, universities, polytechnics, and colleges or institutes of higher education; within adult education, local authority services, university extra-mural departments, and voluntary bodies; and so forth. Any one of these institutions or agencies is likely to provide a wide range of courses involving tens or hundreds of subject headings, leading to a bewildering range of qualifications. The conditions of access, the methods of delivery and teaching, the modes of attendance, and the patterns of assessment may all vary considerably. And all this refers only to what is called 'formal' provision; beyond it lies a vast hinterland of less formal types of teaching and learning, including on-the-job training, in-the-community projects, the educative work of libraries, galleries, museums, and the mass media, the incidental learning involved in many leisure and social activities, and the largely hidden domain of private study: activities which shade off in various directions into work, recreation, social relationships, politics, therapy, reflection, and, indeed, any of the familiar activities of the average adult.

This rich diversity and complexity suggests that any model of the curriculum beyond school will not be simple, and will be a good deal less compact than the three-dimensional cube displayed in Figure 1 above. Many, and perhaps most post-school courses have a specific purpose, orientation, or leaning, and that specificity is indicated by the terms and labels that are commonly used. In higher education, many courses are officially or informally labelled 'academic', and there are frequent references to academic standards, academic freedom, and academic values. There is a Council for National Academic Awards (CNAA) which validates courses in public sector higher education. Equally, there are frequent references to professional courses, which may be partly planned or influenced by professional bodies. We habitually speak of the medical, legal, engineering, and teaching professions, not to mention others. In the further education sector, the term 'vocational' is widely used, as in the new Certificate of Pre-Vocational Education (CPVE), and for adults there is the current emphasis on Post-Experience Vocational Education (PEVE). The term 'liberal' is enshrined in the terms of reference of university extra-mural departments and the titles of liberal studies departments in further education colleges, while the term 'recreational' is contained in the paragraphs (see below) of the 1944 Education Act relating to non-vocational post-compulsory education. The Adult Literacy and Basic Skills Unit (ALBSU) stimulates and co-ordinates much of the work in adult basic education, and the importance of role education for adults was spelled out in the Russell Report (1973). Finally, the education or preparation of people to teach in all branches of education is referred to as 'teacher education' and is the concern of the relevant professional and statutory bodies such as the Council for the Accreditation of Teacher Education (CATE).

All these headings appear in Figure 2. There are also three other, rather vaguer headings: social education covering a wide range of things from discrete social skills training, through social studies to community education or development; personal education which refers specifically to courses which aim to develop personal effectiveness or awareness, but which spills over into counselling and is an aspect of many other courses; and general education referring both to general education courses taken after compulsory schooling (such as O levels) and courses which have a more generic purpose or scope.

The headings that are used in Figure 2 are thus ones which are either institutional ones, or are commonly used in writing or talking about education beyond school. The model therefore matches the reality reasonably well, and indicates the range and specificity of most post-school education. Models, however, are more useful if they not only describe but help one to analyse, and it is in this sense that the model is more problematic. The three key dimensions of general education – knowledge, culture, and ability – can still be

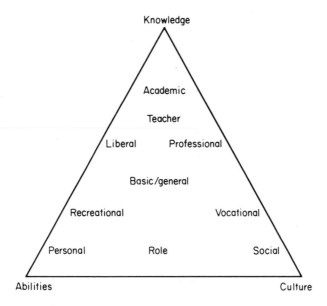

Figure 2   The curriculum beyond school

used. Academic education is clearly conceptualised in terms of bodies of knowledge, disciplines, or interdisciplinary fields. The criteria used in planning and assessing courses are primarily epistemological criteria, to do with reasoning, evidence, argument, verification, logic, and so on. At the other points of the triangle, the planning of social education courses of whatever kind is clearly carried out with prime reference to society, or in Lawton's terms, culture; and courses in personal development with reference to concepts such as ability, capacity and potential, growth or development.

It would be a nonsense, however, to suggest that the curricular reality is uni-dimensional or two-dimensional; that academic courses exist in a social vacuum, or do not involve abilities and potential; or that there is no knowledge content or development of skills in social education. This model is presented in two-dimensional form in order to emphasise the characteristic specificity of post-compulsory education in both purpose and scope, as compared with the schools; but there are always three dimensions involved, and the reality of the curriculum beyond school lies somewhere between the two models, in a tension which is impossible to represent graphically. Likewise, the headings in the models should not be seen as discrete or isolated; they are, rather, identifiable points in a complex field of force. The curriculum, beyond as well as during school, is a locus of tensions. In any engineers' or teachers' course, there will be a tension between academic and professional criteria; vocational courses involve social and role elements; recreational courses may involve personal and social elements; and the concept of liberal education can be interpreted in personal and social as well as purely academic terms. The model, like most models of social reality, is inadequate; but it will be used here because it seems to relate the existing institutional or conventional categories of post-school education to the more abstract issues of curriculum theory. With the above qualifications in mind, therefore, we will devote the rest of this chapter to a fleshing out of the headings used in the model, in order to develop a more powerful language and framework for talking about post-school curricula in subsequent chapters.

Academic education

The term 'academic' in the United Kingdom is applied, broadly speaking, to higher education. This is evident from studies such as Halsey and Trow's *The British Academics* (1971) or Startup's (1979) more recent work.[1] Within higher education it is used more often of universities than of public-sector higher education, though how far this is simply a matter of habit or snobbishness is not clear. And within the universities, it is most often applied to courses which are not obviously professional or applied in orientation: single or joint honours degrees in English, history, mathematics, chemistry, sociology, and so forth. The term is also sometimes used to describe those lines or streams of upper secondary education which lead directly on to higher education, though the words 'pre-academic', 'grammar', and 'general' are also used. And of course it can have a pejorative connotation, as when someone says that a problem is 'purely academic', meaning that it has no practical implications.

Despite the fact that the term is so widely used, it is not without ambiguity. It is of course an ancient word, carrying with it echoes of earlier usages (the groves of academe, the dissenting academies) and bearing relations with other terms and phrases: scholars and scholarship, dons and donnishness, clerisy and the *trahison des clercs*. But the fundamental ambiguity has to do with the nature of the activity, or activities, as now conceived and practised. There would probably be general agreement that the word 'academic' refers to the advancement and transmission of knowledge at a high level, though some might also want to add the connotation of reflection or reflectiveness, a disinterested contemplation of the world. Advancement connotes research or scholarship; transmission connotes teaching; and it is the relationship between these two activities that is at issue. At one extreme the academic is primarily a researcher or scholar who makes his work visible or accessible to students, so that they can follow his train of thought or line of research. This is less teaching in a didactic sense than exposing, or allowing participation in the process. The model is rather like a craft one, with the master surrounded by his willing and curious apprentices. At the other extreme, the academic is primarily a teacher, who is aware of, and can draw on research and scholarship in what he teaches. He transmits and interprets, rather than discovers or invents. In between these two extremes of the academic as researcher and the academic as teacher, there is every shade of grey; and the shade may change not only from one discipline to another, but at different stages in an academic's working life.

The 'balance' between teaching and research, and the relationship between them is a live and contentious issue in higher education in the United Kingdom. On the one hand, there has been a long-term historical trend, which some date from the eighteenth-century Scottish universities, and others from the nineteenth-century German ones, for research to be seen as *the* essential element of academic work. This has manifested itself in the elaboration of post-graduate research structures (the advent of Masters and PhD degrees) and also in the numbers of students, and proportion of staff time, devoted (notionally or really) to research. It is with something of a shock that one remembers that much nineteenth-century research in the United Kingdom was carried out by eccentric geniuses such as Darwin and Galton quite outside the higher education system, and that the PhD was an early twentieth-century import. Research has become almost entirely institutionalised, and most funding bodies will not even consider making grants to researchers who do not have an institutional affiliation.[2]

The impact of the growth of research has had three main effects on the undergraduate curriculum. First, it has tended to reinforce the boundaries of disciplines, since although there is some interdisciplinary research, it is often perceived as being a high-risk enterprise, and peripheral to the mainstream of work in each discipline. Secondly, research imposes a gradient of specialisation. If one is going to do doctoral research in a very specific aspect of a discipline, one cannot long delay specialising in that discipline, and prior to that, in a handful of disciplines. This gradient is particularly steep in the United Kingdom, which has a very compressed system in terms of age, and its effects reach down into the lower secondary curriculum, to the ages of 12 or 13. Thirdly, research reinforces the importance of methodology and procedure. One facet of the growth of the research emphasis in the nineteenth century was a concern not simply with problems, but with the 'meta-problem' of how to know, how to discover, how to find out. The concept of method or methodology is central to the activity of research, and this rather abstract emphasis is transmitted downwards through the undergraduate curriculum. How many a lecture has been devoted to describing, in loving and painstaking detail, the methodological problems inherent in one's own (or more often, someone else's) research!

The long-term growth of emphasis on research has been countered in several ways. The tradition of the academic as teacher and tutor was and is still alive, though in some cases it was no doubt simply an excuse for not doing any research. More recently, however, the dominance of research has been challenged on both economic and educational grounds. Can a mass, or at least large, system of higher education afford to have every lecturer (notionally) devoting 30 per cent of his or her time to research? Does the country really need so much? Would it not be better to concentrate research in fewer, larger, and better departments or institutions? Can we afford to conduct research on anything and everything, or should we be more selective? Likewise, one may doubt the relevance of research-oriented curricula to a greatly enlarged body of undergraduates. It may have been appropriate when only 2 per cent of the age-group were in higher education; but how can a minority occupation provide the appropriate orientation for 13 or 20 per cent?

The arguments about the right balance or relationship between research and teaching may, however, obscure what is arguably a more profound development in academic education: namely, the professionalisation of academe. Both research and teaching are now overwhelmingly carried out within professional frameworks. The maverick teacher is as suspect as the maverick researcher. Academic occupations are finely demarcated horizontally and regulated vertically. Labels and identities are clearly established and carefully maintained; and upward progression through the system is controlled by a series of gate-keeping procedures (first degree, higher degree, post-doctoral work, publication, and so on). The whole structure is reinforced by the existence of professional societies, conferences, and journals.

All this is very well, except that many academics would argue that they, and the education they provide, is not merely or purely professional: to them, the word 'academic' connotes something else, something that goes under the heading of 'liberal education' or 'general education', or 'knowledge for its own sake'. Paradoxically, too academic a perception of purpose may narrow or limit higher education, as manifest in undergraduate studies, in ways which 'professionalise' it in a pejorative sense. The consequent tensions between academic, professional, and liberal education will underlie much of the discussion in Chapter 5.

Teacher education

The heading closest to that of 'academic education' in Figure 2 is 'teacher education'.[3] This refers to the education or training of teachers, typically teachers in primary and secondary schools. In the United Kingdom, teachers in further, higher, and adult education do not come through the 'normal channels' of teacher education, and in fact many of them are not trained to teach at all, despite recent initiatives in these sectors to institute either pre-service or in-service training. Teacher education in the United Kingdom leads to 'qualified teacher status', which is a professional licence to practise in the schools (there is no similar status in post-school education) and which should be distinguished from the study of education as an academic field. Although for many years many teachers were trained or educated in separate 'monotechnic' teachers' colleges, in recent years the policy has been to integrate such training, and institutions, into broader, polyvalent courses and institutions. Thus teacher education is now institutionally firmly within the ambit of higher education, a tendency accentuated by the move towards longer courses and an all-graduate profession. There has also always been a second post-graduate route into the profession, especially at the higher levels, through post-graduate certificates in education. Despite these precedents and trends, the status of education as a field, and teachers as a profession, has always been a little uncertain. There have been doubts both about the 'academic' credentials of education, and the professional status of teachers. Perhaps it has been a subconscious desire to quell these doubts which has led to the demise of 'teacher training' in favour of 'teacher education'. (A parallel shift has taken place in other fields, such as nursing, perhaps for similar reasons.) 'Education' connotes something broader, more theoretical, more academic, than training, which has unwelcome associations with manual labour.

There are many more teachers than academic researchers in the education system, and because the nature of teaching varies considerably from one sector to another, it is difficult to generalise about teacher education. Like research, much teaching uses the conventional discipline/subject categories and thus tends to reinforce them, though this is less the case in vocational, primary and some adult education. The gradient of specialisation imposed on the curriculum by teaching is less steep than that imposed by academic research: a 'joint honours' degree is often appropriate for secondary school teaching, whereas single honours (specialising in one discipline) is more suitable for research. Teaching, like academic work, also stresses process, but it is the teaching–learning process rather than the process of scholarship or research. Teaching, even more than research, refers back to the education system, and a common criticism of teachers is that they have no real experience of the 'outside world' having moved from school to college/university and back to school again. Teaching in higher education is typically knowledge-centred, but even there a tension between that orientation and an orientation towards society or personal development may be felt. The same may be said of the pre-academic streams of upper secondary education, but the pressure to see teaching in a social or personal light is much greater in other parts of the education system.

It may seem surprising, in view of the analysis of general education in the last chapter, to locate teaching nearest the knowledge point of the triangle (see Figure 2). However, the diagram refers to teacher education rather than teaching, and teacher education is typically more knowledge-oriented than teaching itself. Indeed, a familiar complaint about teacher education is that it is too abstract, theoretical, and discipline-bound, and too little concerned with or derived from the practice or praxis of teaching.[4] The preparation of teachers involves conventional disciplines not only as content (to become a physics/chemistry teacher) but as foundations for the study of education. The latter usually involves some study of history, philosophy, psychology, and sociology. In the light of this heavy emphasis on organised knowledge, it seems appropriate to locate most forms of teacher education in the 'knowledge' corner, while recognising the significant pull of both 'culture' and 'ability'; whether teacher education *should* be so knowledge-oriented is another matter. Nevertheless, it can be noted here that there is often a tension between the 'academic' and 'professional' orientations in the education of teachers, the first emphasising the knowledge base of the activity, and the second the analysis of, and competence in, practice. Less common, but also interesting, is the issue of teacher education as a form of role education, indicating an emphasis not on knowledge, or competence, but on the patterns of behaviour which are expected of teachers.

Professional education

'Professional education' will be used here to refer to preparation for any occupation which has some autonomy in regulating its own affairs, and which has a substantial knowledge base.[5] Professional bodies typically have at least some control over who enters the profession (and often how many) and who is ejected from it. Increasingly, professional bodies also regulate who stays in the profession, through mandatory continuing education requirements. Professional ethics stress autonomy, collegiality, responsibility, judgement, and service. Professions also typically have some form of special knowledge or expertise which only members of that profession are supposed to possess and use. The idea of protection of the public is often invoked to justify such restrictions, although it is not always clear that it is the public's safety, rather than the professional's income or prestige, which is at stake. The growth of do-it-yourself divorce and conveyancing have tested the exclusivity of the legal profession, just as various forms of fringe or self-help medicine have provoked varying reactions from doctors.

Professional education reflects this dual aspect of professions: it is based on some form of special, hieratic knowledge, and it passes on a form of special ethic or set of norms. Both of these are long-established and relatively clear in the case of lawyers and doctors, and the special ethic is actually made explicit in the latter case in the Hippocratic Oath which all doctors, except those in communist countries, take. The other oft-cited profession of engineering is less clear-cut, partly because it is subdivided into sharply differentiated groups (civil engineers, marine engineers, and so on) and partly because, whereas one either is or is not a doctor or solicitor, one can be a 'technician engineer' or 'engineering technician' and, in the public mind, as well as in some job specifications, these distinctions are rather vague.[6]

The term 'professional education' has, however, come to refer to occupations other than the traditional professions in recent years. It is now often contrasted with academic or general education, and covers fields as various as town planning, nursing, management, computing, public administration, social work, estate management, and library science.

Indeed, the terms 'professional', 'professionalism' and 'professional education' increasingly seem to refer to the two characteristics of professions – the special knowledge and the special norms – rather than to the professions themselves. It will therefore be used here in this wider, and less exact, sense.

Neither professional education nor professional-type occupations are concerned solely with the *transmission* of knowledge and norms; in each case, innovation takes place, sometimes through a gradual evolutionary shift (nursing might be an example), sometimes a sudden technological breakthrough (laser surgery) or a radical questioning of practice (such as the rise and fall of modernism in architecture). However, the word 'transmission' does appear to be particularly apt in describing professional education because it embodies two common features and requirements: first, the passing on of a certain necessary minimum level of expertise, without which the student will not be able or indeed allowed to practise; and second, the process of socialisation into the profession, which is evident in both the structure (often relatively self-contained and isolated) and length of studies. It is not surprising that students of law, medicine, engineering, architecture, social work, and other professional fields are often seen as slightly separate from the rest of the student body, with their own timetables, buildings, common rooms, and even societies. Nor is it surprising that the length of studies (including pre-professional practice) is seen as being so important in professional education. Periodic attempts are made to spring-clean professional curricula, and get rid of obsolete knowledge, skills, and practices, in order to cut back on the time and cost involved in 'forming' (to use the French term) an engineer or doctor or architect. But somehow these attempts at rationalisation are never very successful. It may be, as professional people are always saying, that new knowledge and techniques are always knocking on the curriculum door; but equally the notion of 'serving one's time', explicit in vocational education, is implicit in professional education. In part, this may be a reflection of the fact that, however well planned a syllabus may be, professional work is apt to throw up the unexpected very suddenly, and the longer one studies or trains the more likely one is to come up against a variety of problems and to develop a capacity for coping with the improbable. However, it is obvious that the longer the period of study and preparation, the more likely it is that the waverers or deviants will drop out, or be 'cooled out', and that those who remain will conform more readily to the ethos of the profession.

The social nature of professional education suggests that it should be placed somewhere between a knowledge-orientation and culture-orientation in the model. It is like vocational education in its orientation towards work, but distinguished from it by the relative strength of its knowledge base and the autonomy that derives partly from that. It is close to role education in that one 'is' a doctor or engineer or social worker, in addition to doing those things; but it is role education for a specific social and economic purpose.

It is worth noting that many professional courses have deliberately introduced a 'social' element into the curriculum in recent years. Titles like 'The Engineer and Society' or 'Law in its Social Context', or 'Medicine and the Community' indicate an opening up of social aspects of professional practice. In some cases the impetus for this has come from higher education; in other cases from the professional body. Either way, such innovations are nearly always under pressure from the need to 'cover' the essential knowledge and competences of the field.

There are two other major issues that arise currently in professional education. The first is the control of the curriculum. Professional education is education for a purpose, and how that purpose is defined can reflect the influence of practitioners in the field, professional bodies, 'academic-professionals' who teach the courses, academic institutions and bodies (such as the UGC, CNAA) and others. One or other group may feel that a given curriculum is too theoretical, too broad, too narrow, or below academic standards. It is not uncommon to find a certain distrust between those who practise and those who teach, with the practitioners complaining that the academics are 'out of touch' and the academics complaining that those in the field present an impossibly wide range of demands. Such tensions are mitigated by the existence of teacher-practitioners, who perform a dual role, by overlapping membership of significant committees, and by the assimilation of higher education to professional norms in terms of the structure of the academic profession itself. Indeed, radical critics of professional restrictive practices would argue that such dissensions are merely ripples on the surface of an underlying consensus, which aims at maintaining existing relativities of wealth and power. In terms of the curriculum, it may be useful to ask how far professional education is or should be influenced by parties outside the professional domain altogether – for example, consumer or public interest representatives. After all, it is the public which receives or uses the services of doctors, solicitors, town planners, social workers, and the like, and mechanisms for client representation already exist in relation to some of these (for example, transport users' committees, health service consultative committees). It would seem logical to extend such a principle beyond professional practice, to professional formation.

The other major issue in professional education is the updating, retraining and reorientation that become necessary in a period of rapid social and technological change. Such continuing education provision can take many forms, formal and non-formal, and is more common in some professions than in others. A review of developments in the United States has been provided by Houle (1980). In some cases provision is allied to 'recertification': a practitioner may lose his or her licence to practise if the requirements are not fulfilled. There is increasing interest in this field of activity in the United Kingdom, and it will be considered along with other forms of continuing education in Chapter 6.

Vocational education

Of all the reasons why people continue their formal education beyond the end of compulsory schooling, work is the chief one in quantitative terms. More people enrol on post-compulsory courses more often and for longer because of work than for any other reason. Not only does work provide the rationale for nearly all 'traditional' and 'new' further education; it also accounts for a great part of the demand for higher education, and is frequently cited even in supposedly non-vocational adult education as a reason for attendance. The recent policy emphasis on continuing education at all levels is work-related. Government support for post-compulsory education is typically, though not exclusively, related to its proximity to employment and the economy. Even non-formal adult learning is frequently vocational.[7]

If the relationship between post-compulsory education and work is ubiquitous and intimate it is also very complex. In principle, vocational education can be derived directly from the labour market. Manpower analysis indicates how many people in each job are needed, and job analysis (subdivided into task and skill analysis) specifies what each job entails. One should therefore know how many plumbers, software engineers, or radiographers the country needs, and what their training should consist of.

However, the process of derivation is straightforward in neither case. The problems of manpower analysis lie beyond the scope of this book; each of the main techniques of forecasting has its theoretical drawbacks, which have been clearly analysed by Blaug (1970). In practice, manpower forecasting has had very mixed success, even in the centrally planned command economies, where not only education but also the movement of labour can be controlled (Fulton, 1982).

It might seem that even if one cannot determine exactly how many workers are needed in a particular field, it should at least be possible to specify the nature of the work that is done, and to derive vocational curricula from those specifications. In broad terms, job analysis can and does provide the basis for vocational education. There is an external point of reference, which is invoked both in the syllabus headings and the process of teaching ('You'll never get by if you can't do...', 'You'll find this crops up time and again', 'You may as well get used to being on time/clean/well-dressed/precise/organised now because once you get into work ...').

However, there are at least eight reasons why the derivation of vocational curricula from job analysis is not a straightforward matter, and it is worth listing them and commenting briefly on each of them.

(1) *Classification* As Benner (1982) has pointed out, occupational classifications and training classifications do not necessarily coincide, since they have been devised for dissimilar uses: the first for demographic and economic purposes, the second for educational/accreditation purposes.

(2) *Interaction* Over the longer term, the structure of vocational education and qualifications may affect the structure of occupations; the influence is not all one-way (see Lutz, 1981).

(3) *Diversity* The same 'job' may in fact involve different skills and emphases in different environments. Small firms may expect people to carry out a wider range of tasks than large firms; large firms may use more up-to-date technology and techniques than small firms.

(4) *Change* Vocational curricula are expected to equip students for immediate employment, but also to underpin their work for years, if not decades. It is difficult to strike the right balance between present and future needs, and to know what the latter will be.

(5) *Substitution* People do not always work in the jobs they were formally trained for. They may 'lower their sights' and work in a job below their competence; they may upgrade themselves, by learning on the job or taking additional training; or they may

work in areas which are near to or cognate with the one for which they were trained.[8]

(6) *Divergence* Vocational curricula may diverge from job needs for a number of reasons: equipment may become out-of-date and teachers out-of-touch; academic drift may lead to courses becoming more and more abstract and theoretical, in line with educational value-systems; or work practices may become ossified.

(7) *Incompleteness* Job analyses and labour contracts are typically incomplete in that they do not specify the 'intensity' of work, or the attitude or approach to it; there is, as it were, an invisible handshake as well.[9] Hence vocational education is also likely to be only a partial preparation for actual work.

(8) *Level* It is not easy to pitch training at the right level. Whereas too low a level will obviously not prepare trainees adequately for the job, and too high a level may create false expectations as well as wasting money, there are arguments for a slight degree of over-training: it equips people to handle unusual problems, enables them to upgrade processes, may reduce the stress that comes from just coping, and avoids the downtime that results from an inability to do basic repairs or maintenance.

The eight factors described briefly above make the derivation of vocational curricula from job analysis far from straightforward. It must be pointed out, however, that vocational education continues to exist, and indeed to thrive on government and private support, despite these difficulties. To some extent the problems listed above are coped with by institutionalising them: that is, by attempting to represent the various tensions and interests on planning and examining bodies. Such bodies have for a long time contained representatives of a wide range of interests: employers, large and small, trade unions, teachers, government departments, subject specialists, and so on. Thus vocational education policy is characterised by a continual dissatisfaction, negotiation, and jockeying for position which is never wholly resolved, because it never can be: the demands on vocational curricula are inherently multiple. Such curricula are always being criticised by someone as being too narrow, too broad, too short-sighted, too airy-fairy, too old-fashioned, too rigid, and so forth.

The other way in which vocational education seems to cope with the conflicting demands made upon it is by a certain pragmatism. Of all the forms of post-school education in the United Kingdom vocational education is least given to philosophising and reflecting on the nature of the enterprise: there is a strong ethos of 'getting on with the job', of 'hard-headed realism', which pervades the staff and students in the typical college of further education. This is a strength and a weakness. It allows colleges, teachers, and students to respond quickly and flexibly to needs as they arise, and in particular gives the college of further education a key role in relation to local employment. It means that innovation can and does take place on a rolling, incremental basis.

The disadvantage of the pragmatic, no-nonsense attitude is that fundamental questions or changes in conditions are difficult to face, and indeed may not be faced. Such a change has come with the unprecedented rise in youth unemployment. To begin with, one can no longer base provision on day-release from apprenticeships, because the number of apprenticeships has declined drastically. And how does one educate people vocationally if they have no vocation? Joblessness strikes at the heart of the rationale for vocational courses, and students are not slow to realise this. Should one continue to provide fairly narrow, specific courses, as the Germans do? Should one go for broad, polyvalent foundation courses, such as the Youth Training Scheme? Should one educate for unemployment as well as employment? Such questions lie at the heart of the tension between 'traditional FE' and the 'new FE'.

Concurrently, but separately, a fundamental challenge to the rationale for vocational education has been mounted by some sociologists and economists. This challenge rests on two concepts, socialisation and screening. Traditional vocational educators have always recognised that in addition to knowledge and skills, vocational education was about attitudes: attitudes to work, to the company, to the employer, to workmates, to materials, to tools, to the products. Words like 'pride', 'self-respect', 'workmanship', 'loyalty', 'care' expressed something of the affective or attitudinal component of traditional apprenticeships and vocational education. These values often formed part of a paternalistic, essentially conservative outlook, which defined both the opportunities and limitations of life as a craftsman or skilled worker. Indeed in Germany, one can speak of a philosophy of vocational education, as expressed by writers such as Kerschensteiner and Spranger, and going back to Luther (Taylor, 1981). (The term 'technician' is both more recent and more ambiguous as regards attitudes and status.) What is new, however, is the suggestion that the affective aspect of vocational education is *more* important than the knowledge and skills acquired; that in sociological terms the 'real' function of vocational education is to teach people to fit into a social hierarchy, and accept their place and that it is the attitude/behaviour of the worker which is the key element in production.[10]

The economist's 'screening' hypothesis, by contrast, puts the emphasis not on attitudes but on ability. The argument is that education or training qualifications are used often not as direct measures of relevant knowledge and skills, but as indirect or oblique measures of general ability; and that the second might even be preferred to the first. Thus a bank might recruit someone with an apparently irrelevant A-level qualification in preference to someone with the notionally appropriate BTEC qualification. The value of education and training to the employer lies not in what was taught, but in the certification of level of ability.[11]

The relationship between vocational education, employment, and the economy is now recognised to be much more complex than was thought in the 1960s, when education was often thought of simply as an 'input' to production and economic growth. It seems unlikely that one can arrive at a standard model which fits all kinds of education and all kinds of occupation. An added complication is the longitudinal relationship between continuing education and career development: most of the discussion to date has been concerned only with initial education and employment. If one may hazard a generalisation it is that the education–employment relationship is both more complex and more flexible than was previously believed. The question of flexibility in relation to employment will arise again, particularly in the next chapter. Indeed, 'flexibility' and 'adaptability' are currently fashionable terms in vocational preparation. However, it does not automatically follow that courses need to be made more flexible (or broader, or more generic, or process-oriented). It may be that the flexibility is already there, in the power of students to extract different things from the 'same' course, in the habit of some employers of 'not knowing what they want', in the generic or transferable nature of many occupational skills, and in the manifold opportunities for learning on the job.

Social education

What was said in the last section suggests that much vocational education is, or is also, social education. Work is a major aspect of society, and most jobs are inescapably social, in the simple sense of working with or for others. It is only the fictional environment of training that allows us to abstract job content from job context: in reality, they are intermixed. Work is best defined not as a particular kind of activity but as a particular socio-economic relationship. Therefore one can say that much social education is contained in vocational (or professional, or academic) education. It is an education that fits us for and socialises us into socio-occupational niches, and in which patterns of knowledge, skill, values, and relations are all intertwined. Often the latter elements are implicit rather than explicit; they are part of the hidden curriculum of dress, time-keeping, speech, life-style, and affiliations, embedded in the minor rituals of classroom, laboratory, or workshop behaviour, and the major rituals of initiation and certification. However, the social aspect of vocational education sometimes becomes quite explicit, as in aspects of the Youth Training Scheme, which speak in terms of working to deadlines, sharing responsibilities with adults, and personal and life skills (Manpower Services Commission, 1982).

A 'social education' may, however, go beyond vocational socialisation in two ways. First, it may extend to adult social existence outside work: citizenship, community involvement, political affiliations, consumer, contractual, or legal relations, and indeed the whole complex web of interdependences which we refer to as 'society'. Second, social education may refer to education *about* society as distinct from *for* society. This is not always a sharp distinction, but it does point to a continuum with a purely 'reproductive' social education at one end and a 'reflexive' social education at the other. Each of these wider connotations of social education will be explored briefly below.

Some social education, while not directly vocational, is nevertheless very closely related to work. The education of trade unionists, for example, is concerned with the detailed knowledge and skills involved in industrial relations, as well as with the other social and political issues connected with organised labour. Health and safety at work is another topic that has recently grown in importance. While trade-union education in the United Kingdom is usually carried out under the broad heading of adult education, the German *Arbeitslehre* (literally, 'study of work') is carried on in certain secondary and post-secondary institutions. *Arbeitslehre* is an umbrella title which covers everything from vocational counselling to education *about* work and society, and its practice varies widely from place to place (Russell, 1982). However, it seems right to classify it in general as a form of social education rather than vocational education since, at least in theory, it is intended to orient students towards the 'world of work' rather than any specific job.

Social education may of course transcend specific skills and contexts. Civics in the US schools, general or liberal studies in UK schools and colleges, and socialist production in East Germany are concerned with citizenship in its widest sense, belonging to (and identifying with, in its normative mode) the prevailing socio-economic arrangements. The term 'political education' is not much used in the United Kingdom, but in other countries, such as Sweden, a good deal of adult education is both organised by, and concerned with, political parties and groupings. Overt political education is part of the polytechnical model in Eastern Europe and the Soviet Union, and continues into the post-compulsory stage through both formal courses (for example, at university) and 'voluntary' organisations. Much post-school education in Western countries is also political, even if it is not labelled as such. Community education (Fletcher and Thompson, 1980) is inescapably political at the local level, and there is a long-standing tradition of 'current affairs' education in adult education. And it can be argued that many other forms of post-school education – academic, liberal, professional, and so on – have a political dimension. The problem, in the end, is to know what is not 'political', since a term that includes everything tells us nothing.

One issue that runs through all these overt or covert forms of social education is the extent to which they are education for, or education about, society. 'Education for' suggests a normative emphasis, a concentration upon means, and a taking-for-granted of certain social assumptions. 'Education about' suggests an analytic emphasis, a concentration on ends, and a concern with conflicts and controversies. The difference is neatly typified by the tussle going on between 'social skills' and 'social studies' both during and after secondary education. For many years, social education meant social studies, which aimed at a better general understanding of society. Recently, there has been a rapid growth of social skills, life skills, or coping skills courses. Such courses aim to equip the student to live and function as an adult in the social situation most likely to confront him or her.

The growth of social skills courses can be interpreted in two ways. They can be seen as an overt response to the failure of the schools to socialise young people into the attitudes and behaviours appropriate to their socio-occupational status. Thus they emphasise punctuality, appearance, self-presentation in writing and in person, dependability, and, to use the old-fashioned word, manners. Since the breakdown in such forms of socialisation in schools is worst among the low achievers (the relationship is two-way) social skills have tended to become associated with low-ability or low-achieving students. Whether such students cannot get jobs because they lack these skills, or because the jobs are not there, is beside the point here; the rationale for social-skills training is that it gives them relatively a better chance than they would otherwise have of getting a job.

The second interpretation of the rise of social skills is that there has always been a real gap in the school curriculum between personal counselling and social studies (McGuire and Priestley, 1981). Schools have not, to date, deliberately equipped students with many of the skills – communication, health, financial, organisational – which they need as adults in our society. They have not done so perhaps because they assumed that such skills would be picked up as part of the hidden curriculum, or from the wider social context, or could be derived from the more abstract skills of subject-based learning.

It is difficult at the present to dissociate the concept of social skills from the particular circumstances of the 16–19 age group. The 'resocialisation' hypothesis seems plausible. Nevertheless, it is worth remembering that adults may need, and are taught, social skills in quite different circumstances. Problem drinkers are taught how to refuse a drink without appearing a kill-joy; salesmen are taught how to develop their patter; counsellors how to listen or confront; timid people how to assert themselves; actors how to project themselves; officers how to lead. Beyond such communication skills, adults learn, either formally or non-formally, a host of skills to do with managing their budgets, finding out information, coping with officialdom, living with health problems, and relating to colleagues or family. Social skills training existed in all these fields long before it was heard of in the 16–19 context. It is a relatively new concept in the mainstream of education, but not in the education and training of adults. Social education is thus a vague term, and necessarily so, because it can refer to a variety of aspects of our social being, and a spectrum of instrumental to reflective approaches to them.[12]

Role education

The passage from childhood to adulthood is characterised not only by biological change but also by a change in the number and complexity of roles.[13] Where the ten-year-old has only a few major roles – son/daughter, sibling, peer, pupil – and these roles are often, though not always, congruent, the adult of twenty or forty years has many more, and potentially more conflicting roles, to play. He or she may be a spouse, parent, son/daughter, sibling, colleague or workmate, employee, trade unionist, taxpayer, consumer, mortgagee, driver, voter, and a member of political, religious, community, sports, or other organisations. Indeed, adult life is often a matter of trying to negotiate between the demands of different roles, in terms of time, energy, and money. Should one take time away from the children to play more sport? Why does one see so little of one's sister/brother now? Should one's loyalty be towards the company or the union? Is there a conflict between religious principles and political duties?

It is hardly surprising therefore that role conflict, role congruence, and role dissonance feature so prominently in discussion of adult life, and that some post-school education is concerned with adult roles. Many roles are, of course, work-related, and as Figure 2 suggests, the distinctions among vocational/professional education, social education, and role education are often hard to maintain. For example, management education could not take place without constant reference to role and role theory, and the same is more or less true of all the 'people professions' or 'caring professions'. In some cases, particularly in the high-status professions of law, medicine, or professional soldiering, there will be less explicit discussion of roles than implicit transmission of role models – 'style', 'bedside manner', 'leadership'. However, it seems useful to have a separate heading for 'role education' both in order to emphasise the role content of other kinds of post-school education, and to account for those forms of post-school education which are *primarily* concerned with role. There are not perhaps very many of these, but as the Russell Report (1973) on adult education pointed out, a distinct heading is sometimes needed:

> 'Role education', directed not to training for qualification but to providing the background of knowledge, especially in relation to social change, through which the individual's role can be more responsibly discharged in society, in industry, in voluntary service or in public work of any kind. Here again there will be many forms: examples are education for magistrates or policemen, for clergy or social workers, for shop stewards and trades unionists, for managers and local government officers. (page 19)

Role education may also be connected with personal and family life. Ante-natal education, which in pre-industrial cultures was usually transmitted from mother to daughter and father to son, has increasingly become a matter of institutional (though not necessarily educational) provision. It can prepare women, and also to some extent men, not only for the experience of childbirth and the ensuing weeks, but in a more general way for becoming a parent: indeed, in the United States it tends to be called 'pre-parenting' education (Pugh, 1983). Likewise, the notion of 'retirement' hardly exists in pre-industrial cultures, although in some there are clearly demarcated life-stages, in which certain activities are deemed appropriate or inappropriate ('age-roles'). Pre-retirement education is thus a modern phenomenon, necessitated by the often sharp break between full-time employment and no employment. Such education covers not only practical matters, such as finance, health, and housing, but is also aimed at helping people to adjust to the role changes that retirement brings, and make positive use of the opportunities that exist.

Other examples of role education may be more specific. Voluntary work may involve a certain threshold of expertise, and if a person is to become a St John's Ambulance Brigade member, a club treasurer, a voluntary social worker, or a magistrate, role education, always involving a mixture of knowledge, skills, and attitudes, is necessary. Some forms of role education fall under the heading of counselling rather than education, and this reflects the imprecision of the term 'role' itself, which (like 'skill') has become more and more widely used. Roles exist within marriage, yet we tend to speak of marital counselling or guidance, rather than education. ('Co-counselling' and 'therapy' are also sometimes appropriate terms.)

This 'fuzzy set', to use the mathematician's phrase, is worrying if one is to try to delimit what is meant by post-school education, but beyond the taxonomist's or administrator's problem lies an important truth: that post-school education itself is extraordinarily difficult to delimit. The clear framework of compulsory schooling (classes, teachers, institutions, examinations) is in this respect atypical and misleading, for the clarities have to do more with the institutional format than the teaching–learning process. Adult educators alternately agonise and rejoice over their inability to delimit education for adults. But all teaching and learning potentially runs into something else: it is merely an unusually ordered or charged form of processes that go on all the time outside the classroom. It should not be surprising therefore that role education runs, in one direction, into social and vocational education, and in another, into what can best be called personal education.

Personal education

Education is always personal. All knowledge implies a knower, all learning a learner, all work a worker. But 'personal education' implies something more than, or different from this: it implies an orientation towards the student, an emphasis on selfhood, a concern with how 'knowledge' and 'culture' are experienced by the individual. Such an orientation is caught by such everyday phrases as 'it means a lot to me' or 'it means nothing to him' or 'it speaks to me'. Phrases like this point up the double sense of the words 'meaning' and 'meaningful'. One can recognise that something is meaningful (that it accords with publicly accepted canons of coherence or sense) without necessarily saying that it is meaningful to oneself, or for oneself. In the first case, meaning is a semantic matter; in the second case it is part of what Alfred Schutz called the 'structure of relevance' (Schutz and Luckmann, 1974).

The word 'relevance' has been so used and abused in education that one hesitates to bring it in at all, but no other word will quite do; and it does make an important point. In educational discourse, there is often an implicit assumption that all forms of knowledge and all facets of the world are equally important, equally significant. The hidden stance is of a 'God's-eye view'. This is symbolised by the determined impersonality of much academic writing, the use of 'one' instead of 'I', the attempt to be nobody in particular. What Schutz describes rather than argues, is the unevenness of the world as lived from a particular point of view, the lifeworld (*Lebenswelt*). In the lifeworld, some things loom large, and others are remote from us; some are vividly real, others quite unreal; some occupy the foreground, others the background. The configuration of our lifeworld changes over time; facets of it which seemed quite central at one period later seem marginal. How often has one gone back to a book which meant a lot to one twenty years ago, and found, with a mixture of nostalgia and incomprehension that it is not the same? Of course, it is the same: the print has not changed; but one's reading of it has. The same is true of people and places, and helps to explain the uneasiness which often attends the meetings of old friends, or the common adage about places: you should never go back. One comes to recognise that our existence is shot through with time; and that not only do things grow old, but that they change. The sense of transience becomes intertwined with the sense of contingency, of the instability of what one took to be fixed and real.

This sense of the world-as-lived is so familiar that the wonder is that education ever departs from it at all. There are two reasons why it does, one institutional and one epistemological. Education is by and large a collective activity, which typically takes place in groups of anything between ten and several hundred people. Despite admonitions to 'individualise' this process, teachers and curriculum planners find it difficult to treat each person on a case-by-case basis, simply because of the pressures of time and numbers. Hence the personal aspects of learning – the individual's sense of relevance or meaning – tend to get marginalised or suppressed. Students may learn to internalise this suppression and set aside questions about the point of what they are doing. A good deal of teaching and learning is faith-in-a-hurry.

There is also an epistemological reason for the suppression of the personal. Whatever one's position as between realist and nominalist theories of knowledge, the experience of knowledge (or the world, or reality) as essentially other, as not-self, can be a profound and moving one. It is the experience not of immanence but of transcendence, not so much of one's dependence on the other as its independence of oneself. It is an experience caught particularly in the writings of some scientists – astronomers, physicists, mathematicians – and of painters; the experience of beholding rather than just seeing. It would be misleading therefore to assume that what is profound in education is always personal, always bound to the self.

It is in fact around the word 'self' and its derivatives ('self-concept', 'self-image', 'self-actualisation') that concern for the personal dimension of education has most recently clustered. Of course, there have always been more traditional ways of expressing that concern, in terms of 'character' in the schools, 'capacity' and 'maturity' in further and higher education, and 'potential' in adult education. An emphasis on the experience of education has been a feature of a number of famous educational reformers in the past, notably Rousseau, Pestalozzi, and Dewey. However, the modern concern with the self in education dates from what has been called the 'Me decade' of the 1960s, and specifically from the writings of Maslow (1954, 1973) and Rogers (1961, 1969) and other 'humanistic psychologists'. Education, they argued, should be centrally concerned with human growth, relevance, and meaning. Concurrently but separately, Erickson, Kohlberg and Loevinger emphasised the developmental tasks of adulthood in terms of 'life-stages' (see Chapter 6). Perry (1970) has been concerned with cognitive and ethical development in higher education.

The 'Me decade' is now part of the past, and the emphasis in the 1980s is more conservative, employment-oriented, and perhaps impersonal. Nevertheless, the recent concern for the self has left clear traces in curriculum theory and practice. Psychologists now stress the importance of the self-concept as a mediating factor in long-term educational achievement (Burns, 1982). The need for personal counselling at every level of education is now ritually stated, though implementation is another matter. The value of project work, real-life placements, and small-group teaching is as often argued in personal terms (responsibility, self-organisation, relating to others) as in instrumental, vocational, or academic terms.

In adult education and 'fringe' education there are also classes concerned directly with personal growth and personal relationships, though fewer than there were ten years ago. The emphasis has moved to the body, which is of course not entirely unconnected with the self. Yoga, for example, which is now a settled feature of the adult education landscape, is concerned with the body-mind. Some forms of personal education – encounter groups, stress situations – have been vocationalised, and are now found in management education and mid-career professional courses.

It is difficult, in these matters, to distinguish the longer rhythms of educational change from the shorter-term swings or movements of fashion. In some ways, personal education is less at the forefront of curriculum thinking than it was ten years ago; but the arguments advanced by Pring suggest that it is still a serious concern. As he notes, it is (like social education) an umbrella concept which covers a lot of things, and therefore not easy to translate into formal curricular terms. It is closely related to role education, since a person's self-concept is (to some extent at least) an aggregation of roles and the feedback from others about these roles. It is also related to the commonsense notion of ability discussed in Chapter 1, since we conceive of ourselves partly in terms of actualised or unactualised potential: and discussion of that potential typically leads back to the kind of intelligences listed by Gardner (1983). The more concrete the idea of personal education, the more it involves discussion of identifiable abilities, aptitudes, or skills.[14]

The word 'person' or 'self', however, seems to connote something over and above this aggregation of roles and abilities, as if there was, at the minimum, an 'executive' function which organised and related the parts, or at the maximum, a relatively stable and enduring 'I', the proverbial little man (or woman) in one's head. The difficulties with such an idea are well known, but equally it is difficult to do without it if one is going to employ concepts like 'responsibility', 'choice', and 'empathy' – concepts which are central to the notion of moral and/or spiritual development.

A discussion of this problem would take us far beyond the scope of this book; it has exercised not only philosophers and psychologists greatly, but also writers: the sense that there is 'nothing at the centre' is a pervasive theme in modernist literature. However, one point can be made in relation to personal education. Nowadays, typically, the relationship between different disciplines or forms of knowledge is bracketed or set aside: few people still accept the positivist hierarchy, and even fewer know of the medieval pecking order. Each discipline is accepted more or less on its own terms, and it is considered philosophically rather gauche, as well as professionally impolite, to suggest that one discipline is more basic than another. Status hierarchies among disciplines do of course exist, but they are complexly determined, and rarely articulated formally. The question is, on the whole, officially shelved; unofficially, snide remarks about neighbouring disciplines are part of the social education of the academic. But there is little emphasis on the personal integration of knowledge.

Similarly, the question of the self-concept tends to be shelved. Education goes on *as if* there were a responsible, executive self; words like 'discipline', 'accountability' and 'option' assume this. But the question of what education does for, or does to, that self is often bracketed, as being too difficult, or too private, or too value-laden, to deal with. It is a question which will be encountered again in Chapter 6, on the education of adults.

Recreational education

Officially, recreational education is a form or aspect of further education for adults. Section 41 of the 1944 Education Act states:

> it shall be the duty of every local authority to secure the provision for their area of adequate facilities for further education, that is to say: (a) full-time and part-time education for persons over compulsory school age; and (b) leisure-time occupation, in such organised cultural training and recreational activities as are suited to their requirements, for any persons over compulsory school age who are able and willing to profit by the facilities provided for that purpose.

The term 'recreational education' is not much used outside the United Kingdom, and even in this country it is tending to be replaced by the newer and more portentous 'leisure education'.[15] To some extent the term 'recreational education' has always had a flavour of marginality, even frivolity, of flower-arranging or dancing on the rates. Just as other forms of post-school education test the distinctions between education and politics, or education and therapy, so recreational education tests that between education and entertainment. The reality is, however, more significant than might first appear.

Recreation, like work, is best defined not in terms of a particular type of activity, but in terms of socio-economic relationships. Whereas work is geared to earning, recreation usually involves spending; and where work is often socially determined in its availability and content, recreation is typically individually determined, within certain constraints of money and time. (Leisure can be defined as the time-frame within which recreation takes place.)

The necessity of defining recreational in these terms, rather than in terms of certain hobbies, crafts, or other activities, becomes evident when one considers activities which can be either vocational or recreational. Sport, a recreation for most people, is nevertheless a vocation for a visible and growing minority. Woodwork classes are 'non-vocational', joinery classes vocational, but the content may be similar. The same applies to other basic crafts such as car maintenance, furniture repair, cookery (which is catering in vocational terms), pottery, and the manifold forms of DIY. Some people turn such hobbies into secondary or even main jobs; contributing to the number of 'cowboys' in the service sector, the growth of the black economy, or what the EEC now calls local economic development. Many more use them to reduce outlays in their budget. In some instances, what was work to a previous generation (fishing, hunting, walking, sailing) becomes a recreation for today's. But like all vocational courses, all recreational courses develop identifiable abilities or skills, and indeed this is seen as their main characteristic.

It is often said that the importance of recreational education will grow as people get more leisure. This assumes both that the real working week (including overtime) decreases in length, as distinct from the statutory working week, and that people have enough disposable income to support their leisure activities. Until recently, the real working week had decreased only a little in the United Kingdom since the war, and the unemployed, who have plenty of 'leisure', usually don't have the money to make much use of it, even if they have the will.

Despite these caveats, however, it seems likely that 'education for leisure' will grow in significance. In addition to the increase in disposable time, another factor may push people to get more involved in various forms of recreation. Many jobs in the future seem likely to be boring and banal. In the past, they were too, but they were often exhausting as well, leaving adults little time or energy with which to pursue other interests. Some recent manpower studies suggest that much future job growth will be in the low-tech or no-tech service occupations (fast food, janitors, cleaning); not very tiring work, but not particularly satisfying either.[16] More people may turn away from their job for their satisfaction. The dissatisfaction that arises from the intrinsically boring nature of some jobs must be distinguished from the concept of alienation arising from lack of control of, or identification with, the work process. The first is more a matter of the internal characteristics of the job; the second of the socio-economic conditions of labour; although in practice they infringe on each other. But, however the socio-economic 'frame' of labour is altered, it is difficult to see how the inherently repetitive, unpleasant, or undemanding nature of some kinds of work can be altered except through the increased use of machines and robots.

This point leads on to a more general one to do with the status of recreational education. Typically, this has been low: education for leisure has been seen as pretty marginal to the main business of educational provision; indeed, something that people should largely pay for themselves. If, however, one argues that abilities and potential are pluralistic rather than unitary, and that most jobs can only utilise or develop some of these forms, it follows that people need alternative avenues for self-development, outside their main vocational role. It is hardly surprising if people want to concentrate mainly in their early adult years on developing vocational skills and constructing a primary adult identity. But is also unsurprising if, having achieved job security and adult identity, they then wish to explore these other aspects of the potential they feel they have in them, to pick up threads of interests which perforce they had to leave aside for a while, and to recognise some countervailing in-stincts and interests in their lives. Recreational education has thus to be seen in relation to vocational and other forms of education. Some people are lucky enough to have work which is broad or interesting enough to fulfil several aspects of this inner potential, and indeed their recreations may be an extension of their job. The business-man's round of golf neatly combines useful communication with physical exercise. For many others, recreation provides a deliberate contrast, or an escape, or a chance to live out what is unlived. In this sense, it can be seen as a continuation or resurgence of some of the facets of general education, an embodiment of the plurality of our desires, and a symbol of that elusive search for the development of potential.

Liberal education

The term 'liberal education' is used in the United Kingdom to describe specific forms of both adult education (liberal adult education as provided by university extra-mural departments and the Workers' Educational Association) and non-advanced further education (liberal studies). It is also used less specifically to refer to a certain orientation in higher education (liberal studies in science, liberal arts). It has also been included in the title of books on post-school education, such as *Liberal Education in a Technical Age* (National Institute of Adult Education, 1955), and is embodied in the names of educational associations concerned with teaching 'liberal studies'.

Despite, or perhaps because of, its wide use, 'liberal' is an extremely difficult term to define. This difficulty arises not only from the above, contextual differences in the meanings given to it, but also from its antiquity. As an educational ideal, it originated with Plato, and successive ages have reinterpreted it in the light of their own conceptions of knowledge, man, and society. At various times, a liberal education has been conceptualised as the education of a particular type of student (the freeman, the gentleman), as an education in particular subjects (classics, the liberal arts), as an education involving certain methods (discussion, analysis, criticism, reflection), and as an education aiming at a particular goal (apprehension of reality or truth, commitment to the values of tolerance or open-mindedness).

There is a large body of literature in the philosophy of education on the original concept of liberal education and its subsequent reinterpretations.[17] What is striking about the notion is not only its capacity to take on the different colourings and emphases of different contexts, to the point of acting merely as a legitimating concept, but also its resilience. Several times in its history, it seems to have become moribund only to be resurrected again in a different form. For all its problems, it appears to be a curriculum concept that is difficult to do without.

It is not easy to know why this should be so, but the answer may lie in the concept's association of two powerful notions – namely, knowledge and freedom. Inherent in the notion of freedom here is the assumption that we are not free; that our natural or at least normal condition is characterised by ignorance, illusion, and limitation. These are the 'givens' of our existence, the epistemological equivalent of original sin. The way out of this condition is through knowledge – 'reason' or 'organised knowledge' – which alone allows us to transcend and work our way beyond the limitations of our condition; the epistemological equivalent of salvation.

The strongest form of this argument is found in the original Greek conception, which, as Hirst describes, saw liberal education 'as freeing the mind to function according to its true nature, freeing reason from error and illusion and freeing man's conduct from wrong' (Hirst, 1974, p. 31). It could do this because knowledge could lead to truth:

> the mind, in the right use of reason, comes to know the essential nature of things and can apprehend what is ultimately real and immutable. Consequently, man no longer needs to live in terms of deceptive appearances and doubtful opinions and beliefs. All his experiences, life and thought can be given shape and perspective by what is finally true, by knowledge that corresponds to what is ultimately real. (Hirst, 1974, page 31)

Contemporary statements of the argument tend to be more muted and equivocal. The growth of nominalist, relativist, subjectivist, or probabilistic conceptions of knowledge mean that few people nowadays are prepared to associate organised knowledge unequivocally with truth, reality, individual virtue, and social good – the original, compact doctrine. Hirst, for example, reformulates liberal in terms of 'mind' and 'public' knowledge rather than reality or truth. Man has, he argues, over millennia objectified and developed conceptual schemata which are subject to publicly accepted criteria of judgement. Such criteria are usually described as rational. Mind is not something which takes on or does not take on these conceptual schemata: they are part of the very definition of mind: they constitute it. The objectivity lies not in some correspondence to reality or truth, but in the existence of public criteria:

> As here reformulated the concept has, again like the original, objectivity, though this is no longer backed by metaphysical realism. For it is a necessary feature of knowledge as such that there be public criteria whereby the true is distinguishable from the false, the good from the bad, the right from the wrong. It is the existence of these criteria which gives objectivity to knowledge: and this in its turn gives objectivity to the concept of liberal education. A parallel to

another form of justification thus remains and the concept continues to warrant its label as that of an education that frees the mind from error and illusion. (Hirst, 1974, page 43)

The problem with basing objectivity on 'public criteria' is that such criteria necessitate an anthropology of knowledge (how it has developed from less to more sophisticated forms) and a sociology of knowledge (an analysis of the social relationships that reside in the concept of 'public'). Hirst hints at such an anthropology:

The formulating and testing of symbolic expressions has enabled man to probe his experience for ever more complex relations and for finer and finer distinctions, these being fixed and held for public sharing in the symbolic systems that have been evolved. ... The forms of knowledge are thus the basic articulations whereby the whole of experience has become intelligible to man, they are the fundamental achievement of mind. ... It is only because man has over millennia objectified and progressively developed these that he has achieved the forms of human knowledge, and the possibility of the development of mind as we know it is open to us today. (Hirst, 1974, pages 40–1)

Such a statement remains little more than metaphor, however, implying a progressive evolution and differentiation akin to biological development. The image of development is gradualist and incremental, rather than catastrophic and disjunctive. As regards the sociology of knowledge, Griffin (1983) has pointed out that it is a short step from 'public criteria' to 'social criteria', and that the use of the term 'public' implies a consensus rather than a conflict model of society. Who decides what constitutes 'public'? Are there not different publics? Is 'public' the same as 'official'?

As with earlier reinterpretations of the notion of liberal education, a proper elucidation of the shifts and emphases would require much more space than can be allocated here. Rothblatt's (1976) account of eighteenth- and nineteenth-century perspectives emphasises change rather than essence. Hirst's reinterpretation is cited only as an example of what seems to be a modern trend, for liberal education to become more problematic and equivocal as it becomes dissociated from metaphysical realism, the idea that knowledge can lead us to reality and truth. Indeed, the contemporary rationales for liberal education seem to be offered less in terms of what it leads to than what it leads from. Implicit in a good deal of writing on the subject is a critique of common-sense knowledge. This critique has three main elements:

(1) Common-sense knowledge is strongly, even oppressively normative; it insists that much is taken for granted, and not questioned. By contrast, a liberal education encourages people to explore assumptions and implicit models, to question beliefs and values, and generally treat the 'natural' or the 'normal' as problematic. It encourages analysis, detachment and critical reflection.

(2) Common-sense knowledge is pre-theoretical. It is based on a culturally accumulated mixture of habits, practices, and techniques. These are often ineffective or purely superstitious, and development is slow, uncertain, and *ad hoc*. Liberal education, by contrast, involves organised knowledge, which attempts to progress through the testing and refinement of theories, models, concepts, and methodologies. It is, or attempts to be, cumulative and progressive.

(3) Common-sense knowledge is parochial, and limited by the horizons of a particular culture or subculture. It does not give access to the general stock of knowledge and expertise that mankind has; it is limited largely to the contemporary and the local, whereas a liberal education widens a person's horizons and releases him or her from the tyranny of the present.

A liberal education, in these terms, is one that liberates people from the characteristic constraints of common-sense knowledge. In general terms, many educators might agree with the three points made above; the problem is that they do not indicate any particular curriculum. It can be argued that some subjects more than others encourage critical reflection, widen horizons, involve theory-building, and so on; but a reasonable case can be made for many disciplines in such broad terms, and it is therefore difficult to know what to exclude.

The above analysis helps perhaps to explain the current paradoxical status of liberal education. As an idea, it still has a considerable attraction and influence, particularly as a basis for criticising other forms of post-school education, notably vocational education. Some of this attraction may be for purely historical reasons, but some may lie in the potent antithesis of limitation and liberation which it embodies. At the same time, it has become a peculiarly shapeless idea, and therefore difficult to translate into a characteristic curriculum. If nearly everything can constitute a liberal education, then it comes close to being synonymous with education itself.

In Figure 2, liberal education has been located somewhere

between a knowledge orientation and an ability/potential orientation. The content of liberal education is typically those organised bodies of knowledge which we know as disciplines, with perhaps pride of place going to philosophy as the discipline that is most directly concerned with 'truth' and 'reality'. But the purpose of such studies is some kind of development of mind and consciousness, of ability conceived in its very widest sense as something that humankind is capable of. This is not the same as the self-development of the humanistic psychologists precisely because the concept of the self does not lie at its centre; rather, it is a concept of the real or the true. And although people from Plato onwards have argued that the leaders of society (whether in the elite, or among the people) could have no better preparation for their role than a liberal education, it is not fundamentally a social concept, because the liberation is primarily epistemological, and only secondarily political.

Basic education

The concept of basic education is more familiar in post-school education than in the schools; and whereas in post-school education it tends towards inclusion, in the schools it tends towards exclusion. The genesis of adult basic education was in adult literacy, and the recognition (not without considerable shock) that even in countries like the United Kingdom which had had universal primary education for decades, there were still many adults who could not read and write at a level which would be considered 'functional' in a modern society.

The definition of what constitutes literacy or illiteracy is not as straightforward as it might seem, but it did not detain the adult literacy campaign that was launched in the United Kingdom in the 1970s. However, once one begins to think about adult literacy, it is a short step to thinking about adult numeracy and hence to the other essential knowledge and skills that adults need to live a reasonable life in society. The notions of 'basic skills' and 'basic education' thus arise fairly naturally, though what constitutes basic education is even more difficult to agree on than basic literacy, and perhaps does not arouse quite the same emotional commitment among volunteer teachers. However, the following list may be taken as being fairly representative:

> a range of educational provisions and associated learning which
> includes literacy and other verbal skills, including English as a

second language; basic skills in number; and a body of general knowledge relevant to the day-to-day lives of adults in society; together with those other elements of education both formal and informal without which an adult might find himself cut off from continuing education, vocational preparation, or cultural or re-creational activity. (ACACE, 1979, page 12)

Lists like these can be criticised for being too prescriptive, too generalised, and too skills-centred. As Bryant (1983) has pointed out in his study of the educational needs of the long-term unem-ployed, the notion of needs is relative, and depends on what a person perceives her situation to be. Moreover, it is just as important to consider a person's self-concept and confidence, as to equip her with specific skills, for unless she will use the skills, it is pointless to equip her with them.

One can see how the seemingly simple concept of basic education can quickly become complex and problematic. However, the in-teresting point here is that basic education, in the adult context, has been an expanding concept, tending to embrace and aspire to more and more. Indeed the problem may be that it becomes too wide, too diffuse, and loses that focus which seems essential for people's commitment. For basic education then generates 'post-basic' educa-tion, which begins to shade into 'general education'. By contrast, the slogan 'back to basics' in the school context has been reductive in the sense that it advocates concentrating on the 'essentials' in primary education, and excluding the 'frills'. It typically implies a greater emphasis on the 3 Rs, with less time spent on dance, crafts, music, and some of the other activities which have become associ-ated with primary schools in the United Kingdom over the last couple of decades.

The term 'basic' raises the question: basic to what? The answers to this question help us to understand why basic can connote one thing in one context, and another thing in a different one. Much education is *basic to other education*: it provides the necessary foundation or grounding for study at a higher level. Thus 'back to basics' in the primary school context implies that primary education is not providing an adequate foundation for secondary education, and that teachers in secondary school can no longer take for granted that pupils come to them equipped with the essential language and number skills that (the slogan implies) they used to. Basic in an adult context is more likely to be *basic to adult life*, including work. Without basic education, adults cannot cope or find work in an industrialised society; they lack the skills even to take proper advantage of welfare. Thus basic education in an adult context is likely to be more society-oriented rather than oriented towards further education. Basic in a 16–19 context is likely to be *employment-oriented* and to aim at equipping young people with the knowledge, attitudes, and skills necessary to find and hold down a job.

It is this kind of orientation that one finds in a recent Further Education Unit (FEU) publication entitled *Basic Skills*. Here the list of desirable outcomes consists of 'language . . . number . . . manipulative dexterity and co-ordination . . . problem-solving . . . everyday coping . . . interpersonal relationships . . . computer literacy . . . and learning' (FEU, 1982a, p. 2). Although such a list does have a distinctly occupational flavour, it is in other respects surprisingly general, and this suggests why basic education, of all the forms of post-school curricula, must be placed right in the centre of Figure 2. At its best, basic education provides a foundation in knowledge (especially in language and number skills), a relevance to social needs, and a development of the self, especially self-confidence. That is not to say that any given course or programme may not lean one way or another: the shift from formal to functional literacy teaching in developing countries is one clear example of a switch from a knowledge orientation to a social one. And basic education in the United Kingdom now often contains a strong element of personal counselling, formal or informal, which was not there in the traditional approach.

At a certain point, basic education turns into something else, variously labelled post-basic, foundation, or general education. This is a matter of level and progression. As it does so, the curricular elements and aims become more differentiated, more prone to lean one way than another. There is no point in trying to draw sharp lines where there are none, and the fact that the centre of Figure 2 is occupied by 'basic' is not meant to exclude other forms of education which can claim to be all things to all ends. Action research projects, for example, might satisfy the demands of all three points of the triangle; and at the micro-level of teaching, from minute to minute and second to second, the focus and emphasis shift constantly: a theory explained, then related to a social problem, then opened up to interpretation in terms of personal experience. Curriculum categories tend to be gross categories, but they are necessary for all that, since they constitute perhaps the main level at which the experience of education is structured and organised. The purpose of the model is to help in the analysis of that level.

Conclusion

It was suggested at the beginning of this chapter that whereas compulsory education is characteristically justified in terms of providing a general education, post-compulsory education is typified by specific orientations, purposes, and effects. The shift from one to the other may or may not be abrupt. In some cases, a student may finish a broad-based school curriculum and then embark on a narrow line of apprenticeship; in other cases, the school curriculum may already have become differentiated, perhaps partly along vocational lines; or post-school education may begin with broad-based foundation courses.

Despite these *caveats*, the general–specific distinction seems a useful one in analysing the curriculum beyond school. The purpose of this chapter has been to map out the major specific orientations of post-school education, in relation to the three-dimensional model of general education used in Chapter 2, and in relation to one another. It has been suggested that the three main headings of knowledge, culture, and ability can still be used, but that the compact, prismatic model has to be broken out into looser form, with the three dimensions becoming three orientations. All curricula involve knowledge, culture, and abilities, but post-school curricula tend to be justified more in terms of one than the others. In some cases the language of justification is couched mainly in terms of knowledge (depth, understanding, research, scholarship); in other cases it makes reference to society or culture (jobs, competence, community, citizenship); and in others again it is framed in terms of the students' abilities and potential (development, growth, liberation). The model allows one to examine the tensions that exist between these.

However, as was pointed out in the earlier comments on curriculum evaluation, it is one thing to say what a course is *intended* to do, but another to say what its effect is, and perhaps another again to say what the student does with it. These possible discrepancies between intentions, effects, and uses mean that the headings in the model are not always mutually exclusive. An academic course may have a vocational spin-off; a vocational course may socialise or politicise; a recreational course may have role consequences; and so on. Moreover, the student's perception of the course may change even during the course. She may begin it in order to get out of the house one evening, and meet people; continue it because she becomes interested in the subject; and in the end use it to facilitate a change of job. The motivation of undergraduates, and their perception of their studies, may change similarly over three years.

In post-school education, perhaps more than in the schools, the curriculum cannot easily prescribe or limit its own effects and side-effects. Adults, being in certain ways autonomous, have it in their power to *use* the curriculum in ways which were not intended; in any case, the effects of education are never wholly predictable or controllable. Post-school education is thus much more an open system than a closed one because the loci of control are more widely dispersed than they are in compulsory education, and because the transactions with the environment are more numerous and more complex. Post-school education is essentially voluntary; the teacher's authority is more limited than it is in school; there are many options if not always within courses, then at least between them; and the adult student brings with him into the class, the manifold roles, connections, and pressures of adult life. So expressions of curriculum aims and intentions in post-school curricula are best treated as one input to the curriculum among others, rather than as determining the outcome. Hence, a course that is labelled liberal or professional or recreational may in fact be and do other things as well. Short of turning post-school education into a compulsory activity in a total institution, with the complete array of institutional and peer-group rewards and sanctions, this inherent polyvance or waywardness (however one views it) can never be altered. Nor would it necessarily be desirable to do so.

If, however, the model and the headings are taken as indications of the intention and primary orientation of curricula, they can still serve a useful purpose in analysing the great diversity of curricula beyond school. In particular, they can be used to analyse what is provided *in curricular terms* by the institutional categories of post-school education. It quickly becomes obvious that there is no one-to-one match between sectors and institutions on the one hand and aims and curricula on the other. Higher education is obviously concerned with academic, teacher, and professional education. There may be tensions between these. But to what extent does higher education provide a liberal education or a personal education? Traditional further education (non-advanced) is clearly to do with vocational education. But how is one to view the 'new FE'? As role education? Social education? Basic education? As for adult education, it was clearly identified in the past with liberal education, recreational education, and remedial education. Nowadays, the scope of adult education has become enlarged to the point where it excludes nothing in the diagram. And suddenly, as Wittgenstein put it, the solution to the problem is seen to lie in its disappearance. Adult education no longer refers to a type of education, but to a type of student.

The purpose of the last three chapters has been to establish a conceptual framework for the analysis of the curriculum beyond school. This has involved exploring what is meant by curriculum, what constitutes a general education, and the different forms of specific education that exist after the end of compulsory schooling. The remainder of the book will consist of an analysis of post-school education in terms of this framework. Chapter 4 will deal with the years immediately following the end of compulsory schooling, variously referred to as post-compulsory, tertiary, and 16–19. Since there is no really suitable title for this part of the system it will be referred to as the 'consecutive phase' since it normally follows on from the compulsory phase without a break. In UK terms, the consecutive phase comprises sixth-form work in schools and colleges, non-advanced further education, the Youth Training Scheme, and other forms of initial training.

Chapter 5 will deal with higher education – namely, advanced studies (in UK terms post-A level or equivalent) in universities, polytechnics, colleges of higher education, or other 'advanced' institutions. Although higher education is not as easy to delimit as it used to be, it is still relatively distinguishable from the rest of the system, not only in curricular but in institutional terms. Chapter 6 addresses what will be called 'education for adults', rather than 'adult education', which has specific connotations in the UK context. It will deal with all kinds of education for adults, vocational and otherwise, formal and non-formal. In all cases, the main reference will be to the UK system, but passing reference will be made to post-school education in other OECD countries, particularly in Western Europe.

NOTES

1   The literature on the nature of higher education is of course very large, but the concept of the academic is perhaps clearest where it is defined in opposition to other possible emphases – in particular, professional or service ones. Levine (1978) gives useful summaries of a range of views, but the ideas of Ortega y Gasset (1946), Veblen (1957), and Jaspers (1960) are central to any discussion of modern thinking on the subject.

2 For an historical perspective on the growth of postgraduate studies
   and in particular the PhD, see Rudd (1975) and Simpson (1983);
   and for a general account of current trends and issues in research,
   see Oldham (1982). The distinction between research and scholarship is ambiguous: in some cases the former connotes science
   and technology, and the latter the arts; in other cases, scholarship
   means keeping up with research (for the purpose of teaching)
   without actually doing it. The distinction, to my mind, confuses
   more than it clarifies, but it is worth noting its use by policy-
   makers who want to reduce the amount spent on research, either
   by segregating 'useful' scientific research from the rest, or by
   concentrating research in 'centres of excellence'.

3 For an historical overview see Dent (1977). The major landmark in
   recent years was the James Report (1972). For an overview of
   comparative developments, see Goodings (1982). Much of what
   can be said about professional education in general applies to
   teacher education in particular, and I will therefore tend to treat it
   here as a specific form of professional education, rather than a
   wholly unique category. However, I have kept the separate
   heading for the sake of clarity.

4 The relationship between theory and practice is of course a central
   issue in all forms of professional education, but it has been
   particularly problematic in teaching perhaps because the 'theory'
   itself is problematic; indeed, some argue that there is no theory.
   The traditional view, that the practice of education should draw on
   foundation or constituent disciplines, was perhaps most forcefully
   advanced by Tibble (1966). The counter-case made by Schwab
   (1969) for more emphasis on practice has already been mentioned
   (see recent issues of *Curriculum Enquiry*); but for somewhat
   different perspectives which also stress the centrality of practice,
   see Golby (1981), Anderson (1982), Hirst (1983), and Eraut
   (1985).

5 Although professional education and its problems have existed for
   a very long time – indeed, one can argue that the real tradition of
   higher education is professional rather than academic (see Bell,
   1971) – interest in the subject seemed to reach a peak in the 1960s
   and early 1970s. Perhaps the reputation of the professions was at
   its peak then, before the attacks of Illich (1973) and others on their
   monopolistic and 'disabling' effects became current. The literature
   on the professions is very large, but Jackson (1970) provides a very
   useful inroad. On professional education, see Schein (1972), Cook
   (1973), Turner and Rushton (1976), Jarvis (1983), and Goodlad
   (1984).

6 Evidence for this is given in the Finniston Report, *Engineering Our
   Future* (Finniston, 1980), but the problems of engineering as a
   profession in the UK (as compared to other countries) go back
   much further and seem to lie much deeper; indeed as Finniston

notes, his report is only the latest in a long line of enquiries into the subject. One explanation of the relatively low status of engineering over the last century and more is advanced by Wiener (1981) in terms of an anti-industrial ethos among certain sections of the upper and upper middle classes, an ethos which he claims was aided and transmitted by higher education. Sanderson (1972), however, provides a good deal of evidence of the involvement of universities, particularly the civic and Scottish ones, in engineering. My own view is that Wiener's thesis, although overstated, is substantially correct, and that this has led, among other things, to a preference for the pure (science) over the applied (engineering) in education generally. However, I suspect that the perception and status of the new technologies is quite different from that of the older ones, and that information technology in particular has achieved a remarkable elite and popular status in a short time. Whether this translates into policy and provision is another matter.

7 It is important to remember that many forms of general education have vocational value (O-level English, Mathematics, for example), and I shall follow Evans (1971) in defining vocational education in relative terms, as an education which makes a person more employable in one occupation than in others. Since the distinction between vocational education and training seems to me to be one of degree (of scope, reproductiveness/reflectiveness, transferability) rather than kind, I shall use the two terms fairly interchangeably, although preferring one or the other connotation where it seems appropriate.

8 Of all the factors which complicate the education–employment relationship, this is surely the most difficult to analyse. The elasticity of substitution of educated manpower depends on two classes of variables: those to do with the education/training received, such as its level, scope, polyvalence, transferability (in psychological terms); and those to do with the labour market, such as restrictions on entry (specified qualifications, union demarcation, professional memberships) and the demand for labour in particular sectors, occupations, and regions. As if this were not enough, it is likely that the whole process is also mediated by cultural assumptions about transferability, which may vary from country to country (e.g., UK to France) and also within countries from sector to sector or level to level: for example, the belief here in the trained mind at graduate level does not seem to have any parallel at craft or technician level, although there is a tradition in some crafts of being able to 'turn your hand to'; and the MSC has recently emphasised transfer and 'learning to take it with you'. In view of the complexity of the problems, it is hardly surprising that there are no general data in the UK on substitution, although there are studies of what happens to particular categories of graduates, and a good deal of anecdotal evidence that substitution occurs

widely, particularly at very low levels of skill (construction work, cleaners) and at very high levels (cabinet ministers, top managers). The only general implication that can be drawn is that the education–employment relationship is more flexible than has been often thought in the past, and certainly does not always require a 1 : 1 match between what the education system produces and what the labour market needs: and that people in the business of formal education and training typically underestimate the potential for learning on the job.

9   This kind of argument has been spelled out recently by Blaug (1983) as part of what he calls a 'second generation' in the economics of education. If labour contracts are incomplete in the aspects he describes, this opens the way for the readier admission of 'economic culture' factors in the analysis of production – i.e., attitudes, norms, and traditions and rituals. For a critical review of Blaug's arguments, see Mace (1984).

10 This kind of argument has been advanced by Gorz (1972), and Gleeson and Mardle (1980), who have stressed the socialising and affective aspects of further education as against its cognitive or skill components. A classic French study is Grignon's *The Order of Things* (1971) as yet only summarised in English. Grignon comments not only on the content of courses, but on things such as dress, behaviour, and types of humour; and in one passage illustrates how even the choice of literary texts in the 'cultural' component of the vocational course mirrors and reinforces the expectations of technical precision and competence.

11 There is disagreement over the validity and extent of the screening hypothesis: for a recent overview of the issues see Atkinson (1983). My own view is that the importance of screening is a function of the degree of relatedness between studies and work. Where there is overt direct relevance (for instance, with nurses), qualifications are used as direct measures of knowledge and skills; where the relationship is oblique (entry to general management, for example) qualifications become used more as an indirect measure of inferred ability and attitudes. In the extreme version of the screening hypothesis, education or training make no difference and add nothing; but the modified and more common version will allow some 'process' and hidden curriculum effects (see Chapter 1) while discounting content *per se*. The use of the concept of ability/ aptitude by some economists is rather simplistic; likewise the clear distinction between knowledge and attitudes implied by some proponents of the socialisation hypothesis (see note 10).

12 While social education is not an official or statutory phrase in the UK, it is nevertheless an important theme in 16–19 and adult education; see, for example, the Russell Report (1973) on adult education, or some of the recent publications of the Further

Education Unit. See also Pring (1984) in relation to the schools. On political education for adults, see ACACE (1983).

13 Role, although a pervasive concept is an elusive one: indeed, it may be a redundant one: for a general discussion see Jackson (1972). Despite these difficulties, I will argue in Chapter 6 below that the increased number and complexity of roles is one of the defining features of adulthood. It should also be pointed out that role education (and social and personal education) may have a strong moral or ethical element. This is true to a greater or lesser extent of all the headings used in Figure 2; which is why I have not given moral or ethical development as a separate heading in the curriculum. Moral concerns, at the level of the curriculum as distinct from in the abstract, tend to be couched in terms of the other headings, rather than in isolation: in operational terms, they are a facet of the personal, social, vocational, academic, professional, and so on; morality tends to be morality *about*. This is not of course to deny the need for thinking about moral or ethical education *per se*; only to argue that it tends to exist 'across' or 'through' the curriculum.

14 A point similar to the one made in note 13 can be made here about the notion of the self. While one can talk in general terms about the self, self-concept, self-development, personal education, individual potential, and growth, and these notions are certainly broader than what many psychologists understand by 'ability', such talk, in practice, soon refers back to, or is stated in terms of more specific abilities. Potential must be potential for something, growth must be growth of something, development must be development of or towards something; and those 'somethings' typically fall under one or more of the types of ability distinguished in Chapter 2. This is simply to restate the familiar problem of talking about the self in the abstract: as with God, the analysis tends to fall back on external reference, metaphor, or analogy. However, the notion of personal or self development does go beyond the notion of ability (even widely construed) in that it points to an organising, integrating, or executive sense which relates abilities to one another, and presumably constitutes what we mean by identity.

15 Some adult educators regret the use of the term 'recreational' in the 1944 Act, believing that it gave adult education a distinctly light-weight reputation in the eyes of many. Words and labels seem to be peculiarly important in the development of adult education; for one view of the 1944 provisions, see Lowe (1970).

16 Whether the new technology will tend to upgrade, downgrade, or polarise jobs in terms of skill levels is partly a matter of policy, not just a consequence of deterministic social and economic trends. See Commission of the European Community (1984) for a discus-

sion of policy options. Boyer (1983) cites several US studies, and suggests that many new jobs will be in the less glamorous low-tech occupations.

17 See, *inter alia*, Hirst (1974), Barrow (1976), Brent (1978), and Strike and Egan (1978). Its centrality in some form of adult education means that it is a recurrent topic in the relevant journals, such as *Adult Education* and *Studies in the Education of Adults*. For a traditionalist statement, see Wiltshire (1983); for a revisionist view see Crombie and Harries-Jenkins (1983).

4 The Consecutive Phase

Introduction

Of all the parts of the education system, the provision in the years immediately following the end of compulsory schooling is the most complex in both institutional and curricular terms.[1] Indeed, the provision in the United Kingdom for this phase of education has been aptly described as a jungle (Locke and Bloomfield, 1982). There are various reasons why this should be so.

First, although education at this stage is by definition no longer compulsory and therefore universal, high and often increasing proportions of the age group continue to be enrolled. A recent OECD report notes:

> Enrolment rates of 16 year-olds increased regularly in most countries; a similar, though less clear-cut trend, is observed among 17 year-olds. This shows that in the course of the 1970s a common pattern within the OECD area was for young people to prolong their studies one year after the end of compulsory schooling, but no longer. There are indications, however, that two years of post-compulsory education or training is gradually becoming the norm in a number of countries, as in fact has been the case in North America and Japan for some time now. (OECD, 1985, page 17)

If various forms of non-formal training are included, the participation rates are even higher. The increase in enrolments in this phase of education seems to be due to various factors: higher female participation rates; government schemes which encourage education or training as an alternative to unemployment; and the inflation in qualifications which leads young people to try to get higher qualifications, or to have a second go at getting school-level qualifications. It should also be noted that continuing part-time education is compulsory in some countries (such as Germany) and was proposed many decades ago in the United Kingdom, though never implemented. Whatever the exact mix of factors in any one country, the result is that educational provision (including training) in every country has to cater for both a larger number, and greater diversity of students, than it did in the past. This scale and diversity in ability, motivation, and circumstances in themselves lead to more complex patterns of provision.

Secondly, provision in this phase of education is complex because of the 'jagged edge' of compulsory education. The most obvious aspect of this jaggedness is the difference in compulsory school-leaving examination achievements. Even if all students emerged, by some miracle, from the compulsory system with standardised achievements, their needs, directions, and destinations would still be diverse; but they do not. Some have learned very little, some a lot. Some are turned off or against education; some are addicted to it. This diversity points to the need not only for different levels of courses in the consecutive phase, ranging from remedial and recuperative to pre-academic and pre-professional, but for different forms and styles of education. There is no way in which post-compulsory education can simply continue the schooling mode for everyone; some young people want to get as far away from school as they can.

Thirdly, education in this phase is strongly influenced by the gravitational pull of higher education. The 'top-down' influence is strong, not least in the role models and expectations of teachers, who are themselves often products of higher education. In the United Kingdom, higher education has a strong influence on the examination system at this stage, and attempts to alter that system have in the past sometimes failed because they did not conform to the needs of higher education, even though these are minority needs (Holt, 1980). It has been observed that the needs of those who transfer to higher levels in the education system tend to take precedence over the 'terminal' needs of those who are about to leave it (OECD, 1977). Education, in the consecutive phase, both is and is not part of a hierarchical structure whose internal priorities exercise a powerful, objective hold on curricula and qualifications. The subjective hold on teachers' values is much more difficult to assess, but may influence students through both the formal processes of counselling, in which a certain pecking-order of choices may be implied, and informally through the existence of the teacher as a role model which the student may imitate or reject.

Fourthly, education in the years following the end of compulsory schooling is subject to the demands of the job market. Some young people leave school and go straight into work; some continue work and part-time training/education: some continue to receive full-time education, and their entry to the job market is delayed, either for a short time or for a longer period. But even with long-cycle academic education, job considerations are never entirely absent, and in the majority of cases, they loom much larger, affecting both the content of the curriculum and the students' response to it. And since the job market is itself an exceedingly complex phenomenon – highly differentiated, shifting, and presenting often competing or conflicting demands – it is not surprising that this complexity is mirrored in the structure and content of much education at this stage.

Fifthly, the consecutive phase of education has had to respond in recent years to the problem of youth unemployment. This has reached unprecedented levels, both in absolute terms and, in some countries, as a ratio of adult unemployment. In the 12 countries reviewed in the OECD Employment Outlook recently, it was forecast that, on average, one in every six of the youth labour force (aged 15–24) would be unemployed in 1984. And although there has been some levelling off or decline in the ratio of youth to adult unemployment, youth unemployment was expected to account for 41 per cent of the total in the same year (OECD, 1985, pages 33–8). Moreover, the percentages are much higher among certain sub-groups of youth; the educationally and socially disadvantaged, immigrants, resident racial minorities, and the handicapped. Thus economic marginalisation compounds any existing problems of alienation among the young.

The initial and minimal policy response to rising unemployment, and especially youth unemployment, is to provide some form of training, as an alternative to unemployment. This is usually seen as being 'better than nothing', both for individuals and for governments. Trainees or young people on work experience/job creation schemes can be subtracted from aggregate unemployment figures, and however poor the training or limited the work experience, are arguably gaining more from it than if they were simply on the dole. Beyond this initial broad response, however, the policy options become more complex, and will be analysed later in this chapter.

There are two other general factors which contribute to making the consecutive phase of education extremely complex. One is that late adolescence/early adulthood is widely regarded as a complex stage in any individual's development. In popular terms, this is referred to in terms of 'growing up', 'maturing', 'coming of age', and 'finding yourself'. In the psychological literature, it is conceptualised in terms of transition and the search for identity (Erickson, 1968). Although we are now moving away from the simple traditional view of adulthood as a stable plateau, which once having been reached, one remains on till one falls off at the other end, there is still a feeling that the late teens are, in industrialised societies at least, a period of particular upheaval and uncertainty. More will be said of this later, but for the moment it can simply be noted that the complexities of 16–19 provision have a personal dimension which is intertwined with their educational dimension.

The other general factor which makes the consecutive phase complex is that it typically involves not only the education ministry, but ministries of labour and social services; not only governments, but para-statal and private organisations; not only employers but also unions. It is at this point that the 'radical monopoly', to use Illich's phrase, of the education system breaks down, and a plethora of institutions and interests becomes involved. Within this, the education service may still be the major force, in terms of both numbers enrolled and control of qualifications, but the consecutive phase is characterised, at the official level, by endless calls for liaison, co-operation, and consultation, and at the unofficial level by a complex and shifting struggle between sectional interests with truces, alliances, parleys, and the occasional pitched battle.

All this is familiar ground, particularly to those who work in this part of the education system, or are otherwise concerned with young people in the years immediately following their exit from the compulsory school. What is interesting, however, is that talk about this stage of education *as a whole* is a relatively new thing (MacFarlane, 1980; Edwards, 1983). It is only in the last decade that terms like '16–19', 'tertiary', and 'post-compulsory' have become current. Before that, the various strands of provision tended to be considered in isolation from one another. The academic streams of upper secondary education (in UK parlance, 'sixth form') were discussed primarily in relation to higher education; technical education, leading to ONC/D and HNC/D awards was seen as another well-defined stream; courses and apprenticeships leading to City and Guilds or Royal Society of Arts qualifications were another strand; and then a lot of young people simply left the system altogether and went into work.

One recent attempt to take a more comprehensive view of this phase has been the guide entitled *Signposts* by Pratley (1985), who divides 16–19 provision into three broad types: general education; job-specific education or training; and vocational preparation. First there are general education courses entailing no particular vocational choice, and often leading on to higher education. The obvious examples here are the GCE O and A level courses, and from 1988, the General Certificate of Secondary Education (GCSE) which will replace O levels and CSEs. Pratley also mentions the Certificate of Extended Education (CEE) under this heading, although this was never officially more than a pilot qualification, and its future is currently uncertain: it may become absorbed within the framework of the CPVE (see below). While such courses, typically composed of discrete single-subject examinations reflecting the academic categories of higher education, are not vocational in the relative sense (see Chapter 3, note 7) they are often used as general qualifications or screening devices for employment: for example, O level English and Mathematics are minimum requirements for some jobs. And as Pratley notes, possession of O levels (and even more, A levels) denotes evidence of a certain level and a certain *kind* of ability – in Hargreaves' terms, cognitive-intellectual.

Secondly, there is full-time or part-time job-specific education or training for those who have made a definite career decision, or who have actually started work. The typical qualifications here are those of the City and Guilds of London Institute, the Royal Society of Arts, the London Chamber of Commerce, and the Business and Technician Education Council; there are also regional examining bodies. These courses are the traditional provision of further education, and the examining bodies date from the nineteenth or early twentieth centuries, although B/TEC is a much more recent arrival, replacing the familiar national certificate scheme (ONC/D, HNC/D) upon the recommendation of the Haslegrave Report (1969). Students who study part-time do so on a day-release or block-release basis, and the studies are often related to apprenticeships, which have latterly declined sharply in number. The level of studies goes from craft through advanced craft and technician levels to technologist level, which is roughly equivalent to a pass degree. Two trends worthy of mention in this type of course are the development of very specific skill competence certificates (for example, grill chef as against catering) and the prevalence of modular or unit structures.

Pratley's third category is broad vocational preparation courses for those who have not yet entered employment or who have not made a specific occupational choice. Examples of these in recent years have included the City and Guilds' Foundation Courses, the RSA basic level schemes, and the Certificate of Further Education, but the two main current frameworks are the Youth Training

Scheme (YTS) and the Certificate of Pre-Vocational Education (CPVE). The one-year YTS aimed to provide broad-based training with an emphasis on work experience, and opportunities to develop social skills and personal competence. The main mode (A) was employer-based, and the secondary mode (B) community, local authority, or college-based. The YTS did not usually lead to any qualification, but the plan is now to extend it to two years with the second year being more specific and leading to a recognised qualification. The CPVE is in some ways the education system's answer to the YTS, and is firmly based on schools and colleges. The curriculum has three elements (core + vocational studies + additional studies) organised in about five basic occupational categories. The YTS and CPVE are the newest and most controversial additions to provision for 16–19 year olds, and in part cater for young people who in more prosperous times would have gone directly into relatively unskilled jobs, without any further education or training. They were thus in the short term a response to the rise of youth unemployment, but now look like becoming part of a general strategy to delay entry into the labour market until the age of 18.

These three types of provision are not as clearly demarcated as this brief description may suggest, and there are other developments as well. The Technical and Vocational Education Initiative (TVEI) is a project which aims to develop such studies across the compulsory line, from age 14 to 18, although preliminary unpublished results suggest that many students are dropping out at 16. Nevertheless, there is some debate now about whether policy should be conceptualised in terms of the 16 to 19 age-group, or a broader 14 to 18/19 span. In another recent development, a general review of vocational qualifications has recently been completed. This has suggested some degree of co-ordination and rationalisation, in terms of levels and equivalences, without going as far as the new Scottish system, in which almost all non-advanced courses are being reorganised in 40-hour modules, leading to a single national vocational certificate for the 16–18 age-group (SED, 1983; Roebuck, 1985). These modules are grouped in nine broad occupational fields, and can be taken in one or several institutions, continuously or intermittently. There is talk of eventually bringing pre-academic 'higher' courses into the scheme as well, and an expectation that the flexibility of the modular-credit structure will attract greater numbers of adults to continuing education and training. Indeed, such a structure begins to blur the distinction between consecutive and continuing education; such a development has much to recommend it, and will be discussed in more detail in Chapter 6.

It is clear from Pratley's description of 16–19 provision that education and training at this stage are complex and diversified, so much so that it is difficult to think of the system as a whole. The picture is particularly confused and confusing in England and Wales, where a series of major initiatives has been taken without the formulation of any general policy for the sector. Thus the relationship between the YTS and the CPVE is not clear, and both may be pre-empted in some respects by the TVEI. The implications of the new GCSE for the years and courses that follow have only been partly thought through. The relationship between the new, two-year YTS and the more traditional vocational qualifications is still unclear, and indeed the whole structure of qualifications at this stage remains unco-ordinated and problematic.

Policy and provision at this stage of education are more complex and confused in England and Wales than in the majority of OECD countries, but the fact is that it is an extremely complex stage or sector in any country, for the kinds of reasons outlined at the beginning of this chapter. How then can it be conceptualised? Is there anything that unifies or characterises the great diversity that exists?

The fundamental fact about education at this stage is that it moves into a closer and more direct relationship with the society or culture around it; in terms of Figure 2 there is a marked shift towards the right-hand side of the diagram, towards professional, vocational, social, and role education. Of course the schools reflect the nature of the society they exist in, but their relationship with it is to some extent generalised, oblique, or indirect; they maintain a certain distance from it, partly because, as Chapter 2 suggested, they are oriented towards knowledge and ability, as well as culture, in the name of 'general education'. Higher education also maintains a certain distance from society, though in different ways and for different reasons. The emphasis on knowledge for its own sake, the long-term nature of much research and scholarship, and the indirectness of the relationship between the curriculum and the graduate labour market (which will be explored in the next chapter) all allow higher education to stand back a little from society, although that stance is always contested, not least by governments which would like to gear higher education much more closely to what they see as national needs and priorities.

However, at the consecutive stage, neither the arguments which allow the schools to generalise their relationship with society, nor those which allow higher education to maintain a certain distance from it, apply in the same way or with the same force. Hence the curriculum at this stage reflects, more clearly and directly than it does in other sectors, the nature of that society and culture. It becomes more *applied or instrumental*, reflecting the major tasks which society faces or sets itself. The task of defence is reflected in the military service which exists in many countries at this age though not in the United Kingdom. The task of production (in its widest sense, as in 'gross national product', and including the production of knowledge) is reflected in the prevalence of vocational, technical and professional, or pre-professional courses. The tasks of social organisation, and the social relations that accompany them, lead to an emphasis on education for citizenship, role education, education about work, and social and life skills.

Secondly, the curriculum carries a strong *affective* loading, reflecting the importance of social norms in both the workplace and adult life generally. Post-compulsory education is concerned not only with knowledge and skills, but also with attitudes, values, and habits, and this emphasis is manifest in, for example, the significance of role models at this stage: the master craftsman, the work supervisor or foreman, or, in A level courses, the academically oriented upper secondary-school teacher. It shows itself also in the current debate about learning environments at this stage (sixth form versus college versus workplace) and the insistence of the MSC that vocational education/training be 'work-driven'. In some cases (the YTS, for example) attitudes, values, and norms are an overt part of the curriculum, but typically they are part of the hidden or informal curriculum, though none the less important for that.

Thirdly, education at this stage reflects the *stratification* of society into social classes or strata, with concomitant differences in access to wealth, power, and information, and differential status. Pratley's tripartite classification is only one national example of the characteristic tripartite division in industrialised countries, which the OECD labels general/technical/vocational. Although the exact pattern varies from country to country, the flow of students through the system tends to reproduce this stratification in broad terms. Within each stratum, there are sub-strata, and hierarchies and 'pecking-orders' exist within, for example, types of subject (more or less academic), types of vocational course (more or less theoretical/practical), types of institution (more or less selective) and types of apprenticeship (size of firm). The selective and allocative role of the educational system does not of course begin at the post-compulsory stage, but it has been accentuated in recent decades by two converging trends: the tendency to delay or postpone selection, in the name of equality of opportunity and comprehensive education, which tends to move it up from the age of (say) 11 to rather later; and the tendency for educational qualifications to play a larger and larger role in initial job selection (Berg, 1973; Dore, 1976; OECD, 1977). Both these trends make the post-compulsory years the crunch years as far as selection and stratification are concerned, as is evident from the intense concentration of key public examinations in this period.

Fourthly, the curriculum at the consecutive stage becomes more *differentiated* than it is in the preceding years of schooling, in that it becomes subdivided horizontally (in terms of the scope and content of courses) as well as stratified vertically in terms of level and length. Compared to the lower secondary stage, there is a veritable explosion of course headings and qualifications, many of them very specific in content and orientation. This ultimately reflects the division of labour in modern society, though some recent labour-market trends have led, in some countries including the United Kingdom, to a search for more generic or transferable forms of education and training. Such trends have also affected the structure of the curriculum at this stage, and have lain partly behind a shift from linear structures (discrete, unbroken, prescribed lines of study) to more open-ended and optional modular schemes. Both these aspects of differentiation will be discussed below.

Fifthly and finally, the curriculum at this stage reflects the fact that these years are, in a modern industrial society, years of *transition*. In fact, they compound various kinds of transition (financial, legal, personal, and so on) which vary in their importance for different kinds of students, being sharpest for those who leave the education system at this stage, and less dramatic for those who see it primarily as a bridge to higher education. Nevertheless, transitions are marked in various overt and subtle ways in all curricula at this stage, not only in the structure and content of courses, but in teaching styles, ethos, and environment. All stages in life can of course be regarded as transitional, and it will be suggested later in this chapter that the transitional theme has been somewhat overplayed in relation to the 16–19 age-group. However, the fact remains that many crucial choices are and have to be made in these few years in our society. This has obvious implications for curricula, teaching, and, perhaps most important, counselling, which will be explored below.

It has been suggested that the basic fact about education at this stage is that it moves into a closer, more direct, and more immediate relationship with society than is the case either before or after. As a result, the major features of the society or culture are reproduced in the curriculum in relatively overt and pronounced ways. The remainder of this chapter will be devoted to an analysis of each of these features, the tensions and contradictions that lie within and between them, and their implications for curriculum policy.

The applied curriculum

It is difficult to find a term which exactly expresses the orientation or emphasis in the curriculum at this stage with which we are first concerned. 'Harnessed', 'focused', or 'task-oriented' give something of the right sense, as do terms such as 'preparation' and 'foundation', which are commonly used to describe post-compulsory courses. In curriculum theory, 'instrumental' is perhaps the nearest term, though it tends to have a pejorative ring to it which is not intended here. 'Applied' seems to be the best compromise, indicating as it does an education that is for something or towards something.

The word sits easily on most vocational courses, but it may initially seem odd to describe O and A levels in such a way. In particular, O level English and Mathematics seem to be the very antithesis of applied courses, both in their content, and in the generalised way they are used by students and employers. Perhaps O levels are best seen as the final stage of a rather academically inclined model of general education; the fact that they perform a general vocational function is due as much to the fact that employers use them to screen for general ability, as to guarantee certain knowledge and skills. A levels, however, are another matter. The close links between A levels and higher education which are evident not only from the nature of the examining boards but also from the history of attempts to bring about change (Holt, 1980) suggests that they are effectively preparatory courses for higher education, which happen to have other, incidental uses in gaining employment. It will be argued in the next chapter that higher education itself has become thoroughly professionalised; hence it makes sense to see A levels as pre-professional courses. They are obviously not as specifically applied as most vocational courses, but that is simply because they are part of a longer cycle of study which ends with a degree rather than a certificate or diploma. If the rest of this section concentrates on technical and vocational courses rather than such supposedly 'general' ones, it is not because they are more obviously applied, but because there have been many more changes in the labour market than in higher education in recent years, creating many more curricular issues and problems.

The applied or instrumental nature of the curriculum at this stage is, however, most visible in technical and further education. In much of the more traditional literature on this field, such as Peters (1967), Bratchell (1968), and Cantor and Roberts (1972, 1979), it is assumed that education at the consecutive stage is typically education *for* something: business, industry, commerce, agriculture, or the wide range of service occupations. Courses and teaching are harnessed or dedicated to the central social tasks of production, distribution, and exchange. This does not preclude some concern with wider issues, with knowledge or skill for its own sake, or with the development of individual potential, but where time or resources are limited, as they usually are, it is the instrumental goal which will take priority. The connection between the content of the courses and the productive tasks is often very direct indeed, and the list of qualifications offered by the City and Guilds of London Institute (CGLI), Royal Society of Arts (RSA), London Chamber of Commerce (LCC), the Business/Technician Education Council (BTEC) and the regional examining bodies is in effect a list of productive categories and roles.

However, the applied rationale of post-compulsory curricula raises a number of issues, some long-standing and some more recent. Perhaps the main long-standing issue has been whether education at this stage should only be instrumental, or whether it should to go beyond instrumentalism and vocationalism: whether it should in some measure be general, liberal, or non-vocational. For many years, vocational courses in non-advanced further education contained an element of liberal, general, or complementary studies, which were intended to counteract any tendency for the vocational element to become too narrow. In A levels too, a 'general studies' element has complemented what is, by international standards, an extremely restricted and intensive diet of two or three academic subjects. However, in both cases, the general or liberal studies element has tended to be marginalised: the central, instrumental priorities of the courses leave little time or energy for apparently less urgent demands, a tendency exacerbated by more intense competition for jobs and places in higher education. Besides, it is not clear how far students themselves want to continue with generalised or divergent studies at this stage. Some theorists, such as Spranger (Taylor, 1981), have argued that at this stage in a person's development, the need for convergence and focus tends to take precedence over more divergent, general interests, because the acquisition of adult identity is closely linked to a sense of competence, of being able to do something. Such a view implies a stage theory of educational development, in which a broad general education at school is followed by a relatively focused vocational or professional education, which subsequently opens out again into the pluralistic needs and interests of the adult. There are problems in applying such stage theories in contemporary society; for example, some women marry early and begin their vocational education in their thirties; and some graduates do not really begin their professional education until their mid-twenties. The fluidity of life patterns nowadays makes it increasingly difficult to think in stages at all. However, the fact that models like Spranger's have made little impact on British thinking may be due less to these obvious criticisms, which apply in Germany also, than to a cultural difference between the two countries (Hearnden, 1976). It is noticeable that whereas in Germany there are philosophies of vocational education, drawing ultimately on the teachings of Luther, which regard work as a central element in and means of human development, as something which both focuses and express- es adult identity, in Britain the ethos of vocational education is much more pragmatic and down to earth. Indeed, educators tend to write as if human development takes place outside or even despite work, and vocational education is therefore often seen as something 'narrow' and 'limited', which has to be supplemented by liberal studies of some kind. In the education world, training is typically thought of as a rote-like, routine, rudimentary activity, ignoring the fact that most training involves complex skills, decisions, and judgements, not to mention an induction into a particular kind of culture associated with a craft or occupation.

The distinctions between the instrumental and the liberal, or the vocational and the non-vocational, may thus be much less clear-cut than they appear. But even if it is accepted that education at this stage is or should be mainly applied and instrumental, further questions arise about the nature of that instrumentality. How far is it vocational-instrumental, developing the knowledge, attitudes, and skills necessary to do work, and how far is it social- instrumental, equipping the young person to function as an adult in a more general way? In recent years, themes such as social and life skills and coping skills have entered the curriculum at this stage (McGuire and Priestley, 1981), often at the behest of the MSC, and often for low-achieving students. Such developments suggest a growing social-instrumental emphasis in educational and training policy, which may be seen either as a response to a breakdown of socialisation in the schools, or as a substitute for the socialisation that would have occurred if the young people had gone directly into employment, as they used to in large numbers. In some other countries (as dissimilar as Japan, the United States and Italy) there is currently a good deal of emphasis on 'education for citizenship'; and in all courses in all countries a good deal of what is in effect role education goes on, although that concept is much more familiar in adult education than in the 16–19 sphere.

Some of the issues raised by a greater 'social-instrumental' emphasis will be taken up again in the next section, but there remain several problems associated even with the more traditional vocational-instrumental one. How far should the curriculum take into account differences between local and national labour markets? Lower-level courses will tend to relate to the former, and higher-level ones to the latter, but although it may be sensible to plan courses in the light of local job opportunities, there is a danger that such a policy will lock young people into local labour markets, and eventually accentuate disparities in regional development. Since training provision is often linked to work experience with local employers, a vicious circle of declining numbers and types of opportunity may result if some attempt is not made to train 'ahead of' the market. The development of open learning packages, and the projected 'College of the Air' could help to spread training resources more evenly across prosperous and declining regions.

Training ahead of the labour market is in fact evident in the increased emphasis in recent years on education for self-employment rather than employment, a policy which first emerged, curiously, in the United Kingdom and the Mediterranean European countries, but which is now strongly endorsed by the EEC. Economic comparisons with the United States and Japan suggest that a greater emphasis on self-employment in Europe might be a good thing, in terms of both economic growth and employment statistics: many large firms are using increased profitability to become increasingly capital- and technology-intensive. However, the problem is to know when training for self-employment is likely to be most effective, and common sense suggests that it may be more useful for people in their twenties, who have had some work experience, and a chance to accumulate a little capital, than for teenagers who have only recently left school, unless they have a quite specific and viable proposition in mind. However, it is too soon yet to evaluate this particular trend in vocational education.

The major challenge to the applied curriculum is of course

unemployment, which undercuts the basic rationale for vocational education. What is the point of preparing or equipping people to work if they cannot work? What is the point of an applied curriculum if there is nothing to apply it to? The response to such questions involves assumptions and issues which go well beyond education, and it has been stated quite forcefully by the OECD, for example, that unemployment is essentially an employment problem and not an educational one. In the long term, of course, the nature and quality of vocational education may have an effect on economic performance, which in turn may affect the level of unemployment. Since this is one of the major issues in education and curriculum policy at the present, it will be taken up in the conclusion of the book. Here, it is sufficient to note that, beyond a certain point, training only becomes a substitute for employment, and a means of keeping people out of the labour market and off the dole. This leads to a perversion of the applied, instrumental role of the curriculum at this stage, which is quickly perceived by young people, and can only undermine further the already low status of vocational education in the United Kingdom. Where there is no realistic possibility of vocational education and training leading to work, the direct relationship between education and production described at the beginning of this section no longer exists. This suggests that a different kind of relationship needs to be envisaged, and hence different curricula (Watts, 1983; Dale, 1985).

The affective curriculum

For many educators, a phrase like 'the affective curriculum' is more likely to suggest the development of fantasy and feeling in primary or secondary education through creative artistic and social activities than the kind of thing that goes on in a course for, say, gas fitters or receptionists. But the description of affectivity given in the introduction to the *Affective Domain* of the *Taxonomy of Educational Objectives* (Krathwohl et al., 1964) makes the relevance of the term in the 16–19 context quite clear:

> the continuum progressed from a level at which the individual is merely *aware* of a phenomenon, being *able to perceive it*. At a next level he is *willing to attend* to phenomena. At a next level he *responds* to the phenomena with a *positive feeling*. Eventually he may feel strongly enough to *go out of his way* to respond. At some point in the process he conceptualizes his behavior and feelings and *organizes*

these conceptualizations into a structure. This structure grows in complexity as *it becomes his life outlook*. (page 27)

The authors of the *Taxonomy* classified affectivity in five levels, each more complex and internalised than the previous one: receiving (attending); responding; valuing; organisation of a value system; and characterisation by a value or value complex. It is in these senses that affectivity is a central element in education and training at the consecutive stage.

It was suggested earlier that this emphasis on affectivity stems from the greater proximity of education at this stage to social norms. Obviously, all education of every kind and at every stage is permeated by the norms of the culture within which it operates. However, post-compulsory education is influenced not only by general social norms but by the more local or specific norms of particular groups and subcultures. The student on a craft course – for example, plastering – will be exposed to norms and values which are to some extent peculiar to that particular trade, and will to some extent distinguish him from members of other craft groups, such as joiners or electricians. On technican or pre-professional courses, likewise, something of the 'culture' of each occupation will be imbibed. This normative element in technical and vocational education has long been recognised, and traditionally was held to be one of the most valuable aspects of it: the relationship between master and apprentice, however idealised, was intended to go much wider than a mere transmission of knowledge and skills. As the Germans put it, the aim was to turn carpenters into men, not men into carpenters. (The male emphasis in traditional vocational education was until recently taken for granted.) Latterly, writers concerned with the negative aspects of this differential socialisation, such as Grignon (1971), Willis (1977), and Gleeson (1983), have been much more critical of the outcomes of this process, but there is no dispute that an affective education is taking place. And though there has been less analytic writing on the affective aspects of general (i.e., pre-academic) education at this stage, the frequent references to the special relationships, atmosphere, and ethos of the sixth form, and how this is becoming or might become diluted in tertiary colleges, suggests that the process described above by Krathwohl and his colleagues occurs there just as pervasively as in vocational and technical courses.

If anything, the emphasis on affectivity in the curriculum at this stage has increased in recent years. For example, the value of the *Meister* as a role model in the German apprenticeship system has been recognised by a number of British writers, and efforts are being made, with the support of the Further Education Staff College, to develop a similar role and status for 'industrial tutors' in this country (Flower and Russell, 1982). The differences in the work culture of the two countries which were referred to earlier may make this difficult, but at least there is now an awareness that 'modelling' in this sense is an important aspect of education and training at this stage, when the young person may be searching for examples of adult behaviour and adulthood to imitate or react against.

There has also been a good deal of debate about the learning environment, with the MSC insisting that the bulk of training should, if possible, take place in a work rather than college setting (MSC, 1981a; 1981b). The implication of this is that colleges are not environmentally neutral, but transmit certain values which belong to the educational system, and which may be inappropriate or even counter-productive in the workplace. The current discussions about the appropriate institutional forms for post-compulsory education (sixth form, sixth-form college, tertiary college, work-based training, community placements) are in an oblique way a debate about cultures and affectivity, and raise not only the 'big' questions about authority, conformity, autonomy, and individuality but also more subtle issues to do with work habits: the perception of time-frames, the rhythm of work, the modes of working alone or with others, the criteria of judgement and satisfaction.[2] There may of course be a conflict between the values and habits required in one work setting and those in another, or between immediate and longer-term requirements. In this way, socialisation into a particular work setting may prove dysfunctional in the long run if it makes employees less flexible and adaptable. The notion of vocational socialisation contains its own tensions and contradictions, quite apart from those arising from the educational connection.

Much of the contemporary concern with affectivity is thus to do with what might be called differential socialisation: the influence of different kinds of role models and environments on the habits, attitudes, and values of the student or trainee. One reason for this is perhaps the growing realisation that in all except the most tightly controlled jobs, the worker has an element of discretion in how he or she works. Some economists in recent years (Blaug, 1983) have stressed the incompleteness of labour contracts, which do not and cannot specify exactly how the employee shall work, and have to be complemented by an 'invisible handshake'. How people work is influenced by their habits, attitudes, values, and self-concept, all of which constitute the 'work culture'. There is some evidence, which will be referred to in the conclusion of this book, that the United Kingdom's poor economic performance is due at least in part to such cultural variables, as distinct from more purely economic ones. Hence whatever goes to shape the work culture and the attitudes of workers is an important factor in production, and this leads back to the affective element in not only vocational education but 'general' or pre-academic education as well (Wiener, 1981). To what extent does a 'liberal' education socialise young people away from certain kinds of work? To what extent does it transmit anti-business or anti-industrial attitudes?

Is it only a question of differential socialisation, of one set of attitudes as against another? Of the culture of education as against the culture of training? Of both against the cultures of the workplace? In the educational world, there is often an assumption that education is not simply one subculture among others, but that it in some way stands outside or back from the culture. Both left-wing sociologists and right-wing economists have tended to undermine that assumption, by arguing for quite different reasons that education is not culturally 'neutral': it inculcates and transmits a whole range of cultural norms and values which (depending on the point of view) reinforce an unjust society or impede a free market. There are two main defences against such arguments. The first holds that one cannot simply conceptualise knowledge in cultural or social construct terms (that is, subsume the top of the triangle in Figure 2 within the right-hand point), and invokes the concept of objectivity in either a strong or weak form. This argument has been rather unfashionable in recent years in education, but is no less powerful for that; such problems have occupied philosophers for some thousands of years. The second defence depends on the concept of consciousness. Culture, it is argued, is mediated by and through consciousness to the extent that the person is aware of the categories it employs. Education develops such awareness through its emphasis on rationality, autonomy, and reflexivity; thus, although it cannot stand outside the culture, it can certainly stand back from it, in a much less determinate relationship than concepts like socialisation and acculturation seem to imply.

Such arguments and counter-arguments are rarely encountered in their abstract or pure form in discussions of curriculum policy. Nevertheless, they do underlie many of the current debates about education and training at this stage, debates which have taken on an institutional dimension through the involvement of differing and to some extent competing agencies, such as the DES, MSC, LEAs, and examining bodies. The least that can be done on all sides is to recognise the importance of the affective dimension in this sector of education, even if the possibilities of consensus about attitudes and values are slim.

Stratification

Modern industrial societies are stratified vertically into strata or classes which have differential access to wealth and power, and this stratification is typically founded on different economic circumstances: not simply how much people earn, but whether they employ or are employed, can dispose of capital as distinct from income, and so on. The socio-political analysis of this phenomenon is of course very complex, and here we will concentrate only on looking at its implications for the curriculum at the post-compulsory stage.

The general issue that stems from stratification can be expressed in educational terms as equality versus selection. At the consecutive stage, curricula are typically stratified in OECD countries into three strata (general, technical, and vocational) with various streams within these (OECD, 1985). (These strata or 'tracks' also reflect the differentiation of the curriculum at this stage, and ultimately the division of labour, underlining the typically economic and occupational basis of stratification; hence there is a close relationship between what is said in this and in the next section.)

In the OECD countries, the debate about educational stratification in recent decades has been about when rather than whether it should occur. In some countries, such as France, Germany, and the Netherlands, the subdivision of the general curriculum into particular streams and strands begins relatively early (often around the age of 13/14), whereas in others, such as the United States, Sweden, and Japan, it appears to be delayed until the age of 16–18; 'appears' because in fact internal and to some extent hidden stratification exists even in systems and institutions which are nominally comprehensive. The argument for early stratification is based both on economic rationality (the need for effective manpower allocation) and on student motivation (some students do not want a general curriculum beyond the age of 13/14). The arguments for delaying stratification are partly social (equality of opportunity), psychological (late development), and economic (the need for polyvalent skills in a fast-changing economy). Such arguments have been widely used, and do not need rehearsing here.[3]

However, the issue is not simply whether or when; many questions turn on the question how. One may accept that both the range of student achievement and the demands of the labour market make stratification inevitable by the age of 16, but given that, what *progression* opportunities are there for students to move up from lower to higher streams at later stages? The Further Education Unit's concern with 'progression' at the post-compulsory stage has been voiced in several documents, in terms such as the following:

> There requires to be a public commitment by the training and education systems to the principle that the wider opportunities apparently associated with the various plans for vocational preparation, must be accompanied by opportunities for progression. The responses in this document suggest that this commitment exists and dissenters should be required to publicly 'contract out'. (FEU, 1982c, para. 33)

Such views tend to receive wide general approval in this country; they attempt to mitigate the harsher effects of curricular stratification by creating 'alternative routes' and 'second chances', and by avoiding educational 'dead-ends'. Some of the support for continuing education and training also stems from the belief that it can help to modify the effects of selection at earlier stages. However, the existence of opportunities for progression on paper is no guarantee that they can or will be taken up by significant numbers of students. Those who would like to progress further may be deterred by the extra time it takes (compared to the normal route), and institutions and lecturers have all sorts of subtle ways of 'cooling out' students they would rather not have. At the policy level also, there is a potential contradiction. Too much progression might deprive the labour market of some of the lower- and middle-level manpower that it needs.

The notion of progression also runs into a more profound problem. If progression from the lowest to the highest curricular strata is possible, then any qualification except the highest is a relative failure; whereas if progression is impossible, the top of each particular stratum can be seen as a relative success. The existence of opportunities for progression tends to assimilate all kinds of courses to the central hierarchy of educational qualifications, and the values and norms associated with these. It was argued in Chapter 2 that these values are primarily cognitive-intellectual; hence the attempt to create opportunities for those in vocational and technical education to progress to higher education risks assimilating the "he(augane ty"

somewhat distinctive cultures of the former into the dominant culture of higher education. An example may make this clear. It is usually reckoned that a Higher National Diploma is equivalent to a pass degree. However, if all HNDs were reclassified as pass degrees, they would merely become poor degrees rather than good technical qualifications, and might begin to be thought of as rather deficient in truly academic content. A similar problem would arise if a craft course were seen merely as a lower form of technician course.

The basic issue is the one raised in Chapter 2, to do with the unity or plurality of types of ability and types of educational objective. If a truly comprehensive and unified system of post-compulsory education were created, it would tend to position all courses and students on a single hierarchy of educational values, in place of the rather chaotic but multiple hierarchies that currently exist; and as long as higher education was seen not simply as a more advanced form of academic or professional education, but as the apex and ideal type of all education, that problem would remain.

The unity/plurality issue also manifests itself in the way employers select young people for jobs. There is a widespread belief among employers that there is such a thing as general ability, and that the education system is quite good at sorting and grading people in terms of it: thus they will often prefer the bright but untrained candidate to the less able one who has had a 'relevant' training. Such decisions, of course, depend on the potential cost of training to the employer, but they raise a basic policy problem: what should the education/training system do for the less able students, in order to maximise their chances in the job market? Rather than providing them with a watered-down form of general or pre-vocational education, which will inevitably compare unfavourably in employers' eyes with the 'real thing', it might be better to give them marketable skills in a specific area which could tip the 'ability/skills' trade-off in their favour. In other words, if they are not 'bright', make sure they are well-trained. This kind of reasoning underlies the German and French systems, with their emphasis on relatively specific but quite rigorous skills training, in contrast to the UK one, with its current emphasis on generic, pre-vocational preparation in the one-year YTS and the CPVE. But as the next section will suggest, current labour-market trends themselves are affecting the generic/specific balance for quite different reasons.

The issues of stratification and progression, and selection and equality, have also led to concern in recent years with the methods of assessment and selection. This has taken the form of an increased interest in continuous or coursework assessment, stimulated partly by the two arms of what is now BTEC, in criterion-referenced as against norm-referenced procedures (embodied in the new GCSE), in profiles of student achievement as against traditional marks and grades (encouraged by the FEU), and by a growing interest in the accreditation of experiential learning, which will be referred to in Chapter 6. There is not room here to discuss any of these trends in detail; but perhaps they can all be seen as attempts to ensure that if selection and stratification have to take place at this stage in education, they do so in as fair and as sophisticated a way as possible.

Differentiation

It was suggested at the beginning of this chapter that education at this stage begins to reflect the division of labour in a much more direct and immediate way than it does at earlier stages, and that this leads to the horizontal differentiation of the curriculum into large numbers of relatively specific courses. This specificity has always been greater in shorter, lower-level courses (vocational) than in long-cycle higher-level ones, which tend to lead on to higher education.

In the past, this led to as many as a thousand distinct lines of study in some countries, reflecting in particular the many different kinds of craft occupations, each with its own specific apprenticeship or training. However, in recent years, several kinds of changes in the structure of occupations have led to modifications in this highly specific pattern. First, many of the distinct craft occupations have either disappeared or shrunk into rarity, with the advent of modern industrial processes and technologies. Secondly, the need for multi-skilled workers in some occupations has grown, reflecting both technological changes and changes in the demarcation of jobs. And thirdly, the scale and rapidity of change in post-war industrial economies, together with the recent rise of unemployment, has made it very difficult to know what to train young people for, undercutting the simple instrumental rationales which used to exist.

Education and training systems have responded to these changes in the labour market in four main ways: by moving from pre-determined to flexible course structures; by broadening the scope of courses; by introducing certain 'key' subjects or skills; and by emphasising process rather than content. Each of these responses will be examined briefly below.

The change in course structures has occurred in some countries but not others. In Germany, for example, vocational and technical education are still organised in distinct and self-contained lines of study, of which there are now about 450 at the craft level. This linear approach makes it difficult to move sideways, or combine elements of different lines, and it leads to a largely prescribed curriculum, with little student choice. Moreover, the system is rather bureaucratic, and changing the syllabuses is a slow and sometimes difficult business. The system overproduces some kinds of skills (for example in bakery) and underproduces others (such as in electronics), but since nearly a third of apprentices find work in an occupation which is not related to their training, these mismatches appear to matter less than they might. On the credit side, the linear system produces large numbers of well-trained young people, the majority of whom find relevant work. There is rigorous control of coverage and standards, on both the theoretical and practical sides. Young people have a clear identity and status, though they are not paid much, relative to adult workers. The opportunity exists for further work and study in order to become a *Meister*, which usually assures a reasonable financial and social status. And whatever the specific content of the line of study, there is the assumption that it will produce a trained worker; the affective implications are strong (Jochimsen, 1978). Attempts to broaden the training base have met with strong resistance (Russell and Neale, 1983).

At the other end of the spectrum of structures is the new Scottish system, which is modular. Here, all non-advanced vocational courses are organised in standard units, leading to a single vocational qualification. There is a great deal of choice among units (of which there are already several thousand), although some restrictions are built in for reasons of continuity and coherence. The student can take the units in one or several institutions, since there is a common currency of course credits, and the system allows initial choices to be modified in the light of experience or changed circumstances, either individual or economic. The Scottish system is very new, and as yet no large-scale evaluations of it exist, but it is open to the standard criticisms of modular schemes: that it fragments knowledge and skills; that it places a great burden of choice on both students and counsellors; that it discourages specialisation; and that it takes little account of the affective dimension. Whether such criticisms turn out to be justified remains to be seen.[4]

 The second response of education and training systems to the changes in the job market has been to alter content rather than structure. There has been a trend in many industrialised countries in the last decade to broaden the base of initial training, leading to 'foundation' courses, 'study-by-stages', and 'occupational training families'. Such broad-band courses, it is argued, allow gradual and considered specialisation, facilitate teamwork among specialists, and make subsequent retraining easier. They also allow both individuals and institutions to hedge their bets in an uncertain economic world. In this country, the occupational training family approach has been associated mainly with the work of the Institute of Manpower Studies, and the policies of the Manpower Services Commission (Hayes, 1985).

Broad-based training, however, runs into certain problems (Kaiser and Werner, 1979; Benner, 1982; Johnson, 1984). It may fail to supply the labour market with adequate levels of the specialised skills which are still widely required, especially in the manufacturing sector. It may leave students without a real sense of competence and identity. And it is not easy to arrive at broad training families which make both educational and occupational sense. Clerical skills, for example, are found in all occupational sectors, as are management and interpersonal skills. To the extent that skill categories and occupational groupings do not coincide, the classification becomes problematic. Also, as Deforge has pointed out, an empirical analysis of transfer and mobility in the labour market suggests a central/marginal basis for organising training, rather than the generic/specific one characteristic of more taxonomic approaches:

> there is no need to invent new types of training courses which are syntheses or combinations of others, or to embark on a painstaking search for 'broad bases' or 'common cores', for there already are a number of traditional training courses which may be affirmed, from the subsequent careers of their 'products', to provide firm foundations or platforms for future development. We need only identify and make greater use of them. (Deforge, 1979, page 10)

The difficulties of arriving at any standardised pattern of training arise from the fact that the structure of tasks within each occupation varies. In some occupations, such as construction, the tasks that are performed are essentially discrete and self-contained. Thus the bricklayer, plumber, joiner, electrician and plasterer work separately, and have little to do with one another beyond (sometimes) holding one another up. By contrast, there is a strong linear relationship between tasks in most production and processing occupations, and an even stronger interactive relationship between the tasks in many service occupations, for example in office work.

These variations in the structure of tasks from one occupation to another suggest that whereas broad-based training may suit some, others will require a more specific pattern.

The arguments about the relative breadth or specialisation of vocational and technical courses can also be applied to pre-higher education courses such as A levels. Here, there has been less debate, mainly because higher education has changed less in the last decade than the labour market has. But the current role of A levels corresponds more closely to Deforge's central/marginal approach than to the generic/specific one. It is widely believed that certain subjects at A level provide a good 'platform' for degree studies: hence the popularity of a relatively small number of subjects such as English, Mathematics, History, Geography, and Physics. The broad-based foundation concept is found in the alternative entry patterns provided by some FE colleges (for example, higher education preparatory courses) and in the foundation courses of the Open University. It is striking that in all the long-running debate about the reform of A levels, the discussion has been mainly in terms of the number of discrete subjects to be studied, rather than arguments about the relative advantages of discrete subjects or interdisciplinary foundation courses. There has been little analysis of what might constitute appropriate 'academic families'; and this despite the fact that correlations between A-level performance and degree performance have been known to be low for some years (Choppin, 1973; Goacher, 1984).

The two other responses to labour market change and uncertainty can be briefly described. The first attempts to identify certain key skills or subjects which underpin a very wide range of possible future occupations or studies. At a basic level, this leads to the identification of 'basic skills' which should be covered by or incorporated in whatever training is provided. The FEU has again been prominent in advocating such an approach, and it has been a key element in the design of the CPVE. However, such a strategy can be applied to higher levels of study as well, where it can lead to requirements that all students should study, for example, some mathematics (in teacher education), information technology, communications skills, and (in other countries) a second language. Such subjects can be seen as providing the essential codes of organised knowledge in our time, rather as Latin and Greek did in previous ages.

Finally, labour market uncertainties can lead to an emphasis on process rather than content: on generic intellectual and other skills which are likely to be useful in virtually all possible jobs and adult roles. This kind of 'process' approach leads to an emphasis on self-management, self-analysis, self-evaluation, working in teams, time-management, problem-solving, and ultimately on 'learning how to learn', topics and headings which are important in both the YTS and even more so in the CPVE (Joint Board, 1985). There is no doubt that such skills or capacities are likely to be very useful in jobs and outside them; the problem lies in finding concrete and meaningful ways to develop them. They can seem rather abstract and generalised to the student who, at this stage, wants above all to get down to something.

Transition

As was mentioned earlier, this stage of education – and, indeed, of life – is often thought of as a stage of transition. That theme has figured prominently in the literature on the consecutive phase. The Coleman report, *Youth: Transition to Adulthood* (Coleman, 1974) was a landmark in US thinking. In this country, the series of Youthaid reports, *Study of the Transition from School to Working-Life* (Sawdon et al., 1979–81) analysed many similar issues. The major study of post-compulsory education in Europe by King and others (1975) emphasised the transitional and therefore provisional nature of young people's development at this stage. West and Newton (1983) speak of the confusion and uncertainty involved in the transition from school to work. Neave (1978) has discussed research perspectives on the theme of transition, and a bibliography has been compiled by Willis (n.d.).

The idea that the years immediately following the end of compulsory schooling are years of transition in fact conflates several kinds of change. There is the change in student status, from compulsory to voluntary, although the abstract freedom of the latter is often severely modified by various kinds of pressure: examination pressures, pressure from family or peers, financial pressures, pressure to get a job or a place in higher education. There is also a change in financial status, though the traditional shift from dependence to wage-earning has now been undermined by youth unemployment, and confused by inconsistencies in student and trainee support policies: some kinds of courses attract grants, whereas others do not. The transition has also to do with the change from studying to working, though this is by no means as clear-cut as it used to be: Kallen (1983) notes that one French report shows a higher percentage of students working part-time during school than working full-time within six months of leaving.

There are of course other aspects of transition, not necessarily to do with education. At this stage, the young person may leave home, either to work or study. The daily routine will in any case change. Other 'marker events' can be noted: the right to drive a car, to buy cigarettes and alcohol, to open a bank account on one's own, to set up in business, to marry without parents' consent, to vote, and so on. This conglomeration of rights, roles, and responsibilities goes a long way to defining what we think of as adulthood.

However, two general points should be made. First, the whole notion of transition has, at least since the Industrial Revolution, been closely bound up with entry to employment. The current high levels of youth unemployment thus call into question many of the conventional assumptions about transition; it may be clear what young people are leaving behind, but not what they are moving towards. This raises particular problems for vocational education at this stage, since its whole rationale depends on the general availability of paid work. Secondly, transition is a more important theme for some young people than others. For those who enter technical or vocational streams at this stage, there is likely to be a significant change in environment; and the same is even more true for those (now a minority) who go directly into a job. But students doing 'general' courses (O and A levels) may experience, and want, more continuity than transition. For them, these years are the bridge between the lower secondary stage and advanced studies. The transition may still be accommodated and marked in certain ways (for example, the peculiar ethos of the sixth form) but for many of these students, the real break comes after graduation, and not before.

There is no doubt that transition is an important aspect of the curriculum at this stage, reflecting the multiple transitions that young people are undergoing. It has implications not only for the structure and content of the curriculum, but for teaching and learning, and above all for counselling and guidance. Nevertheless, it is perhaps unwise to abstract it from the other themes that have preceded it in this chapter; after all, it is always a transition from and to something. The theme of transition does not, in itself, provide a sufficient conceptual framework for analysing the curriculum at the consecutive stage; and the somewhat rhetorical treatment of it in some of the literature cited earlier tends to abstract it from its context. After all, transition is socially and institutionally determined, rather than being a psychological constant, and a concern with it should lead to an analysis of the concrete situation of young people, whether students, trainees, or employees, in our society.

Implications

It has been argued in this chapter that education at the consecutive stage moves into a much more direct and immediate relationship with the society around it than is the case either before or after. Hence the curriculum at this stage reflects in a fairly overt way some of the major characteristics of that society. It becomes harnessed or applied to the social tasks of production and organisation. Its affective emphasis – the inculcation of attitudes and values – reflects both general social norms, and the norms and 'cultures' of particular occupational and other groups. It becomes increasingly stratified and differentiated, reflecting 'vertical' social stratification and the 'horizontal' division and subdivision of labour. It displays some of the transitional features of this stage of life-span development.

Pratley's account of the UK system and OECD analyses of international patterns suggest that this sector of education is more complex than any other in organisational terms. The relatively brief analysis in this chapter suggests that it is extremely complex conceptually and thematically as well. The implications drawn from that analysis in this final section must therefore be rather tentative, and the aim will be only to suggest the general directions that policy might take, not to enter into detailed prescriptions.

A good deal of the debate about this sector is centred on the type of institutions which can best provide for the age-group: sixth forms, sixth-form colleges, tertiary colleges, community colleges or schools, education-based or work-based training, community projects, and so forth. The institutional debate mainly lies outside the scope of this book, but the preceding discussions of the affective dimension of 16–19 provision, and of curricular stratification, have implications for the kind of institutional environments provided for young people. The general problem is how to provide both a measure of diversity and a measure of unity. The needs of students at this stage are more diverse than they are at earlier stages in their educational development, and there are strong social and economic pressures also towards diversification. However, a measure of unity is also desirable in order to mitigate the harsher effects of stratification, to allow progression and avoid dead ends, and to facilitate some degree of co-ordination among providers. This tension suggests that some kind of federation of the institutions and agencies concerned with this age-group might strike the right balance. In fact, the reality may not be very far from this in some cases. The upper secondary 'integrated' schools in Sweden which appear to embody the demands of 'unity' at this stage are in some cases rather loose aggregations of pre-existing institutions, often on a variety of sites, with relatively little contact between the different lines of study. By contrast, the diverse pattern of provision in some UK local authorities is in fact linked together by formal and informal committees and networks, with much more co-operation and collaboration than might appear on paper. Federal structures are not easy to operate, but perhaps it is better for the inevitable tensions to exist within such a structure, rather than between autonomous institutions.

The curricular structure is, however, at least as important as the institutional structure. Here, the analysis points to the need for a common currency of courses and qualifications at this stage, in order to make the system comprehensible to students, counsellors, employers, and even providers, and to create the flexibility that is necessary in a period of transition for students, and of uncertainty in the labour market. Such a currency would need to classify all courses as regards level, and equivalent qualifications, and indeed there is already EEC agreement on the former. There are also well-recognised academic/vocational equivalences in this country, such as BTEC National equivalence to A level. It may also be that some standardisation of the 'size' of course units, such as now exists in Scotland, would have long-term benefits in terms of a simpler and more accessible system, for adults as well as young people. Variations in teaching patterns from subject to subject, and in the lengths of terms from institution to institution, make such standardisation difficult to achieve (Squires, 1986). However, a three-week or six-week unit (or its equivalent in total study hours) might fit in reasonably well with educational, training, and employment calendars. It has to be remembered that many employers and some MSC courses operate on a 48-week year (excluding public holidays) compared to the shorter 39 or 36 weeks found in the education sector. The size of unit is not as crucial as might appear, since double and half units exist in most modular systems. However, size does matter in terms of the impression that the structure gives, and small units are more open to the charge of fragmentation than large ones. In this respect, the use of short units (40 hours) in the Scottish post-16 scheme, while it may suit the motivation and learning rhythms of many vocational students, may prove to be an obstacle to the eventual incorporation of pre-academic courses into the overall plan.

The diversity of current course structures and sizes may, however, point towards a less homogenised 'tariff' system, rather than a full-blown modular one. A tariff system standardises credits, without standardising courses, and one is already in operation among a number of polytechnics in the south-east of England (Squires, 1986). For example, if it is agreed that a full year's study earns 60 credits, then it does not matter much if that total is made up of three 20-credit courses, four 15-credit courses, five 12-credit courses, six 10-credit courses, or any combination of these. (There is no educational significance about numbers such as 60 and 120; it is simply that they can be easily divided by most numbers up to 12.) Such a system avoids the difficulties of imposing a standard size and shape on all course units, although it is less flexible for the student in terms of choice and timetabling.

A less than total modular system might also be preferable in another respect. The need to build up adequate levels of compe-tence implies continuity and concentration in courses, and this is particularly true where skills have to be 'confirmed' (that is, practised and overlearned) not just acquired. The affective emphasis in many courses also implies a certain stability in the learning situation and the learning group; socialisation seems to depend on a degree of continuity and identity, even isolation. Free-choice 'pick and mix' systems, on the other hand, optimise choice and student autonomy. It may be that something in between the traditional linear structures and the new modular ones – a core-plus-options pattern – would strike the right balance. That balance will in any case differ from course to course: the structure of occupations and the tasks they involve varies greatly, and whereas in some jobs (and subjects) there has to be a substantial prescribed core, in others the core requirements are relatively minor. The needs of individual students may also vary in this respect, with some wanting to concentrate their efforts at this point, and others preferring a more divergent pattern.

As regards the structure of the curriculum at this stage, a variable core-plus-options pattern within an overall, standardised credit system might accommodate the conflicting demands implied by the analysis in the earlier sections. Issues of content are much more difficult to resolve, and the nature of the resolution depends on much wider educational and ideological stances. One fundamental question is whether education should in all circumstances and at all stages attempt to strike a balance between various kinds of general goals, to do with individual development, transmission/critique of cultural patterns and norms, induction into organised knowledge, preparation for work, and so forth, or whether the emphasis on these should vary. A good deal of the writing on curriculum theory assumes that all such goals are desirable in all circumstances, perhaps because it is grounded in the generalised nature of compulsory schooling.

The alternative view, and the one taken here, is that a lifelong perspective on education allows a differential emphasis in different sectors and stages, as long as the total educational package, over the lifespan, adds up to a balanced or desirable one. Thus there is no harm in education at the consecutive stage having a mainly applied emphasis, or higher education having a mainly academic one, as long as they are both preceded by a truly general education at the compulsory stage, and a truly pluralistic one at the continuing stage. Compulsory education should not attempt to be vocational, since that will compromise its general aims, and post-compulsory education should not attempt to be general, since that is likely to interfere with its applied and affective tasks.

Such a view points away from any required general or liberal education at the consecutive stage, although of course a core-plus-options pattern would still allow students to opt for it. It would not preclude, and indeed it would point towards some transition-related role and social education within the required curriculum, perhaps along the lines of the German *Arbeitslehre* courses (education about, rather than for, work) (Russell, 1982). There are two main problems, however, with 'stage' theories of the curriculum. The first is that not everyone conforms to the simple linear models that they imply, particularly in a society in which life-patterns and life-styles appear to be getting more and not less fluid. Flexibility within the system can to some extent accommodate such variations. The other problem is that if education at different stages and in different sectors has different goals or emphases, one is left wondering what, if anything, binds the whole enterprise together. Is there any common or characteristic emphasis? Anything which would characterise the activity as an educational one, as distinct from training, or indoctrination, or recreation, or socialisation?

It was suggested earlier that 'reflexivity' – the turning of the mind back on itself and what it is doing – is perhaps one thing which distinguishes an educational activity from others akin to it. That implies knowledge about knowledge, thinking about thinking, and learning about learning. In the 16–19 context, it points towards education about education and education about work. There is a real tension between such ideas and the applied and affective emphases of the curriculum at this stage, since some forms of anticipatory socialisation require precisely that students take certain things as given, and do not question the questions. The hidden curriculum is no longer hidden if it is reflexive, and the pressures not to reflect are particularly strong in some vocational contexts. Indeed, it may be that there is a fundamental tension between education and society in this respect, which becomes sharpest when the relationship between the two is closest – that is, at this stage. Perhaps such tension is part of the price that a society has to pay if it wishes to espouse pluralistic, and potentially conflicting, goals.

The other major issue to do with the content of the curriculum at this stage relates to the theme of differentiation. It was suggested that rapid change and uncertainty in the labour market had led to broader and more process-oriented courses in recent years, particularly in technical and vocational fields. A few general points can be made here. First, the dangers of too narrow a training must be balanced against the less obvious dangers of training in nothing in particular. Classifications of occupations, created for economic and demographic purposes, run into tens of thousands, and traditional vocational training categories into some hundreds. By contrast, the occupational training families used in Western Europe in recent years usually number fewer than 20 (11 in the United Kingdom). They thus conflate training and occupational categories to an extreme degree, and it may be that policy-makers have overreacted in this respect. A larger number of somewhat narrrower categories (about 30–40 lines account for the vast majority of German apprentices) based on an empirical analysis of employment patterns, and allied to a flexible core-plus-option structure, might meet both labour market and individual needs better than the rather abstract groupings currently in vogue. In any case, there appears from OECD analyses to be a good deal of labour market mobility and transfer of learning *already*. Such mobility is likely to be enhanced more by a sound general education at the compulsory level, than by rather superficial broad-spectrum vocational courses, which tend to fall between two stools, providing neither general understanding, nor marketable skills (Gleeson in Dale, 1985).

It is unemployment, however, rather than employment, whether of the employee or self-employed variety, which presents education at this stage with its most urgent problem, and subverts the traditional vocational rationale which in the past underpinned not only overtly vocational courses, but a good deal of general education as well; a point noted many years ago by Becker in *Human Capital* (1964). The response to this problem depends very much on wider assumptions and values.

In my view, a society must judge itself not only in terms of the level of goods and services it provides, but also in terms of its activities, relationships, institutions, and environment. Work, like education, and like many leisure pursuits, is an activity, not simply a socio-economic relationship, and just as a society should aim to make the activity of education available to its citizens, so it should aim to make work available to those who want it. In concrete policy terms, this means distinguishing between short-term, medium-term, and long-term unemployment. Short-term unemployment (up to three months) is a normal feature of a changing economy, and should be accepted as such. People at this stage need information about job opportunities, both locally and nationally, and help in finding and taking them, in the form of job application and interview skills, and advice about mobility. If at the end of three months or so, a person has still not found work, it is unlikely that he or she will do so without retraining; so the medium-term unemployed (three months to a year) should be provided with retraining, based on initial counselling. The pattern and nature of such training would of course vary greatly. If after a period of retraining the person is still unable to find work, it is unlikely that more retraining is going to solve the problem, which must lie in the aggregate shortage of jobs or opportunities for self-employment. For the long-term unemployed therefore (more than one year) the state should provide some work (say, half-time) and opportunities for educational and leisure activities (access to sports facilities, subscriptions to certain clubs, and so on).

It is this last suggestion which is most problematic, since to provide all the long-term unemployed with half-time work would currently mean finding the equivalent of half a million jobs. The task does not seem impossible to me;[5] but the main point to be made here is that different kinds of education and training provision are required for different kinds of unemployment situations. Simply lumping together all the unemployed as one undifferentiated mass does nothing to clarify policy.

Finally, some comments must be made in relation to the theme of transition. Just as education at this stage reflects the other major features of the society it exists in, so it cannot but be affected by the transitional nature of these years in the young adult's development. Even when in the past large numbers of school-leavers entered the labour market at the age of 15 or 16, they typically entered secondary labour markets, moving in and out of a series of short-term jobs before in many cases settling down to something more permanent. That provisionality, as King (1975) puts it, affects the curriculum also. It implies a certain degree of flexibility, the opportunity to 'sample' courses (as is now common in major consumer purchases), to move sideways or even backtrack on original choices. Such flexibility poses problems for teachers and even more so for administrators, and it runs counter to some of the affective aims referred to earlier. Socialisation and shopping around are not always compatible. But if the system does not grant such flexibility, the students are likely to take it anyway: their participation, however constrained, is fundamentally voluntary. It is surely better to facilitate such chopping and changing than to cause what may be irreversible drop-out.

Transition also has major implications for counselling. This is a major field in its own right, which goes well beyond the scope of this book, but one point can be made here.[6] Despite its wide use, the term 'comprehensive' is somewhat ambiguous in education. It may refer to institutions, or to the curriculum which they offer. The drift of this chapter has been away from a comprehensive model of post-compulsory education in both these senses, pointing towards a looser institutional federation, and a relatively differentiated and stratified curriculum, though with opportunities for movement and progression. By contrast, a comprehensive counselling service at this stage seems not merely desirable but essential, if students are to relate their own complex needs to the complexities of what is provided.

NOTES

1   This chapter draws heavily on recent and on-going work for the OECD (Squires, 1985), and on other OECD reports such as *Policies for Apprenticeship* (1979), *The Future of Vocational Education and Training* (1983b), and *Education and Work* (1983c), together with some as yet unpublished studies of developments in Western European countries. As regards the UK, there has been room in the bibliography to cite only some of the many useful reports and papers published by the Further Education Unit and the Further Education Staff College. I am also indebted to colleagues who work in this sector in Humberside for helpful discussions over a number of years.

2   It is worth pointing out that training is sometimes slightly removed

from the main production process in the workplace, and sited in special training workshops, because it would interrupt the flow of production, or create unacceptable risks. Where small employers come together to provide training which they could not offer separately, in group training associations and the like, training is also inevitably distanced from the work process. It cannot therefore be assumed that work-based training always involves direct experience of the production environment.

3   Perhaps the most systematic and sustained attempts to postpone selection and create equality of opportunity, at least in the OECD countries, have been those in Sweden over the last two decades (see OECD, 1981; Turner and Rawlings, 1982; Boucher, 1983). A recent, as yet unpublished study by Lundgren suggests to me that while education policies can make some difference to the patterns of selection and equality, they do so only within limits which are socially determined, and a stratified society will find ways of stratifying educational outputs, however comprehensive or egalitarian the curriculum. The issue then becomes a general social and political one, rather than a specifically educational one. As Willis (1977) has noted in this country, stratification and differentiation become internalised at this stage, in different perceptions of what policy-makers like to call 'provision'.

4   It is interesting to ask to what extent the language of aggregative or modular structures implies a 'market' model of the curriculum, as against the more familiar 'planning' models. The emphasis on units, options, choice, credits, currency, accumulation, and transfer all suggest a change of metaphor. Transposing Hayek's (1944) economic thesis to the educational sphere, it can be argued that unlike compulsory education, which is suspectible to rational planning derived from general goals, the 16–19 stage is subject to such a range of demands and pressures that it is best thought of as a curriculum market in which the various forces work out their optimum relationship. The policy-makers' task is no longer to plan and prescribe, but to simply to create the conditions in which a market can operate: a stable, common currency; adequate market information; adequate distribution of purchasing power; absence of supply-side rigidities; absence of monopolies and encouragement of competition. At the very least, such ideas force a reappraisal of the assumption, common in educational writing, that curricula always have to be planned, designed, or developed.

5   Not all the long-term unemployed would want to take up the opportunity of half-time work, although it would seem sensible to offer some incentives to do so, without going as far as the compulsion of some US 'workfare' programmes. The main problem in creating or subsidising more jobs seems to me not the overall cost, which has to be balanced against the direct and indirect costs of unemployment, but the danger that subsidised labour will

displace full-cost labour, thereby simply shuffling the jobs around. Strict limits on the percentage of subsidised employees in any given organisation might help to limit this problem; the experience of the Community Programme suggests some guidelines. Any depressant effect on wages is to be welcomed, since it is becoming increasingly clear that wage increases are not being depressed by aggregate unemployment; the long-term unemployed are effectively outside the labour market altogether.

6   The work of the Educational Counselling and Credit Transfer Information Service (ECCTIS) is relevant here (Toyne, 1983), as are the attempts to establish guidance services for adults, which attempt to provide cross-institutional information and counselling on the whole range of education and training opportunities in a locality (Butler, 1984a; 1984b). Such services often operate on a centre-network basis, with full-time advisers and a wide range of contacts or representatives in providing institutions and agencies.

5 Higher Education

Introduction

In the United Kingdom, 'higher education' is taken generally to refer to advanced courses provided mainly though not exclusively by the universities, polytechnics, and colleges or institutes of higher education. 'Advanced' in this context usually means beyond A- level standard, and in fact entrance requirements are typically stated in terms of A levels: one for higher technical or business courses; two for most polytechnic and college degree courses; and three for university degree courses. There are variations in this pattern, with 'waivers' in particular for mature students, but in general terms the curriculum in higher education is concerned with studies between A level and degree level, and beyond that with post-graduate studies and research.

Much of the debate on higher education in recent years has been about things other than the curriculum. There has been a good deal of discussion about the size of the system and there is now the prospect that the steady expansion of the last twenty years may be partially reversed in the coming decade, for a combination of demographic and policy reasons. Since 1981, substantial cuts in funding have been imposed, and there is increasing selectivity in the allocation of those funds.

There has also been a recurrent debate about the structure of higher education, much of it turning on the advantages or otherwise of having a non-university sector alongside a university one. The extent to which the former has developed a distinct identity and function is a matter for argument (OECD, 1973; Neave, 1978, 1979b). Access to higher education has also been a major theme in recent years, both in terms of the traditional 18-year-old school-leaver intake, and 'non-traditional' applicants of various kinds (Fulton, 1981; Squires, 1983). And perhaps the major current policy emphasis is the relationship between higher education, the labour market, and the economy, a topic which has featured strongly in research studies (Lindley, 1981) and government statements (DES, 1985).

Questions about size, structure, access, and output all have implications for the curriculum in higher education, but there has been surprisingly little direct discussion of the overall pattern and content of undergraduate studies in the United Kingdom. Indeed, much of the basic data which might inform such studies has not been collected. The poverty of the data-base is reflected in, and is a consequence of, the absence of substantial centres for research into higher education, a gap filled only partly by individuals and small groups working in the field, and the efforts of the Society for Research into Higher Education (SRHE). The last major governmental enquiry into the system (Robbins, 1963) devoted only a few pages to the curriculum, and the most recent government policy document (DES, 1985) compressed even those few pages into a few lines.

It is not easy to explain this general absence of attention to what is taught. Perhaps the relatively abstract nature of some of the writing about the aims of higher education does not translate easily into curricular specifications; perhaps the curriculum is left vague so that it can easily reflect changes emanating from research.[1] It may also be that the fissiparous nature of academic institutions (faculty entrepreneurs held together by a common grievance over car-parking, according to Clark Kerr) precludes much general discussion of undergraduate or postgraduate studies. Whatever the reason, there is nothing in the British literature which corresponds to the kind of general surveys that periodically appear in the United States, of which Levine (1978), Chickering (1981), and Gaff (1983) are only recent examples.

There are, of course, books on specific aspects of the curriculum. Some of the literature on professional education was referred to in Chapter 3. Sandwich courses have attracted some interest (Smithers, 1976). There have been accounts of specific innovations, such as the Keele foundation year (Iliffe, 1968), the independent study schemes at Lancaster University and North East London Polytechnic (Percy and Ramsden, 1980), and also books about new or innovative institutions, such as the 'new' universities, the polytechnics, and in particular the Open University (Tunstall, 1974). But neither Powell's bibliography (1966; 1971) nor the ongoing series of SRHE abstracts yields much on the specifics of the curriculum, and there is virtually nothing British on the curriculum in general. In this chapter, therefore, it is necessary to start with a basic description of the curriculum in higher education, before we can embark on any analysis of issues and policies.

The pattern of undergraduate studies in the United Kingdom depends on two things: *where* one studies and *what* one studies. The first of these subdivides into national, sector, and institutional variations. The Scottish, and to a lesser extent, Northern Irish pattern is broader than that in England and Wales, largely for historical reasons (Davie, 1961). The Scottish undergraduate will typically enter higher education earlier than his or her English counterpart, and take four years over a degree that in England and Wales would take three. Admission is initially to a faculty rather than department, and in the first year, four or five subjects are likely to be studied, rather than two or three. Specialisation in Scotland tends to come in the third of the four years, and a much higher percentage of students take ordinary or general degrees than in England or Wales.

These national variations are to some extent overlaid by variations between the university and public sectors. Degree courses in the latter (the polytechnics and colleges) are validated by the Council for National Academic Awards and should reflect the Council's principle that the student 'must learn to perceive his or her main studies in a broader perspective' (CNAA, 1986, p. 3). There is no corresponding commitment to breadth in the university sector, nor could there be, since each university validates and awards its own degree. However, there are institutional variations within each sector. At Cambridge University, for example, the undergraduate curriculum is divided into two stages, Part I and Part II, with some opportunities for transfer between subjects, usually at the end of the second year. At Sussex University, all students take a two-term preliminary course, before deciding on their major field within a relatively broad 'school' rather than department. Some institutions, notably Oxford and City Polytechnics and the Open University, have large-scale modular schemes, and many others have modular structures in some faculties or departments.

However, the main variations in curriculum pattern derive not from where one studies but from what one studies. This is much less easy to categorise than the first set of variations, but following Figure 2, a broad distinction may be drawn between professional and academic courses. Professional courses lead to a recognised professional qualification and licence to practise in one of the older well-established professions such as medicine, law, and engineering, or in one of the newer professions or semi-professions such as pharmacy, social work, architecture, teaching, town planning, accountancy, or management. It is of course difficult to define what is or is not a profession, but in terms of the curriculum the crucial factor is a direct and substantial manpower relationship between the subject(s) of study and the eventual occupation. Professional degrees can be subdivided into two types: the sandwich degree, in which the element of practice occurs during degree studies, and the 'end-on' degree, where the practice comes after graduation.

With academic degrees, the direct, external manpower relationship is replaced by a much stronger internal relationship with academic structures and occupations. The student of history, English, sociology, mathematics, or physics may or may not go on to use his knowledge and skills directly in a subsequent job; what is certain is that the way he studies the subject will reflect academic priorities and norms, and will indeed lead naturally on to postgraduate work, if he can get a first class or upper second class degree and a grant. Academic degrees can also be subdivided into two subtypes: single honours, in which most of the time is spent on one subject, and joint or combined honours in which two subjects, usually cognate, are studied in parallel. Both are useful for entry to the teaching profession.

The professional and academic patterns account for the great majority of first degrees in the United Kingdom, but there are some degree courses which do not fit either of these moulds easily. Their underlying orientation can best be described as general or developmental, in that their main aim is to give the student a relatively broad, general-purpose higher education, and/or to help the student to develop his or her general intellectual and personal potential. Some of the broader public-sector degree courses in the humanities and social sciences fall into this third, residual category, but it must also be stressed that the notion of 'development' is often a powerful if secondary rationale in many other courses (Lane, 1975). Much of this emphasis depends on the hidden curriculum, and the less overt aspects of the teaching–learning relationship, and is thus difficult to pin down. But the particular emphasis on individual care and attention in the UK system (evident in favourable staff–student ratios, the tutorial tradition, and the collegial aspirations) must caution us against a too syllabus-bound interpretation of what is actually taught (Squires, 1980).

This brief description of the patterns of curricula in higher education suggests some themes and issues which will be explored in the rest of this chapter. First, the basic distinction made above, between professional and academic courses, will be examined in the light of what seems to be the increasing professionalisation of the academic world. Following that, three aspects of academic and professional courses will be discussed: the balance between breadth and depth; the nature of disciplines and interdisciplinarity; and the relationship between theory and practice. The final section will explore the implications of each of these for current policy.

Academic and professional

Higher education as professional education or education for the professions is both a very old, and very recent theme in analyses of the curriculum. It can be argued that higher education in the Tudor period, the eighteenth century and the nineteenth century should be seen as being primarily professional in the sense that it equipped young men for careers in the church, court, or civil service of the day. This does not necessarily imply a direct relationship between the content of studies and subsequent employment, although in the case of the clergy this was often the case. In other instances, however, the curriculum-employment link was of an indirect or surrogate nature: classics would inform young men about ancient Greece and Rome, rather than Victorian England or the India of the Raj, but it was nevertheless considered to be an appropriate preparation or screening for the job. To label all this 'professional education' is perhaps to stretch the term, but the point has to be made that universities in past centuries were far from being places where education was justified or pursued entirely 'for its own sake'. As Bell has pointed out, Newman's *Idea of a University*, so often taken as a key statement of English university tradition, constituted in its own time, an idiosyncratic, not representative point of view.

> Newman also believed in a breadth of curriculum totally unaccept-able to the vested interests and superstitions of contemporary academics even in Scotland. Moreover, he was opposed to profes-sional studies, perhaps the one genuinely traditional element in the contemporary university and a major spur to nineteenth century reform. (Bell, 1971, page 65)

The historical argument about the nature and functions of universities in the past is a complex one, and cannot be pursued here. The point being made is merely that professional education is not a new element in higher education. Nevertheless, it seems to be receiving particular attention at the present. It is the subject of much recent debate, both in the United Kingdom and elsewhere. In Italy, *professionalità* is something of a buzz word in educational circles. In Sweden, the undergraduate curriculum has been restructured along professional lines, so that, on paper at least, all studies are professional studies. The main growth in US higher education in recent years has been in professional subjects, with business and management degrees comprising 22 per cent of the total number awarded. In the United Kingdom, student demand for 'professional' courses (such as medicine, veterinary science, and law) has been high for some years.

It is common to conceptualise what is taught and learned in professional education courses as *expertise*, a word which Archer, in her *Social Origins of Educational Systems*, has placed at the centre of analysis:

> The principal resource commanded by the education profession is its expertise (i.e. the specialist knowledge possessed by teachers, their capacity to impart skills and to inculcate values). Basically, internal initiation involves the profession exchanging the expert services it can offer for other kinds of resources which it needs, namely the financial means and legal rights required to translate its own goals into reality. To do this it depends on getting a good rate of exchange for educational services against the financial resources supplied, in return, by external interest groups. But these transactions themselves may be subject to political veto so the profession also has to increase the value of its expertise to the political authorities in order to prevent their imposing such embargoes. The latter is merely one aspect of a broader negotiation with the polity in which expert services are exchanged against increments in autonomy. (Archer, 1984, page 122)

Archer is describing here how the education profession trades expertise in exchange for resources and autonomy, but the concept of expertise as she uses it has wider application in the understanding of professional education. Expertise, to have exchange value, must remain scarce. Scarcity is assured partly through intrinsic 'difficulty' (the hieratic coding of technical terms, the inexplicable mysteries of arts, the slow process of acquiring judgement) and partly through restrictive organisation (gate-keeping at entry, licences to practise, limited memberships). There is a constant tension in expertise, and thus in professional education, between making it available and keeping it scarce, between opening it up and closing it off, a tension which is evident not only in arguments about numbers and access, but in the curriculum, with its carefully controlled sequence of

revelation, and the teaching–learning relationship, with its overtones of apprenticeship, transmission, and 'handing on'.

All this may seem to be characteristic of the traditional
professional fields (law, medicine, engineering) and perhaps of the
newer emergent or aspirant professions (social administration,
management, town planning, and so on). But what of the 'academic'
lines of study, of the single honours or joint honours degree in
(say) biology, history, mathematics, or economics? Lane, for
example, draws a distinction between academic and professional
courses, implying that they differ not only in their orientation but
their process (Lane, 1975). The distinction may be expressed in
terms of the difference between 'knowledge' and 'expertise'. In
professional courses, 'expertise' seems the appropriate term to
describe the outcome and the use to which it is put. But in the more
academic courses, 'knowledge' is perhaps the word that is more
readily used; although that knowledge, in the context of an
academic career, constitutes the expertise of the person concerned.
In terms of the analysis in Chapter 1, it seems appropriate to
describe much of the higher education curriculum as being concerned with organised knowledge, a concern that transmits itself
'down' through the various levels of secondary education, in the
form of conventional disciplines or subjects.

Even courses which are thought of as non-professional or
academic may in fact be professional, because their main aim is to
prepare students for an academic career. One way to test this is to
ask: if one wanted to prepare students for an academic career, what
kind of preparation or apprenticeship would one design? One can
then see how far existing courses conform to, or depart from, that
model. An academic apprenticeship would first of all have to
observe the professional demarcations of academic work. These are
largely though not wholly, subject boundaries: an academic *is* a
chemist, or zoologist, or sociologist, or philosopher. Secondly,
apprenticeship within that field would progress from a relatively
broad base (to give competence in terms of coverage) to increasing
specialisation (competence in terms of expertise). Thirdly, the
apprentice would be inducted not only into the content but also into
the process of work: the master's teaching would be partly a
'display' of how he proceeds, and the student would have to imitate
or simulate this on a smaller or less ambitious scale. Fourthly, the
apprentice would be socialised into the norms and values of the
profession, a process which involves intense contact within the field,
and segregation from those outside it. Fifthly, there would be stages

or hurdles at which people who had been inappropriately selected could be weeded out.

The above paragraph describes, fairly exactly, the conventional 'single honours' degree course in an English university. Apart from one or two first-year 'ancillary' courses, studies concentrate entirely on one subject, moving from broad first- and second-year coverage to specialisation and options in the third year. The process of academic work is mirrored in library/laboratory work, essays, seminars, and probably a long essay or project in the final year. Much of the teaching is in the nature of a display of the methods and procedures of work. The student is socialised into the 'culture' of the department, and external contacts are limited both physically and intellectually (Becher, 1984). There is little weeding out on the way, but students may be given to understand that they are not really suited to an academic career, and should think in other terms. In departments which have tutorial teaching, there is an intimate contact between 'master' and 'apprentice', which serves to induct the student not only into the subject, but a way of thought and even a way of life. The tutor, like the *Meister*, is sometimes a moral tutor as well, *in loco parentis*.

In what way do 'academic' courses depart from this 'apprentice-ship' model? A student who does a combined/joint honours course in two subjects is clearly crossing professional demarcations. It is difficult, without detailed research, to discuss the place of such students in the system. They appear to be less likely to get first-class degrees, and they sometimes claim that they have to study not 50 per cent, but more like 66 per cent of each subject. In the eyes of some academics they are perhaps not 'pure' students, with whose aspirations they can identify; they are neither fish nor fowl.

However, even single honours courses may depart from the apprenticeship model in a more subtle way, through the 'hidden curriculum'. I remember one of my tutors giving me to understand quite clearly that the syllabus we were meant to cover was something of an irrelevance to the true business of education (for a similar view, see Broady, 1978). As for examinations, they were, at best, a necessary evil, something to be forgotten about until the last possible moment. In any case, they were in the nature of an oblique test, not so much of what one knew, as of the kind of mind one had. Everything in the formal curriculum was in fact treated as a pretext for our meeting together, and having, as diplomats put it, wide-ranging discussions. He made me work: essays were frequent and had to be in on time. But the atmosphere was best described as

amateur, in the old sense of doing something for the love of it.
And with the benefit of hindsight I now realise that I picked up
from him a certain attitude (not quite distrust, more a distancing)
towards all that is expert and professionalised. Amateurism is
not perhaps the innocent and charming phenomenon which it is
sometimes painted, once one locates it as one of a cluster of elite,
privileged assumptions. But the example given here must make one
cautious about describing courses in terms of their overt curriculum
only. The reality may be three-levelled; courses which are labelled
academic may in fact conform to a professional pattern, but may be
taught in an amateur way. One cannot, in the end, abstract the
written curriculum from the setting it is taught in and the people
who teach (Powell, 1985).

Nevertheless, it does seem as if the distinction between academic
and professional courses is open to question, because academics are
also professionals (Perkin, 1973; Neave, 1979a). But are they a
special kind of professional, different in some fundamental way
from, say, doctors, lawyers, or engineers? There is some doubt as to
whether one should speak of an academic profession, embracing
all academics, or academic professions, which are subject- or
field-specific. However, the same ambiguity exists in engineering,
with its subdivision into civil, mechanical, electrical, marine, and so
forth; and to some extent with the various specialisms in the medical
profession. Certainly, the academic profession displays many of the
characteristics of other professions: it has considerable autonomy as
regards recruitment and promotion; it has its own professional
bodies and journals; its own methods of licensing; and its own
mechanisms for negotiating with the state. To some extent,
academics have become 'unionised' rather than 'professionalised' in
recent years (more emphasis on collective bargaining, explicit
regulation of conditions of service, and so on), but that is true of
other professions (such as doctors) as well. And one must not forget
the common root of the words 'professor' and 'profession'.

If the academic profession is atypical, it is because of the nature
and use of its expertise. This expertise does not lie in teaching: the
mechanisms for selecting, training, and evaluating academics as
teachers are either weak or non-existent in the United Kingdom
despite attempts in recent years to formalise this aspect of their
work. Whereas other professions are expected to apply their
expertise, the academic profession is expected only to make it
available, either in the form of published research, or public
teaching. This emphasis on public availability is inherent in both

the academic journal and the academic lecture. Both are exercises in exposure.

The argument so far can be summarised thus: higher education consists largely of academic or professional courses; but since academics are also professionals, albeit slightly odd ones, nearly all higher education courses may be regarded as professional courses, although the hidden curriculum may emphasise non-professional outcomes. As noted earlier, this is not what higher education is usually said to be about. It implies that higher education is in no sense a liberal or personal or social or general education. To constitute any of the latter, higher education would need to be not only about knowledge, but about knowledge about knowledge; not only about expertise, but about consciousness. There are four broad reasons for arguing that higher education should attempt to 'go beyond' knowledge or expertise.

The first is social. It is knowledge/expertise that distinguishes the graduate from the non-graduate, and typically gives her differential power, wealth, and opportunity. It would seem socially desirable that the graduate should be aware of the nature of the thing that distinguishes her from her fellow-citizens, so that she may use it responsibly. Secondly, special knowledge/expertise may in turn create special, intellectual limitations: Veblen's 'trained incapacity'. Learning to analyse the world one way may preclude, or at least make one unsympathetic to, analysing it in other ways. One can only realise the explanatory power of a discipline by immersing oneself in it, and becoming part of its culture; and yet that culture, like all cultures, imposes limitations on thought. This is not to say that all ways of seeing create equal and opposite blind-spots, but being 'inside' a discipline makes it difficult to see it from the outside. This affects not only how the professional uses or applies his knowledge, but also how he works with other professionals with different backgrounds. The third argument for 'knowledge about knowledge' is that it may stimulate the development of that knowledge. Kuhn has argued that a great deal of research takes place within the limits of what counts as 'normal science' at the time (Kuhn, 1962). To the extent that academics may become aware of the norms, models, and assumptions that currently underpin their work, one would expect them to be able to relativise their approach, and perhaps perceive alternatives to it. Finally, since professionals are defined in terms of their knowledge ('He's a geologist'), knowledge about knowledge has a personal dimension, to do with self-concept and identity. One's professional identity may conflict with other sources of identity, or simply come to seem an inadequate expression of one's existence. Indeed, some of the mid-life crises that some professionals experience may be related to their identification with their expertise, and the way it becomes modified over time.

It has been suggested that if higher education is to go beyond professional education, it has to define its curricula in terms not only of knowledge, but knowledge about knowledge. Another way of putting this is to say that it needs to be concerned with *consciousness* as well as *expertise*. The implications of this will be explored in the final section of this chapter, after some other aspects of higher education curricula have been considered.

Breadth and depth

The issue of the appropriate breadth or depth of undergraduate studies has run like a thread through the debate on higher education in the United Kingdom for at least two decades now. The Robbins Committee not only placed it firmly on the agenda; it made the broadening of studies a condition of expanding the system:

> The present distribution of students between different types of honours course is therefore unsatisfactory. A higher proportion should be receiving a broader education for their first degree. This in itself calls for change. But if greatly increased numbers of undergraduates are to come into the universities in the future, change becomes essential. Indeed we regard such a change as a necessary condition for any large expansion of universities. (Robbins, 1963, page 93)

Yet seventeen years later, in 1980, Lord Robbins could see little progress in this direction:

> In my opinion prevalent thinking on these matters in England has got itself into a thorough mess. It is quite absurd that young persons at the tender age of fourteen or fifteen should be asked to choose whether they want to be humanists or scientists – or much worse still 'social scientists'. And it is equally absurd that so large a proportion of the enlarged university population should be taking highly specialized first degree courses, only directly suitable for future careers as university teachers or branches of extreme expertise. Too many English professors seem to assume that the only way to

reputation is to have a flourishing honours undergraduate department, ruining school education in its later stages and neglecting the
very considerable number of students who would do better with
broader degrees. Educationalists who boast that the English system is
the best in the world in this respect must be either very innocent or
very insular. Other areas including, thank heaven, Scotland, must, in
their judgement, be all out of step. (Robbins, 1980, page 22)

Even more recently an ex-Vice-Chancellor of Keele University,
noted for its broad foundation year, could write:

Educational history in British schools and universities is almost
littered with declarations in principle in favour of breadth of studies,
of diversity and flexibility in undergraduate education, and of the
fruitfulness of research possibilities at the interdisciplinary contact
points between subjects. But the history is not so strong with
evidence that such declarations have been associated with real
changes in practice. The position of the single honours subject
associated with an entrenched Departmental structure is still strong
in Britain, and it appears to continue to be well regarded and well
rewarded by funding bodies like the UGC and the Research
Councils. (Harrison, 1984, unnumbered)

There appears, therefore, to have been little change in the
distribution (in terms of breadth and specialisation) of undergraduate studies since the Robbins report. Certainly, new subjects and
combinations of subjects have appeared (many of the latter under
interdisciplinary headings) but there seems to be no evidence of a
more general shift towards breadth of the kind that Robbins
recommended.[2] Such a statement must remain tentative, because a
detailed analysis of the data on distribution does not exist. Even
non-quantitative analyses of the breadth/depth issue are relatively
rare, considering the centrality of the issue, and the atypicality of
English universities in this respect (Squires, 1976). In this section,
therefore, the discussion will necessarily be in qualitative rather
than quantitative terms. There are four main types of argument
which bear on the issue, related to (1) student demand; (2) labour
market demand; (3) postgraduate needs; and (4) intrinsic value.

The question as to whether students prefer or would prefer
broader or narrower undergraduate courses is difficult to answer in
the absence of any systematic survey of attitudes and preferences on
the matter. In the absence of this, two indicators are often cited:
student choice of A levels; and student choice of undergraduate
courses. Both of these choices are, however, heavily constrained,

and are in no way indicators of 'pure' demand. Students can choose which A levels to study, but even here their choice is constrained by the number offered in the institution, by timetabling clashes and by earlier choices. The trend towards more 'mixed' A levels (mixing arts and science) is sometimes cited as evidence that such students would like a 'mixed' higher education, crossing faculty boundaries. However, in an era of intense competition for places, a student's choices of A levels may be dictated partly by what he thinks will result in the best average grade. Moreover, the student has little choice in the number of subjects studied: two are essential, three desirable. We simply do not know if students would opt for (say) five or six subjects at a slightly lower level, because such an option does not exist. The choice is institutionally constrained, and a circle of reinforcement operates between higher and upper secondary education.

Student choices within higher education are also a cloudy indicator of breadth/depth preferences. In most professionally-oriented courses, the scope of studies is largely determined by professional 'needs'. Questions of breadth and depth thus do not arise for students of engineering, medicine, law, social work, or business studies, except in terms of the spread of options, often in the final year. Again, short of a detailed survey of the range and choice of such options, it is difficult to say if 'professional' students in general feel limited or overspread by the scope of their studies.

The pattern of choice in 'academic' courses might be a better indicator, but here again other things enter into the equation. All institutions will offer both single-subject and some double-subject degrees; beyond that there may be a few tripartite or interdisciplin-ary degrees drawing on several subjects. In Scotland, a wider range is usually available in the first two years. But in all cases, the choices are choices within strict limits; and there are not only limits but pressures. Whether it is the case or not, rumour often has it that double subject degrees involve more work; that there is a low percentage of first-class degrees in them; that such students are not, in a vague way, 'pure'; that essay deadlines often coincide; and so on. In most institutions, it is simply not possible to choose pairs of subjects which are very dissimilar: most of the common pairs are said to be 'cognate'. Nor is it possible to do 'one-off' courses in remote or contrasting fields. And there is perhaps a general, if often unspoken, suspicion of anything that looks like a 'cafeteria' or 'ragbag' curriculum.

If student demand does not provide a clear guide to distribution preferences, do the demands of employers and the labour market?

Here again, caution is needed. The curricular distinction between 'professional' and 'academic' courses is mirrored by the labour-market distinction between 'specific' and 'general' intake. The scope of professional-type studies leading to specific intake is regulated largely by the initial demands of the job itself. This still leaves scope for argument about the right breadth or depth of courses, not only between academics, employers, and professional bodies but also within each of the three groups. Such arguments concern not only the breadth of undergraduate studies, but the role of initial on-the-job training, and of continuing professional education; indeed it makes no sense to discuss the breadth of undergraduate studies without reference to the other two. Thus, for example, the desirability or not of a broad, first-year engineering course is affected by the provision (or not) for later specialisation and updating. As Harrison has noted, 'it is always more difficult in programmes offering a wider range of studies to satisfy the detailed requirements laid down by professional bodies at the same time' (Harrison, 1984). 'Specific intake' thus tends to set outer limits to the breadth of professional courses, but within those limits there is still scope for disagreement.

It is in 'academic' courses leading to 'general intake', however, that the breadth/depth issue really comes to the fore. Here there are three broad interpretations of labour-market demands: that employers would prefer broader graduates; that they don't really care; and that they are looking for other things anyway. Each of these three views will be examined briefly in turn. Holloway (1972) is representative of the first view. He argues that whereas the universities (in the early 1970s) were producing 85 per cent specialist graduates and 15 per cent generalists, only 30 per cent of jobs requiring 'graduate-level intelligence' required specialists and 70 per cent of them required generalist knowledge and skills. Even if these figures were true then, which some doubt, the question arises as to whether they are still true now. The increasingly technological content of some jobs might suggest that the proportion of specialists needed by the graduate labour market has increased. However, the specialist/generalist ratio may also be affected by the proportion of the age-group graduating. Here, one can argue that the higher the proportion of the age-group graduating, the higher the appropriate proportion of generalists to specialists, since the increase in graduate output is unlikely to be matched by an increase in specialist graduate jobs. More graduates are likely to end up in jobs which have only an indirect or oblique relation to their specialism.

The suggestion that employers don't care very much whether the graduates they employ have had a broad or deep education is backed mainly by negative evidence. The *Expectations of Higher Education* project (Kogan and Boys, 1984: Roizen and Jepson, 1985) typically implies that whereas employers select with reference to the class of degree, or the institution where it was obtained, the actual breadth or depth of the course of study is usually of less interest to them. This tends to corroborate a good deal of anecdotal evidence (and criticism) that employers don't know what they want or, when asked what higher education should do for them, can only formulate their needs in the vaguest of terms. This vagueness is, in fact, quite explicable, if one assumes that the degree is being used in such cases as a screening rather than a selection device. Hence, the generalist/specialist argument is largely irrelevant; what is relevant is the associated status of each type of course. If generalist degrees are associated with weaker students (as they currently are), then employers will tend to prefer specialised students, not because of the specialisation, but because of the student.

This argument leads on naturally to the third interpretation of graduate labour-market needs: namely, that employers are looking for, or looking at, other things altogether. Much, of course, depends on the nature of the job, and the importance of specialist expertise within it. Some of the literature on the subject distinguishes between general intake and specific intake, a distinction we have so far used here, and which perhaps derives partly from Becker's original distinction (Becker, 1984). However, it may be more accurate to see jobs in terms of a spectrum going from those in which specialist expertise is virtually everything, to those where it is virtually non-existent. Where specialist expertise is crucial, employers (and colleagues) will often put up with what would otherwise be considered outrageous behaviour and attitudes (turning up late or not at all, idiosyncratic dress and manners, extreme egotism, absent-mindedness, disorderly work habits) because they cannot afford to do without the expertise. The stereotypical god-like hospital consultant, mad scientist, dashing general, unworldly scholar, and rebellious artist are all extreme cases in point. But in most jobs, specialist expertise is only one factor in the equation, even if the most important one: and the capacity to work with people, or under them or over them, to be reasonably organised, to sustain effort over the long term, to think clearly and systematically, to adapt when necessary, to be committed and yet detached enough to analyse where one is going wrong – all these are qualities that the employer will look for in the graduate along with, or even above, his or her specialist expertise. Hence, it is no surprise that employers place such an emphasis on face-to-face selection techniques – interviews, residential weekends, trial periods – and on extra-curricular evidence, in the form of references and signs of non-academic activity, for both of these are ways of gauging what the graduate has to offer beyond his or her expertise.

There is another sense in which employers may be looking for something else. In many jobs, there are certain competences which are necessary or desirable: a basic grasp of mathematics or computing, the ability to communicate effectively in either oral or written form, or to process and summarise large amounts of information quickly, knowledge of a foreign language, or of the rudiments of law or accounting. These skills are not *expertise* in the sense in which the term has been used here; rather they are competences, added on to expertise, which allow the graduate to apply his expertise more widely, or to work more effectively with other people, or which make him trainable in a shorter time than otherwise. Thus a graduate who has a degree in history or politics or geography, but who also possesses some of these competences, might be in a better position to get a job than one who can offer only his specialist expertise. Indeed, employers might prefer added competences to added subjects.

The breadth/depth issue is affected not only by student and labour market demands, but by the needs and influence of post-graduate studies. It is important to distinguish between needs and influence here, since on the face of it, the 'needs' would only apply to the 13 per cent or so of graduates who currently go on to postgraduate work. While this is an increase on the 6 per cent of pre-war days, it is still a small minority (Welsh, 1979; Simpson, 1983). However, the influence of postgraduate studies may be more profound than these figures would suggest, because of the vertical or hierarchic nature of the education system.

The literature on postgraduate education in the United Kingdom is relatively limited, and very little has been written on the relationship between postgraduate and undergraduate studies, whether in terms of the content of courses, or the attitudes of staff and students. No systematic survey exists which would prove or disprove Lord Robbins' assertion that 'a great many professors look upon their jobs as being the manufacture of dons to produce further dons or of high experts in the professor's own specialization' (Robbins, 1971). However, the question of the structural rela-tionship between undergraduate and postgraduate studies has been raised by suggestions that undergraduate education could be restructured on a 2 + 1 or 2 + 2 years basis, with two generalist years followed (perhaps by only some students) by one or two specialist years. Scottish and American patterns are typically invoked in support of such arguments, but they founder (at least at present) on the twin reefs of limited expenditure and reduced access: it is unlikely that governments will be able to afford to lengthen higher education by a whole year for everybody, and if it is not for everybody, then some people are going to get less than the three years they get now.

In curricular terms, the length of the Masters degree is important. If a Master's degree only takes one year, the pressure to specialise on the undergraduate curriculum must be greater than if it takes two years, since there is less time to reach the necessary depth of study. In the United States, professional graduate schools typically involve two years of study (although sometimes this can be accelerated) with the first year consisting of pre-dissertation course work. In the United Kingdom, the Master's can often be obtained after one year's study, usually involving course work and a dissertation over a 12-month period. (Oxbridge and the Scottish universities award an MA on different grounds.) With the Master's coming so quickly on top of the Bachelor's degree, it is hardly surprising that the pressure for undergraduate specialisation remains intense, and attempts to broaden the curriculum often fail. The greater breadth of undergraduate studies in the United States may be partly due to the distancing of that pressure.

There is thus a structural pressure on the undergraduate curriculum which affects the depth/breadth issue. Much more difficult to gauge is the professional pressure, arising from the fact that lecturers are academics who have themselves typically come up the postgraduate route. It would only be human for lecturers to consider it 'natural' for undergraduate work to lead on to postgraduate studies, and to identify most strongly with students who aspire to such a progression. Such considerations might well also influence what they consider to be the minimum coverage or depth or level of studies in any particular discipline at the undergraduate stage, and any attempts to reduce or modify that minimum would therefore be resisted, as a lowering of standards, or an attack on the integrity of the discipline.

Such professional pressures on the undergraduate curriculum are often couched or justified in intrinsic terms. It is alleged that one cannot reach degree 'level' unless one commits most of three years to studying the subject(s) in question; and that the intellectual advantages of reaching such a level are very great. Indeed, not only is there less advantage in reaching lower levels, there is a positive risk. Pope's 'a little learning is a dangerous thing' is often cited. The argument is that only through study in depth can one achieve a right understanding of the relationship between the constituent parts of a discipline and the discipline as a totality, and, perhaps even more importantly, of the relationship between what is known and what is unknown. If one studies only part of the discipline, one may fail to see how one part draws on or reacts against others. *Hamlet* will not be located in the tradition of Elizabethan revenge tragedies, Joyce will not be seen in reaction against the Celtic Twilight. Worse still, the other side of the argument (if there is one) will not even be encountered: and the student will be quite unaware of, for example, the case *against* positivism, or empiricism, or social construct theories of knowledge. Of course, exposure to all sides of the argument and the full complexity of organised knowledge can, as Perry (1970) has observed, induce a kind of intellectual paralysis in which choice and commitment become impossible. But Perry argues that the stage of 'seeing all sides' is one that has to be gone through and transcended; it is worse never even to get to that stage. But depth also implies an encounter not just with the other side, but with no side: with not knowing. This has been powerfully described by Bernstein:

> By the ultimate mystery of a subject I mean its potential for creating new realities. It is also the case, and this is important, that the ultimate mystery of the subject is not coherence but incoherence; not order, but disorder; ... knowledge is permeable ... its orderings are provisional ... the dialectic of knowledge is closure and openness. (Bernstein, 1971, page 57)

Study in depth, then, is the study not of discrete topics, writers, or themes, but of a complex and internally conflictful tradition, the sense of which comes only when a certain 'critical mass' of understanding has been accumulated; it implies a grasp not only of what knowledge is, but how it changes. Even more, it inculcates in the student a profound sense of the difficulty of knowing, and of the uncertainties and limitations of our understanding; a sense which persists even when one is engaged in producing what the Americans call 'quick and dirty' work, which the pressures of time and resources make necessary in many jobs. It is these aspects of study in depth which give the term 'discipline' its full resonance, which goes well beyond the referential connotations of 'subject'.

Yet the resonances of, and arguments for, depth do not stop even here. We pointed out in an earlier report that the idea of depth was closely linked to the idea of transfer of learning: the belief that, as Thorndike once put it, 'learning to do one thing well will make one do better things that in concrete appearance have absolutely no community with it'. In the British academic world, this is usually referred to as 'training the mind', or 'learning to think'.

Both lay belief and systematic research on transfer of learning are contradictory and inconclusive. Belief in transfer is a cornerstone of curriculum thinking in British higher education, set firmly in place by Robbins' reference to 'the general powers of the mind'. It is rarely articulated and often taken for granted, and only a few writers, such as Hajnal (1972) have explicitly questioned it. However, it appears to be a peculiarly Anglican tenet. In most other countries, doubts about the transferability of learning tend to lead to either a broader-based curriculum (as in the United States) or a more direct matching of study and application-in-work (as on the Continent). In neither case is there much faith in 'breadth-through-depth'.

Systematic research on transfer is also rather inconclusive. The transfer issue may appear a purely theoretical one, but it has direct implications for the curriculum. For if transfer does occur, specialisation can be defended and even promoted on the argument that breadth (of application) comes through depth (of study). If transfer does not occur, or only in a limited fashion, a broad education necessitates a broad curriculum. The newer cognitive or information-processing models of transfer seem a distinct advance on the older behavioural model with its emphasis on identical elements of content or procedure. The new emphasis is on what we bring to the world, rather than what it presents us with, perceptually and conceptually; what we make of it, rather than what it stubbornly 'is'. It seems therefore more likely *a priori* that study in depth can yield transferable effects, and that specialisation is not necessarily as narrow in its outcomes as it may look. However, two *caveats* must be entered. First, if one does not learn something in the first place, it cannot be transferred; so the nature of the initial platform or base for transfer is crucial. An undergraduate curriculum which contains no mathematics will produce no mathematical transfer effects. Secondly, it has been assumed here that it is the transfer of knowledge and skills which is mainly involved. The 'trained mind' argument may have, however, a powerful affective or value component; and it may be less a case of learning to think in any purely intellectual sense, than of learning to survive and prosper in a particular social and economic milieu. Learning to think, in that case, may mean learning to talk, dress, react, and behave in a manner which is, to use that deceptively mild word, appropriate.

The 'intrinsic' arguments for depth appear to be quite powerful. Depth not only inculcates a proper sense of the difficulty of knowledge; it gives a balanced perspective on the discipline as a whole; and probably produces valuable transfer effects as well. What of the intrinsic arguments for greater breadth of study? To some extent these are critiques of the arguments in favour of depth, but there are positive points to be made in favour of breadth of studies in higher education as well.

One argument in favour of depth was that it allowed one to grasp the discipline as a totality, and to see the parts in relation to the whole. But what if the discipline does not constitute a totality, what if it is only a collection of loosely-linked sub-fields? In that case, it would not only be possible to study one of those sub-fields in relative isolation from the rest; any attempt to conceive of the discipline as an integrated or unified whole would produce either vacuity or confusion. Of course all disciplines claim that they are integrated wholes ('seamless garment' is the phrase often employed) but their unity may be more professional and institutional than epistemological. Is there really something which binds together all the branches of mathematics, chemistry, the biological sciences, the sub-specialisms of sociology or psychology? Is economics all of a piece? Is history? Is philosophy? Where the discipline possesses strong general theories and a ruling class of concepts, the answer must be yes: but the fissiparous tendencies of even the oldest and best-established disciplines make the question a pertinent one. One cannot automatically assume that every part of a discipline is tightly bound to every other part – what is called the 'integrationist fallacy'. At the same time, even disciplines which seem to be divided against themselves may possess an elusive common ethos, a cultural tone, which cannot be dismissed as 'mere style'. The internal structure of bodies of knowledge – the extent to which they cohere or not – is a fascinating subject for research. To date, it has been characterised more by assumptions – such as Bruner's (1968) that each subject *has* an essential structure – than by exploration. Certainly, the notion that there is a minimum threshold of understanding the discipline as a totality which constitutes 'degree level' is open to question. And that this takes exactly three years (in the United Kingdom) to reach in almost all subjects is a suspiciously convenient coincidence. If there is such a threshold, then one would expect it to take a little longer in some subjects, or a little less in others. The likelihood must be that 'degree level' is a function of time available, and not the other way round.

Another argument for depth was that, paradoxically, it allows the student to encounter ignorance, not-knowing as well as knowing. Again, however, one may doubt whether this can take place only after a long, cognitive build-up. Sociologists would see this in terms of the control and release of knowledge: a withholding of the 'real thing' until the apprenticeship has been served, and the socialisation confirmed. Surely it is possible, even in first-year courses or projects, to encounter the limits and limitations which are an inseparable part of 'real grasp'? Much depends on the manner of teaching (the hidden curriculum) and the extent to which it projects superficial certainties and closure or profounder uncertainties and openness. Of course, saying 'we do not know' is one thing; experiencing it in one's bones is another. Perhaps the problem lies partly in the attitude of mind of those teaching first-year courses, and the extent to which this is conditioned by notions of level, and assumptions about unilinear progression. Bruner's spiral curriculum and his assertion that one can teach sophisticated concepts with integrity at several levels, may have more ambition than realisation to it, but it does usefully challenge the idea that the development of understanding is a severely linear process, and that the true state of knowledge can only be revealed or grasped after one has climbed the ladder.

There is also a more positive intrinsic argument in favour of breadth of studies in higher education, in terms of the concept of curricular *contrast*. People often speak of the value of suddenly finding themselves in a different culture. It wakens them up, challenges their usual routines and attitudes, and demonstrates the living possibility of doing things otherwise. Much the same can be said of the value of visiting other disciplines. But such visits must have the quality of *immersion* that a foreign trip has to be really valuable. Flying over the country, and its academic equivalent, the survey course, will not do; one must get in among the natives.

The value of such immersion and contrast is that it throws one's own disciplinary culture into sharp relief. It has often been noted that researchers who have crossed from one academic field to another have sometimes been able to see problems with a fresh eye. The same benefit can arise at the undergraduate level, provided that the subject is in some way experienced rather than simply introduced. Introductory or survey courses do perhaps have a place in higher education, but as part of an orientation/guidance process, rather than an educational one.

Finally, breadth can be justified in terms of just that – breadth. No one subject contains within itself anything approaching the total gene pool of types or procedures of knowing. A subject may be largely quantitative but not qualitative, convergent rather than divergent, 'objective' but not 'subjective', pure rather than applied, concerned with the natural world but not the human world, impersonal rather than personal. Even if transfer takes place, the base from which it takes place may be rather restricted. The demands of, and for, specialisation must be set against the criticism that higher education is turning out intellectual pre-Copernicans, who believe that their own discipline lies at the centre of the intellectual universe, and who are incapable of conceiving that things might be otherwise.

Disciplines and interdisciplinarity

Interest in interdisciplinarity in higher education seems to date from the mid-1960s. That is not to say that interdisciplinary courses did not exist before then. Classics, involving the study of the literature, philosophy, and history of two cultures was for long one of the most prestigious courses of study in English universities. Another long-established field of study, medicine, draws on a number of, if not disciplines, at least areas of knowledge; as do several other applied, professional courses such as engineering, agriculture, and education. It was in the 1960s, however, that the concept of interdisciplinarity began to gain wider currency. This was partly due to attempts to innovate, as well as expand, in higher education in the period of rapid growth which all OECD countries saw from 1960 to 1975; attempts which in the United Kingdom included new curriculum patterns in some of the new universities, as well as unconventional courses in existing ones. By 1975, the first Careers Research and Advisory Centre degree course guide to *Interdisciplinary Courses* could list over 150 courses in a wide range of institutions (CRAC, 1975). But the increased interest in interdisciplinarity was also due to questioning, at a more abstract level, of conventional notions about disciplines and the 'map of knowledge', a questioning which was both focused and stimulated by the OECD report on *Interdisciplinarity* published in 1972 (OECD, 1972). A Nuffield Foundation study of the same name, published three years later, based on 19 case studies in universities and polytechnics, sought to relate some of the more theoretical issues to the practicalities of academic structures and professional identities (Squires, 1975), and several other significant publications appeared around this time also, including a Society for Research into Higher Education Conference Report (SRHE, 1977).

Since then, some of the interest or at least glamour seems to have waned. The value of the academic department embodying the study of a single discipline has been reasserted by, for example, Trow (1976). The conceptual and practical difficulties of interdisciplinary work have become plainer (Barnett, 1981). Recession in higher education has to some extent brought disciplinary retrenchment. Interdisciplinary 'project-orientation' has been an important trend in some continental countries, such as Denmark, Germany, and the Netherlands, but rather less so in the United Kingdom where 'project work' has a pragmatic ring to it, with fewer of the epistemological and ideological overtones that it has abroad. The 'social construct' theories of knowledge which were widely used in the 1960s and 1970s to attack 'artificial' disciplinary boundaries have themselves come under increasing attack. It may be that interest in interdisciplinarity is partly a function of external factors – economic, social, and political – and that the conservative mood of the mid-eighties finds its curricular correlative in the traditional discipline just as the radical mid-sixties did in integration and interdisciplinarity.

Nevertheless, the conceptual and organisational problems and possibilities still exist. Much interdisciplinary work (or work which claims to be interdisciplinary) goes on, and the 'map of knowledge' is different, irreversibly so, from what it was, say, in 1960. Questions have been opened up which will not be closed, and interest in the topic persists (Levin and Lind, 1985). In this section, some of the curricular aspects of interdisciplinarity will be examined; but it will be impossible to do this without making some reference to related issues, such as academic structure, professional identity, teaching methods, and that vague but important factor, the ethos of higher education.

The concept of interdisciplinarity depends on the concept of a discipline, which in turn depends on theories of knowledge. Broadly speaking, people who believe that there is a real world, that that world has a structure, and that that structure can be known, tend to believe that one should maintain and respect the *structure* and boundaries of disciplines, since these correspond to the structure of reality. A modified form of this realist argument holds that even if the structures do not 'correspond' they have nevertheless been very productive of organised knowledge, and should only be replaced if a more productive structure can be discovered.

People who believe that either there is not, or we cannot have access to, such a real world, and who see our knowledge as a social and historical *construct*, which is shaped and permeated by the society we live in, tend to believe that the structure and boundaries of disciplines are artificial or arbitrary, and reflect the knowers more than the known. Changes in the map of knowledge therefore tend to mirror social change, and may even help to bring it about.

What makes interdisciplinarity a complex concept is not simply the complexity of these underlying epistemological arguments, but the fact that the educational (as distinct from the philosophical) debate is carried on at various levels – epistemological, professional, organisational, and curricular. Rarely are the arguments stated in purely philosophical form: typically they are embedded in other kinds of concern. Thus interdisciplinary courses are sometimes criticised as being flabby, inchoate, superficial, or a 'warm mush of good intentions'; and monodisciplinary courses as being compartmentalised, myopic, unreal, or rigid. Many of the so-called practical difficulties of interdisciplinarity are in fact the institutional or professional embodiments of monodisciplinary beliefs about knowledge, education, and the curriculum; the rituals, resources, and practices that express a resistance to any alternative.

The two opposing points of view described above, which one can label for convenience 'knowledge as structure' and 'knowledge as construct' can be partially reconciled in several ways. Strict realists and disciplinarians may allow interdisciplinary work *after* the student has had a solid grounding in two or more disciplines. This then makes it a postgraduate matter, and indeed the resistance to crossing discipline boundaries or attempting to 'build bridges' seems to be rather weaker at that level. This constitutes a form of 'postdisciplinarity'. In addition, some 'disciplinarians' will allow 'predisciplinarity' – the teaching of cross-disciplinary themes and studies at the secondary school level before the disciplines have become fully differentiated and distinct in higher education.

A rather different argument will admit interdisciplinarity in some areas of knowledge rather than others. The assumption here is that the real world can be divided into various levels of complexity or organisation (sub-atomic, atomic, molecular, organic, social, and so on) and that the lower levels exhibit a greater degree of structure than the higher ones. Therefore disciplinary structures and boundaries are 'real' in the natural sciences, which deal with the 'lower' levels of complexity, but become increasingly arbitrary at the higher levels in the social sciences and humanities. While this argument is very problematic, there does often seem to be less resistance to interdisciplinary courses in the latter faculties than in the former. Even within the natural sciences, one senses that the boundaries around and within the biological sciences are less firmly established than in physics or chemistry; although this may be only a matter of historical accident, in that the biological sciences have happened to have gone through a relatively fluid period of development in the last few decades. It is conceivable that major shifts in, say, physics, could modify the sense of it as a cohesive discipline sometime in the future.

Another aspect of the problem is the degree or extent of integration aimed at. In this book, interdisciplinary studies have been contrasted with (mono) disciplinary studies, but the 1972 OECD report used four terms, of increasing 'tightness':

Multidisciplinary ...	Juxtaposition of various disciplines sometimes with no apparent connection between them. ...
Pluridisciplinary ...	Juxtaposition of disciplines assumed to be more or less related. ...
Interdisciplinary ...	An adjective describing the interaction among two or more disciplines. ...
Transdisciplinary ...	Establishing a common system of axioms for a set of disciplines. (pages 25–6)

Of these four, only the first and third have achieved anything like common currency in the United Kingdom, signifying juxtaposed and integrated disciplines respectively. A further complicating factor is the extent to which any particular discipline is perceived to be open to subdivision or disaggregation without damage to its 'essential nature'. It is of course possible to draw up criteria for what one considers to be a discipline, as did Heckhausen in the OECD report: material field, subject matter, level of theoretical integration, methods, analytical tools, applications, and historical contingencies. However, as he notes, these criteria are not applied with equal emphasis in each discipline: in some cases it is the methodology which is seen to be the distinguishing or unifying feature, in others it might be the object of studies or the general models/theories. And, as noted in the previous section, the unity may be a more elusive one of ethos or style.

Enough has already been said to indicate, even in this brief account, that interdisciplinarity is a conceptually complex topic. This complexity is compounded by organisational and professional complexity. The Nuffield Foundation report referred to above is full of examples of the ways in which the location, structuring, and embodiment of knowledge affect, and to some extent even constitute, the 'knowledge itself'. One of the most obvious aspects of this is the difficulty of mounting interdisciplinary courses in departmentally structured institutions.

> A department is not simply an academic or curricular unit. It is a social unit, a research grouping, a welfare centre, a territory, an administrative entity, and a symbol for both staff and students. Institutions which have tried to do away with departments have often found them re-emerging in subtle forms, perhaps because not all the functions listed above have been taken into account. It may also be a matter of habit: most academics have *experienced* departments and anything else is a trifle strange. (Squires, 1975, page 16)

How then does one go about setting up an interdisciplinary course which involves several departments? One solution is negotiate an agreement or 'treaty' between such departments, relying on the fact that departments, at least in British universities, can have a good deal of autonomy. Many interdisciplinary courses depend on such agreements; but they may be unstable. If one department is substantially larger or stronger than the other(s) this may create tensions among those who are contributing. Worse still, if the departments, or the institution, fall on hard times, such courses can be among the first to be cut because they are seen as peripheral to each department's essential work. In this way a number of interdisciplinary courses have become casualties of the 1981 university cuts.

An alternative to the *ad hoc* treaty between departments is the creation of an entirely new and relatively autonomous structure which will underpin the course in question. But establishing such a structure can be a lengthy and tortuous process, necessitating a considerable amount of political skill. Another possible solution to the organisational problem is to adopt a more flexible or polyvalent structure for the whole institution, such as schools of study, a unit/modular system, or a matrix structure with teaching and research along different axes. None of these is entirely satisfactory. Modular structures, for example, bring flexibility but also discontinuity and fissiparousness, which may even exacerbate the problems of integration which already exist in many interdisciplinary courses. The problem is not that there is a mismatch between academic structures and curricular patterns, but that such structures are not entirely neutral: any given structure will facilitate one kind of curriculum and hinder others. The real problem is that different kinds of curriculum pattern are mutually exclusive or at least antagonistic: one cannot easily reconcile the demands of continuity and choice, coherence and flexibility, specialisation and breadth, and where research structures influence the undergraduate curriculum they reinforce – in the name of the indissolubility of teaching and research – the pattern that best suits postgraduate work.

The professional structures of higher education also have a profound influence on interdisciplinarity. It was suggested, earlier in this chapter, that the distinction between academic and professional courses might be false, in the sense that the academic world has itself become professionalised. Such professional demarcations affect not only what academics teach, but what they write, and hence what students read. The implicit boundaries and perspectives of specific disciplines are thus passed on, consciously or unconsciously, to the next generation, even when the course is purportedly an interdisciplinary one.

Even teaching styles may clash. This is not necessarily a disciplinary matter, although to some extent different disciplines and departments may develop norms as regards how one teaches, how one relates to students, how one sets and marks examinations, and so forth. More often, however, it seems a matter of individual style and assumptions. The way that lecturers teach and behave reflects, among other things, their assumptions about their subject, about higher education, about learning, about students, and even about human nature. These are not necessarily disciplinary assumptions: but as long as they remain within the conventional disciplinary boundaries, they tend to remain implicit, unchallenged, and, to a considerable degree, private. Interdisciplinary courses, however, entail an end to isolation: not only one's subject, but one's teaching, is thrown into the public arena. Lecturers may end up quarrelling not over the differences between their subjects, but because of divergent political beliefs, or attitudes to students, or habits of teaching. The lecturer who thinks that, for example, punctuality and neatness are important in students' work will not take kindly to working with a colleague who doesn't care much about these things. Even 'small' matters like spelling or the citing of references can become bones of contention.

Perhaps the main point to emerge from the interdisciplinary experiences of the last two decades has to do with institutions and professions rather than with knowledge itself. This may seem surprising, since interdisciplinarity raises, as no other issue raises, fundamental questions about the nature of knowledge and its organisation into disciplines. But whatever the balance of the epistemological arguments, that balance is always tipped slightly by the existing institutional and professional set-up: it provides an extra justification for the epistemological status quo which has nothing to do with epistemology, and everything to do with the continuity and convenience of higher education and those who work in it.

This is not to argue that all knowledge is merely a social construct; or to imply that all institutions are somehow artificial. It is simply to suggest that the permanence of our institutions must be accompanied by a permanent critique of them, because all institutions and professions, once established, seem to set self-preservation high on their list of priorities, whatever their formal aims. In the academic world, this tends to reinforce the traditional discipline and department (at least in the United Kingdom) *over and above* whatever academic or epistemological justification they may have.[3] It would seem wise therefore to give a certain 'extra' support to interdisciplinary and other non-traditional developments to balance that 'over and above'.

Two other general points can be made, one conceptual, the other practical. We still lack enough detailed analyses of the internal structures and coherence of disciplines which would allow us to answer questions such as: How unitary is this discipline? What parts of it are tightly related, and which parts loosely coupled? What constitutes the mainstream or the core of the discipline? Which parts of it can be described as peripheral? There is a mass of anecdotal evidence about such matters, but little systematic analysis. Yet if disciplines are to be 'subdivided' or 'drawn on' for interdisciplinary purposes, answers to such questions are crucial. For example, it may be argued that whereas one can treat manpower planning as a relatively discrete and therefore isolable aspect of the economics of education, one cannot do likewise with human capital theory, because it involves an understanding of some of the basic concepts of the discipline of economics. Likewise, whereas one might be able to detach a module on skill learning for teachers, understanding the different models of transfer of learning is impossible without a grasp of the basic models of learning theory in general. Some authors in English Literature seem easier to treat in relative isolation from the rest of literary history and tradition than others. Blake, for example, seems to stand on his own more than Pope; Milton more than Donne. These are only examples, and debatable at that: the point is that where we are dealing with anything less than the whole of the discipline (or what is conventionally seen as the whole) the question of 'dismembering' arises. If a discipline is truly an organism, then all 'dismembering' will be difficult, although a limb or two may be severed without fatal consequences. But one suspects that the claims of 'organic unity' are sometimes exaggerated. What is needed is a kind of internal model of each discipline, showing the location of all the major topics and themes, and the strength of the relations between them. Only in this way can we begin to move beyond the simplistic metaphors of 'organism', 'body', 'seamless garment', or 'house' to a more subtle appraisal of the unity and integrity of different disciplines. Such an analysis might also show that different kinds of integration can exist between different disciplines. In some cases, it might be appropriate to speak in terms of boundaries and overlaps, while in others, of different aspects or facets of a phenomenon. To some extent, these differences are already implied in talk about 'bridge-building', 'different angles', or 're-structuring', each of which suggests a different kind of relationship between disciplines. It may be that over time we are moving away from a standard model of disciplines. Certainly, knowledge tends to be organised in entities which we refer to as disciplines or subjects; but we cannot therefore assume that the basis for that organisation is the same in every case. If there is a variety of ways in which knowledge can constitute a discipline, then there will be an even greater variety in the ways in which disciplines can relate to one another.

The final and more practical point has to do with the responsibility for the organisation of knowledge in disciplinary or interdisciplinary configurations. Veblen's notion of 'trained incapacity' has already been mentioned – the inability to understand things one way which may be a consequence of learning to understand them another way. It is also sometimes said that whereas universities have departments, societies have problems; or that all knowledge meets in the knower; or that we must strive to see the world whole. Each of these statements or slogans in its own way tends to subvert the conventional classification and framing of knowledge in terms of a collection of subjects handed down to the student. It has already been suggested that a little extra support for such subversion is a permanent necessity, because of the institutional and professional weight that maintains the disciplinary status quo. However, asking the students to do all the subverting is another matter. Students, like staff, who break out of the cocoon of organised disciplines, face a difficult task, and the responsibility of the teacher who leads the student not along but off the path of organised knowledge is that much the greater. This does not mean that it all has to be sorted out at the research level first, or that a paternalistic profession must exorcise all risks, but it does imply that staff should be aware of the added difficulties of unconventional (to use the word in its strict sense) studies. The enthusiasm for interdisciplinarity and 'breaking down artificial boundaries' or 'doing away with arbitrary distinctions' of the 1960s was accompanied by a certain youthful optimism. Twenty years later there seems to be more caution, and some disillusionment. This may be the reflection of a changed educational, social, and political climate. It may also reflect a realisation that the boundaries between disciplines, even if they are not 'real' or always productive, are nevertheless not arbitrary.

Theory and practice

Of all the curriculum concepts which are used, 'theory' is the oldest. Its origins appear to lie in the Orphic cult, and the term was used by Pythagoras in the sense of watching or contemplating. The concept of 'practice' is first used systematically by Aristotle, and with it begins the tendency to see theory and practice in dichotomous though not necessarily mutually exclusive terms (Russell, 1946). However Lobkowicz (1967) has argued that the dichotomy was not so much the modern one between abstract ideas and their concrete application as between two ways of life, the philosophic and the political; that even this distinction was seen more as a tension between what was divine and what was human in man, and that later Greek philosophers modified this tension further to constitute aspects of a fundamental unity.

The subsequent shifts in the two concepts, and their relationship, in Roman and medieval times, up to Hegel and Marx, have been traced by Lobkowicz; and Marx's treatment of the distinction has since been taken up by a number of writers, particularly Habermas (1974). One consequence of this has been a tendency to distinguish in English at least, between practice, as activity or application which derives purely from theory, and praxis (the original Greek term) as activity which modifies theory or consciousness.

The concepts, and the opposition between them, are thus complex and many-layered historically. There appears to be no study which has traced their educational usage, although they are frequently employed in both formal educational writing and informal discussion. In such discourse, theory and practice often seem to overlap with other sets of distinctions, such as pure and applied, abstract and concrete, and even, obliquely, active and contemplative. It is not possible here to attempt to sort out the meanings and connotations of all these terms, which in any case may vary in relation to the discipline being discussed. Rather, the emphasis will be on how the distinction operates in practice (*sic*) in terms of the structure of the curriculum in higher education.

The distinction impinges on all the three types of curriculum – academic, teacher, and professional – which comprise higher education. In academic degree courses, there is often a part of the course which is labelled 'theory', although the term is rarer in the humanities than in the social or natural sciences. The label 'practice' or 'practical' is commonly applied to laboratory work in the natural sciences, but is rarer in the social sciences and humanities, though one finds 'practical criticism' in literature, and the syllabus may describe certain parts of the course as being concerned with 'practical applications' or 'practical problems' or 'action research'.

In teacher education courses, the relationship between theory and practice often looms large, partly because there is some doubt as to what constitutes theory in education, partly because such 'theory' as is taught is sometimes felt to be impractical, and partly because teaching practice is an integral part of most such courses. As was mentioned in Chapter 1, not only is the relationship between theory and practice at issue; the 'balance' between them, and the sequence, are also problematic (Carr, 1982).

In professional courses, theory and practice may be embodied in taught courses and job placements respectively. In the United Kingdom, many professional courses are of the sandwich type, with the job placements providing the filling between the academic slices. (Where the placement comes after the academic input, as in medicine and law, one might refer to an open, Scandinavian-type sandwich.) Again, the distinction gives rise to worries: are the theory and practice elements properly integrated? Is the practice properly supervised? Is the total load too heavy? Should one have one long, or several shorter, placements?

The distinction between theory and practice also affects the pecking order of subjects as a whole within higher education. Some disciplines are thought to be more 'theoretical' than others, often with the connotation that they are more difficult. Mathematics and physics are examples. In other cases the prefix 'applied' indicates an orientation towards practice. Applied mathematics is more 'practical' than pure mathematics, applied social studies more so than sociology, applied linguistics more than pure linguistics, applied psychology more than psychology. Within disciplines too, there may be specialisms, schools, or trends which are perceived to be more theoretical than the disciplinary norm: structuralism in English, econometrics in economics, and microbiology in biology have a reputation for being 'theoretical' relative to the rest of the discipline.

Even the above brief comments will show the difficulty of arriving at a standard definition of either concept. Theory is typically used to refer to statements of some generality or scope which have some predictive, explanatory, or taxonomic power. But there are problems with even this very loose definition. Much depends on the discipline. In some disciplines, it is arguable that 'explanation' is simply 'prediction' written backwards; and in any case, 'prediction' may be thought of in probablistic rather than absolute terms. In other disciplines, 'explanation' is used in a different sense, that of understanding relationships or connections without necessarily being able to predict them. This is not to say that in philosophical terms 'explanation' and 'prediction' are or are not the same, but simply to argue that the same terms are used in different ways in different disciplines.

The word 'theory' is also sometimes used in the even weaker sense of taxonomies, classifications, or descriptive models of phenomena. Some would argue that the word 'model' is more appropriate here, but 'model' too can be used in different ways: there are predictive models, explanatory models, models which 'represent' reality, and 'working models' which merely provide a better purchase on complexity than one would otherwise have. What all these have in common, however, is a certain, relative generality: they refer to a group or a class of phenomena. There are no theories or models of the particular. However, even this statement is relative. One finds, in many disciplines, a distinction between 'general theories' (sometimes called 'grand theories') and mere 'theories', the latter being somewhat more localised in their scope.

Definitions of practice are equally elusive. Practice is usually associated with doing rather than thinking, but this distinction itself needs elucidating. 'Doing' seems to have several connotations in educational discourse. First, it signals a shift from the controlled environment of the classroom or laboratory to the decontrolled environment of the field, workplace, or community, where things can 'go wrong' for all sorts of reasons. The decontrolled environment is not simply more complex in terms of the number of phenomena, variables, and interactions; it may operate on a different time-scale (more hurried); and the consequences of what one does are not limited or muted; it is 'for real' and a mistake can cost money, jobs, and even lives. Practice, therefore, refers partly not to what one does (which might be thinking) but to the context in which one does it.

Secondly, practice sometimes has the implication of acting without being able to explain what one is doing or why; not being able to 'theorise' about it. This implication is strongest in the creative arts and crafts, in which the musician or actor or painter may have to resort to 'showing' what he is doing rather than trying to verbalise it. It is not surprising that practice plays a large part in the curriculum of such subjects. Conversely, one can learn how to talk about doing something, without necessarily being able to do it: the most obvious examples are people who can analyse tennis, or piano playing, or leadership without being able to perform themselves.

Practice also has the sense of repetition, of confirmation rather than initial learning. This is most often met with in motor skill subjects, where such repetition, sometimes with variation, sometimes without, is an integral part of 'stamping in' or 'chaining' the activity. However, practice in the sense of repetition has a wider significance because it invokes a model of learning which can be applied more generally, beyond the psychomotor domain. This sees learning in terms of levels of strategies, tactics, routines, and subroutines. Any of these can become 'automatic' or 'autonomous' (that is, one can do them without 'thinking') if practised enough, and performed in a fairly predictable environment (Fitts and Posner, 1973). The classic example of such levels of automatic behaviour is driving a car, where each subroutine (such as changing gear, steering) has to be consciously controlled while being learned, but once learned becomes automatic. The importance of automaticity in much behaviour is that it leaves one's mind free to attend to more important strategic or unpredictable matters – which is what is often meant by 'thinking'. Thus doing (in an automatic fashion) releases our minds for thinking; or, to put it another way, practice can free us to theorise.

To summarise: theory has to do with statements which are relatively general in scope, and which in some sense predict, explain, or clarify complex phenomena. Practice has to do with activity in a decontrolled environment, with activity which may be only partly expressible in words or symbols, or which may be to some extent automatised or routinised. Using these extremely loose characterisations, one may nevertheless say that there have been two major, and to some extent contradictory, trends in higher education curricula, in recent years. The first is for subjects to become more theoretical; and the second is for the importance of practice to be reasserted. Each of these trends will be discussed briefly below.

The statement that a subject has 'got more theoretical' often indicates, in the first place, a greater mathematical element in it. Whether mathematics is a theoretical subject or not, many people think of it as such. Not only has the use of mathematics spread in subjects like the biological sciences, economics, and psychology; the kind of mathematics used has widened to include topology and complex modelling as well as the more familiar arithmetic or statistical procedures.

'More theory' may also refer to more science. Where previously subjects like nursing and agriculture were based to a great extent on 'good practice' and transmitted skills, there is increasingly a scientific base for them in chemistry and the biological sciences. Archaeology, geology, and certain branches of psychology also lean increasingly on the natural sciences. Again, one may hesitate to label the natural sciences as automatically 'theoretical', but in the eyes of many students the drift seems to be in that direction. And there is a constant debate within the various branches of engineering education as to how far engineering should be seen as an 'applied science' or as an activity which to some extent generates its own knowledge and procedures.

'More theory' may equally indicate an attempt to establish a sound and unique theoretical basis within the discipline itself. Geography seems to have become much more theoretical in this sense in the last two decades. There is a constant concern in the social sciences with the theoretical basis of the various disciplines, conflicting sometimes with the belief that progress is more likely to be made on narrower or less ambitious fronts. Such issues raise questions about how disciplines evolve, which go well beyond the scope of this book, but suffice it to say that the example of the evolution of the natural sciences is never far away, as a model to aspire to or react against.

Many disciplines in higher education thus seem to have 'got more theoretical' in a variety of ways. The advent of computers and computer modelling may seem like yet another movement in this direction, though, conversely, computer models can be used to concretise or represent what would otherwise remain purely abstract relationships. But how is this drift towards theory to be explained? Is it a natural or inevitable consequence of the advancement of knowledge? Is theoretical knowledge the highest form of organised knowledge, differing from other types of organisation (for example, concepts or aggregated data) merely in the extent and power of its 'organised-ness'?

Three factors at least seem to have been at work in the drift towards theory. The first is the pervasive, persuasive example of the natural sciences – physics, chemistry, geology, biochemistry, and increasingly the other biological sciences. If the 'success' of those sciences is due to their methods (discovering how to discover), it is nevertheless embodied in their theories. Theory, especially theory which will predict events, thus seems eminently desirable, and hence there is a strong inclination for other subjects to adopt not only the content but the form of the natural sciences: experimental methods, formulation of hypotheses, mathematical modelling, excision of subjectivity, impersonal style. Whatever the epistemological doubts about the natural sciences, and the humanitarian doubts about their consequences, there is a widespread feeling that they work: they produce results, and discernible progress. Of course, this simple, positivistic view of science has come under severe attack in recent years from philosophers, sociologists, and some scientists; but such criticism seems to have little effect on the momentum of science.

A second reason for the drift to theory may be connected with the perception of academic status. To say that a subject has no theory is to question its academic birthright. This does not mean that all subjects are described in terms of theory: the word is rarely used in relation to classics, for example. Nevertheless, few academics want to be thought of as representing a subject which is 'merely descriptive' or 'purely practical'. For well-established disciplines like philosophy, classics, or history, there is no problem; but for newer disciplines, which are attempting to establish their academic legitimacy, questions about the theoretical basis of the discipline touch a raw nerve, and a good deal of time and energy is spent in trying to establish precisely such a theoretical base, however problematic. Indeed, if the theoretical base is problematic, so much the better, because a literature can then rapidly develop dealing with the complex and intractable issues thereof.

Do the professional structures of higher education encourage an emphasis on theory? On the face of it, the requirement of postgraduate research, and in particular the Ph.D., that it should constitute an original contribution to knowledge, would seem to point towards theory rather than practice. However, much depends on the discipline concerned, and many pieces of research, particularly at the Master's level, are of an applied rather than theoretical nature. To specify that research should be original does not necessarily entail that it should be 'theoretical' in terms of its own discipline, although perhaps a special accolade is reserved for work which is seen to develop theory. Interestingly, this theoretical bias at the very apex of the educational system is implicitly recognised in the system of *honorary* degrees, which are often awarded to distinguished *practitioners*. Lower down the educational scale, for example, in middle-level technician education, the value of having practitioners teaching students or at least part of their courses is widely recognised in the United Kingdom. But in higher education, it is the exception rather than the rule to find *practising* engineers, businessmen, teachers, or social workers contributing regularly to courses, beyond the one-off lecture or seminar. (It is worth noting that such a dual role is normal in medicine.) The professional 'closure' of higher education, with its highly developed research apprenticeship system, means that in the United Kingdom at least, most lecturers and professors are not practitioners outside the institution, although they may do some consulting. Indeed, the 'second route' into academic life, after a period as a practitioner, may be becoming even more exceptional, as the intense competition for academic posts becomes dominated by the young post-doctoral researcher. The movement between academe, industry, and government is easier in some other countries, particularly in the United States, but what is pertinent here is the influence of this movement, or lack of it, on the relationship between theory and practice, and the legitimacy of expertise which is based squarely on the second. It is interesting to note, in this connection, that 'academic drift' appears to be a British and European phenomenon rather than an American one. While there is a great deal of competition among higher education institutions in the United States, the fact that the community colleges have burgeoned *and* developed a distinctive role in the system beyond that of academic feeder institutions suggests that American higher education is subject to not one, but several gravitational pulls.

There are however, trends in the opposite direction, which serve to reinforce the importance or distinctness of practice, and several of these must be mentioned. In a few cases, the reassertion of practice seems to be a direct reaction against what is seen as an over-theoretising of the subject. This is the case, for example, in management education, where the 'action learning' approach bluntly rejects the usefulness of 'management theory' (Revans, 1982). In the study of education too, there is a reaction against the idea that the student should be taught the various disciplines of education (philosophy, psychology, sociology, and so on) so that she can 'draw on' or apply these in her work. Better, say the critics, to start with practice, and let the disciplines enter as needed, when they can usefully contribute to the elucidation of such practice (Hirst, 1983). Social-work education has always emphasised the need for both theory and practice, so although there has been no comparable reaction against theory in that field as yet, doubts have been expressed about the relationship between the two elements of the course, and the total load. It is obvious that a subject must first become 'theoretised' before a reaction can set in. It will be interesting to see, for example, if such a reaction occurs in the nursing field, in response to current academic trends.

The reinforcement of practice, however, goes beyond mere reaction, and can claim stronger philosophical roots, in both Marxism and pragmatism. Marx's notion of praxis appears to have had greater influence on Continental higher education than in the United Kingdom perhaps because the theory/practice distinction has always been more strongly observed in those countries than here. 'Project-orientation' and 'action research' have, on the Continent, implied a strong concern with *praxis*. In crude terms, this is the belief that only by involvement in real-world problems and situations will the student develop an understanding of the social and historical forces which influence or determine thought and action. Practice, in this sense, is not simply the application of theory; it raises and radicalises consciousness and hence generates theory. The challenge to theory is not so much to the notion of theory as to the use of theory to legitimate and authorise certain forms of political consciousness, which in turn reinforce particular economic and social structures. Thus project-work, which in the United Kingdom is often seen merely as one teaching–learning method among others, to be used as appropriate, is often on the Continent a symbol of the challenge to academic authority, to received knowledge, and to false consciousness. The ultimate repression is the repression of consciousness, and it is only through praxis that the student can break out of the conceptual and imaginative restrictions imposed by a dominant ideology. Praxis destroys the illusion that thought or theory can be 'autonomous', because it forces the student to locate or situate ideas in a social and human context. Knowledge becomes no longer a thing, but an aspect of the way people relate to one another, and of the way societies are structured. And this applies also to teaching and learning: everyone is *in* the situation. As Habermas has put it, 'in a process of enlightenment there can only be participants' (Habermas, 1974, p. 40).

The influence of ideas such as these on higher education in the United Kingdom seems to have been uneven. Certainly, terms such as 'praxis' or 'reflexive' have a fairly wide currency in the social sciences, particularly in sociology and education. In other fields, such as law, literature, and the natural sciences, they tend to identify academic minorities who see themselves as battling against the dominant positivist/technicist/capitalist mentality. Many scientists and technologists have probably never even heard of the concept of praxis. This is not just a question of antipathy: many of their Continental peers would be equally antagonistic to the philosophical and political presuppositions that the term now embodies. It is also a question of tradition. There is something about the language of analysis used (say) by Habermas which seems unfamiliar and alien to the dominant intellectual traditions in the United Kingdom.

If the Marxist concept of praxis has had a limited but obvious influence on higher education in the United Kingdom, American pragmatism has had a wider but less obvious impact. Pragmatist philosophy directs our attention to the consequences and effects of ideas, which may in turn modify our conceptions. John Dewey emphasised the importance of relating the logical aspects of a subject (the subject-matter in itself) to its psychological aspects (in relation to the learner). The two, he argued, are mutually dependent. It follows, therefore, that the experience of the learner, or the subject as experienced, is central to the concept of education.

Since Dewey's *Experience and Education* (1938), the idea that experience is important in teaching and learning has become both more widely accepted and vaguely understood. It is therefore difficult to put one's finger on Dewey or other pragmatists as the source of the many statements one finds or hears about the importance of practical experience, project work, problem-solving, or relevance in education. Yet it is more likely to be Dewey than Marx who is ultimately behind the essentially pragmatic, down-to-earth, no-nonsense justifications of sandwich courses, projects, experiential learning, a year 'out' between secondary and higher education, and mature entry, in higher education. To some extent, what Dewey said reinforced an older tradition in further (as distinct from higher) education in this country of the importance of practical learning as against book learning, or as it is sometimes put, 'the university of life'. The restricting consequences of such practicality (and suspicion of theory) have been cited as one among various causes for the United Kingdom's failure adequately to educate or train manpower (Roderick and Stephens, 1978). However that may be, it is worth noting that it is in the polytechnics, not typically the universities, that one finds the heaviest emphasis on sandwich courses and experience.

One can, of course, theorise *about* practice. The work of Argyris (1982) for example, represents one attempt to elucidate how it is that people actually do things, as distinct from thinking about doing them. There are great problems in disembedding any rules or tactics or tricks that people may use in their decision-making. Such rules are apt to be highly contingent ('it all depends') or barely conscious ('I suppose I did take that into account'). They may blur into personal qualities or characteristics (level-headedness, quick-thinking, sensitivity). Once they reach a certain level of generality, they are apt to turn into general, bland models of rational problem-solving (define the problem, consider alternatives, allocate resources, and so on) or exhortations to openness and trust. Nevertheless, attempts to understand practice and action are important because they counter-balance existing concepts which describe the 'theoretical' style of thinking: concepts such as rigour, depth, precision, grasp, and so forth.

The problems of 'unpacking' practice, and verbalising what it involves, have of course long been recognised in a specific area of higher education – namely, that of the creative and performing arts. In music, drama, art and design, and dance, practice looms very large, and theory has an oblique and often secondary role to play. The fact that the institutions which teach these subjects have an ambiguous place within the system – either outside the main structure, or if in it, then determinedly not of it – may reflect the different balance of theory and practice in these subjects and in the 'conventional' academic ones. If one is to look for ways in which parctice could be revivified or re-conceptualised in academic fields, one could do worse than examine the professional structures, teaching methods, and curricula in such institutions which at the least provide an interesting contrast to 'normal' academic patterns. This is not necessarily to say that physics can be taught like painting, or mathematics like music, but an examination of the reasons why they can or cannot might help to illuminate what is meant by theory and practice.

The issues related to theory and practice are clearly complex and long-standing, and do not allow any simple or neat conclusions, but two points can perhaps be made. First, in so far as there is any institutional or professional bias towards 'theory' in higher educa-tion (for reasons similar to the ones related to the status of disciplines) there may be a need for a permanent, countervailing assertion of the importance of practice. The value structures of higher education are unlikely to be neutral in this respect, and it may be that a greater use of practitioners as teachers, and more opportunities for theoreticians to experience the context of practice, would help to correct any imbalance in this respect. At the same time, it must be recognised that 'balance' itself is not necessarily or self-evidently a good thing here: the evolution of knowledge may require swings towards theory or practice at particular points in the development of disciplines.

The second point picks up Lobkowicz's assertion that the distinction was originally one between two types of activity, or life, rather than two types of knowledge. The analysis of theory–practice relationships in any given field tends to produce many gradations between the extremes: practical theories begin to shade into theoretised practice, and so on. The rough definition of theory given earlier, in terms of scope and power, is after all a relative one. It may be that more progress will be made through talking about theorists and practitioners than about theory and practice: about people whose activity or occupation is primarily to do with theorising, or with practising. The epistemological dichotomy may have over-polarised the occupational reality: after all, no practitioner can operate without some theory (even an implicit one) and no theoretician operates in a total social or occupational vacuum. It may be less a question of the type of knowledge involved than of the intention and context of the activity.

Implications

This chapter has examined four aspects of the curriculum in higher education: the academic and the professional; breadth and depth; disciplines and interdisciplinarity; and theory and practice. The discussion of each of these has perforce been rather brief compared to what it could be, and it should also be remembered that not all curricular patterns or innovations in higher education fall neatly under these four headings. For example, the development of independent study or individually tailored degree programmes impinges on all four of the headings, as does in a somewhat different way the accreditation of experiential learning. Nevertheless, the four themes selected seem to represent major axes of curriculum theory in relation to higher education, and the bulk of debate about what should be taught and learned turns on them.

Whatever the structure of higher education and the labels given to institutions in the different OECD countries, the term 'higher education' is common to all. (In Greece, a distinction is drawn between highest education – universities – and higher education – polytechnic or similar institutions.) While it may be unwise to read too much into the term, it is nevertheless true that this form of education is in all cases seen as being at a more advanced level than the rest of the system. The implication is that students have studied not simply more, in terms of coverage, or longer, in terms of time, but at a higher level, in terms of sophistication or difficulty of the content or mental processes. It is this sometimes covert assumption that may lie behind the deep-seated resistance to the complete modularisation of higher education. This tension may be seen in terms of an opposition between a 'holistic' model of the curriculum, and an 'aggregative' one (Squires, 1979).

The holistic model implies that higher education should be a consecutive and cohesive experience. In the United Kingdom this has traditionally meant an uninterrupted passage from upper secondary school (the sixth form) to university, an uninterrupted course of study (over three or four years) ideally in one discipline in one residential institution, culminating in one set of examinations resulting in a single measure, the classified degree. There are variants on this model, both within and, even more so, outside the United Kingdom. The length of studies can vary, as may their breadth, and the element of residence is largely a matter of national tradition. Nevertheless, the holistic model implies that higher education is a 'total experience', a notion that probably derives from the idea of a university as a communal, collegial, or religious institution.

In the aggregative model, by contrast, the essential element is the course or course unit. Each course is to some extent self-contained and is assessed at its termination, leading to a credit. These credits can be aggregated in a variety of ways, and when enough have been accumulated, a degree can be obtained. Since the essential unit is the course credit, it does not matter very much if the studies are intermittent, or if they take place in more than one institution. The question of residence does not arise. As with the holistic model, there are variants, ranging from the very aggregative 'cafeteria' curricula in some US universities and colleges, to the typically much more restricted credit/modular/unit systems found in Europe (Squires, 1986).

The advantages of the aggregative model are obvious, and frequently voiced. It is more flexible; it allows greater student choice; it seems to allow for either breadth or depth; it suits mature students who want to move around the country, or temporarily interrupt their studies; it may allow rationalisation of teaching provision; it makes higher education less of an all-or-nothing affair. The model is the norm in US higher education (though typically it is *not* a completely free-choice cafeteria) and has spread to many other countries in the last decade. But is it really *higher* education? Are the students going *deeper*, as distinct from studying more, or longer? If they are not, how does this affect the notion that higher education is at a different level, or that it is concerned with special expertise, or that it develops, as Robbins put it, the 'general powers of the mind'?

Depth implies knowing a lot about something. For all the denigration of fact and detail that one finds in some curriculum theory, it is surely true that one sign of study in depth is a detailed and accurate knowledge of the object of study, even to the point of knowing apparently useless, quirky particulars. They may not be useless; they may turn out to be crucial in some years' time, one cannot be sure. But depth implies two other things as well; it implies reflexivity, or thinking about the way one thinks; and it implies a continual returning to the problem. It is particularly this last aspect – the experience of coming back to something, often with a slightly altered perspective – that the aggregative model with its tendency to study, assess and leave behind, may miss out on. In extreme cases, depth leads simply to obsession. But it is not for nothing that so many metaphors about knowledge and study express its almost physical difficulty, in terms of struggle, grappling, coming to grips with, getting stuck, pursuit, going round in circles, getting lost, and the like. Knowledge is difficult: the experience of knowing is the experience of difficulty.

However, the analysis in this chapter has suggested that higher education in the United Kingdom today is largely *professional* education. Many degree courses are overtly professional anyway: this applies not only to the traditional professions of law, engineering, and medicine, but also to the newer professions or quasi-professions of teaching, management, public administration, pharmacy, social work, architecture, town planning, and so forth. But the argument has been that even 'academic' courses are professional in that they prepare students (ideally) for the academic professions. The pressures of professionalisation are felt not only in terms of the emphasis on expertise and depth, but in terms of the status of conventional disciplines and of what is called theory. This broad conclusion must be modified in two ways: first, the curriculum patterns in some institutions allow for deviation from or dilution of the optimum professional prescription; and the manner of teaching may in some cases stress a more liberal or less instrumental approach.

One's reaction to such a state of affairs depends on what one thinks about professions and what one believes about higher education.[4] Clearly, higher education in the past has often had a professional function and purpose, and indeed as Veblen (1957) notes, that may have been its main justification in society. One may also believe that the professions and professionalisation are a positive force in modern society. Such arguments tend to be reinforced in the United Kingdom today by the obvious and urgent need to do something about the country's parlous economic decline; hence the current emphasis on vocational and professional relevance.

The implication of such a view is that the higher education curriculum becomes primarily a service curriculum, not in any narrow sense, because service may involve both contextual knowledge and altruistic ethics, but justified primarily in terms of how well it can prepare students for their future occupations. In terms of the models in Chapters 1 and 2, this means an emphasis on culture rather than knowledge or abilities, or on the professional (including the academic-professional) at the expense of the liberal. It also exposes higher education, even allowing for elasticity of substitution, to economic and manpower criteria in a more direct way than would otherwise be the case, since (despite ritual protests to the contrary) there are no other effective criteria. In such a situation, 'irrelevant' subjects seem likely to be increasingly consigned to the 'consumption' of continuing education, rather than the 'investment' in first or higher degrees.

Is there any alternative? The American pattern, where students divide their time between a major specialism, a collection of elective options, and some prescribed general education is sometimes mooted as a less professionally geared alternative. But recent American writing on the subject suggests that the electives can be bitty and incoherent, and general education is extremely problematic. The only thing that works really well, it seems, is the major, which of course reflects the institutional and professional structures. Another possibility is an aggregative, modular pattern, such as exists in modified form in the Open University and some faculties of some polytechnics. But an aggregative pattern runs counter to the belief that higher education should in some sense be a holistic, cumulative experience; if the student simply collects units, in what ways is his understanding deepening?[5] In what sense is his education higher? How far does he apprehend what Bernstein called the ultimate mystery of the subject, the dialectic of openness and closure? A third possible model, the broader-based Scottish general degree, has been eroded over time by both the dominance of the English pattern, and the increased influence of postgraduate priorities; besides, the Scottish pattern involves four, not three years of study.

The analysis here suggests that if higher education aspires to go beyond professionalism, it must do three things in the undergraduate curriculum: first, immerse the student in modes of understanding disciplines to a depth where he can experience the absoluteness of those modes; secondly, to relativise that absoluteness by exposing the student to several alternative or contrasting modes; and thirdly, to make his understanding of all modes reflexive.

The first requirement of depth is necessary for the student not only to get an adequate understanding of the body of knowledge but also to experience what it is like to see the world that way; to think like an historian, or chemist, or engineer. That experience is absolute not in a philosophical sense, but in the sense of excluding any other alternative at that time. The second requirement, however, challenges the first, in that the student is forced to experience multiple possible perspectives, to see that what seemed like a world was in fact only a frame of reference. Thirdly, the student needs to be encouraged to reflect on the nature of the knowledge that he has acquired, and in so doing reflect on organised knowledge itself and its relation to self and society. He has to begin to treat knowledge itself as problematic, rather than something to be taken for granted in the received categories of the higher education curriculum.

This suggests that, in practice, most undergraduates should have substantial contact with three disciplines, and that all undergraduates should have a common course on 'knowledge about knowledge'. Any more than three disciplines would make it impossible to experience any degree of depth in three years; indeed, many academics might feel that three disciplines is already too many. It is worth remembering, however, that many professional courses already involve substantial contact with three disciplines; depending on how one classifies disciplines, this is the case with medicine, engineering, social work, teaching, management, public administration, and others. Where it is not the case (as in law or pharmacy), it is arguable that graduates might be better educated if it were. Tripartite degrees in 'academic' courses are rarer, but do exist: classics (involving history, literature, and philosophy); modern area studies (involving languages, literature, social history, and other subjects); broad-based social science or humanities degrees; and specific examples, such as PPE (philosophy, politics, and economics) at Oxford. Many more academic degrees involve subsidiary subjects in the first or second year, but one suspects that these have an ambiguous status, and that because they are subsidiary, no one takes them very seriously. Substantial contact entails carrying the three subjects for at least two, and possibly all three years. Fewer than three subjects allows more depth, but weakens the 'triangulation' or relativising effect that is essential if the student is to experience the essential contingency of modes of understanding. The tension is not so much one between depth and breadth as between several kinds of depth; the problem is how to do it all in three years.

That problem may be eased rather than exacerbated by adding one further requirement: that all students follow a common course, perhaps in the second or final year, which encourages them to see their disciplines in the perspective of other kinds of knowledge, and to reflect on the nature of the knowledge involved, its origin, status, application, and consequences. This implies some acquaintance with the philosophy, history, and sociology of knowledge, but just as importantly the opportunity to discuss with others the kind of disciplines one is studying, their peculiar ethos, culture, or style. It is, after all, the organised knowledge which they have acquired which differentiates graduates from other citizens, and there is a social and moral case for asking students to reflect on what it is that makes them different, and often gives them added influence, wealth, and status.

The norm, then, in higher education, might be to study three disciplines, in either an 'academic' or 'professional' framework, together with a common course on knowledge about knowledge. Several consequences of such a proposal should be noted. First, it would leave little or no time for short, elective courses of a contrasting nature: fine art for the biologist, or an introduction to physics for the historian. The three main subjects would likely be cognate, and reinforce one another to some extent, although odder combinations might be possible within timetable constraints. However, there is no need to try to pack everything into three years, and the short elective courses should perhaps be regarded as part of the person's continuing education, and deferred to a later stage. Higher education, like the schools, still seems to operate on a 'now or never' principle, and has yet to grasp the full implication of lifelong education: namely, that the curriculum can be distributed along the life-span.

The kind of model suggested above also leaves little time for short vocational-competence courses in (say) computing, mathematics, languages, or communication. It would still be possible for many students to do one or two such short courses in the three years, either during term, or perhaps in special summer schools (a more sensible proposition than the mooted fourth term) so as to equip themselves for projected occupations.

More seriously, a broadened first degree would have a serious knock-on effect on postgraduate and professional work. It would be impossible for graduates who had studied three disciplines at first-degree level to specialise adequately in a one-year Master's or immediate Doctoral thesis. A broader first degree would necessitate a two-year Master's programme, as is common in the United States, and would probably delay the acquisition of the PhD by a year or two. However, the numbers (and costs) involved are small compared to the total cost of higher education, and such an extension might seem a small and acceptable price to pay for a system which would do better by not only undergraduates but, by extension, upper secondary and even lower secondary pupils as well.[6]

There are thus considerable problems and costs involved in any broadening of first degrees, which is probably why the Robbins recommendations, and subsequent ones, have never been wholeheartedly implemented. The dominant pressures on the higher education curriculum, and in particular the coincidence of professionalised academic values and instrumental government policy, make it unlikely that anything of the kind outlined here will come about soon. The consequence of that may not immediately become apparent; but in the long run, it means that higher education will have no claim to uniqueness, no purposes or priorities which are peculiar to it. It would therefore not be surprising if it became simply the advanced tier in a comprehensive system of initial and continuing professional education; a prospect which leads naturally on to the next chapter.

NOTES

1   I am indebted to the German scholar, Ulrich Teichler, for this point.
2   For a discussion of generalists versus specialists in graduate civil service entry, see Blackstone (1981) and Griffiths (1982/83). Curiously, Blackstone assumes that historians and classicists are generalists; why they should be more so than (say) economists or physicists or engineers raises some interesting questions.

3 Many disciplines are not as traditional as they seem: the map of knowledge, like the map of Europe, looked rather different in 1935, and very different in 1885. The idea that all disciplines have existed since the beginning of academic time, in some vaguely Platonic form, does not survive even a rudimentary knowledge of academic history. When modern history was first introduced in the late nineteenth century as a degree course, it was not considered as a proper subject, and could only be taken along with something else; English is even more recent, and had a major struggle (mainly against classics) to get accepted. Some social sciences only gained a firm foothold in the post-war period; but all disciplines quickly learn to give the impression of having been around for a long time, of being 'necessary'.

4 The following paragraphs reflect Jaspers' (1960) view that higher education should be engaged in three things: professional training, education of the whole man, and research; and that without the second, the first and third lack a moral and existential framework. However, I cannot subscribe to Jaspers' belief in the unity or wholeness of knowledge, based, as far as I can see, on the older German notion of the unity of science (broadly defined). Rather, I believe that a true apprehension of the nature of knowledge is more likely to come from the tension between depth (immersion in a discipline or mode of thought to the point where it becomes a 'world') and relativity (the realisation that that world is only one of many possible ones). In terms of Figure 2, this points towards a curriculum which is neither purely academic nor purely professional. And it is not liberal at least in the strict Platonic sense, because it offers no certainties about reality, only the continuing tension between closure and openness, knowing and not knowing.

5 My distinction between 'holistic' and 'aggregative' models of higher education is spelled out further in OECD (1977, pp. 58–61) and Squires (1979). Clearly, there are things to be said on both sides, and I have a high regard for the Open University. The basic objection, however, is that *if* higher education has as a general and defining aim an understanding of the nature of knowledge, a modular system is not likely to bring the student to the point where the fundamental questions of knowing and not-knowing, depth and perspective, absoluteness and relativity are *experienced,* as distinct from verbalised. However, it may be that, depending on the internal structure of the discipline, it is possible to experience cases of that tension which in some way stand for the discipline as a whole, if it is a whole.I sometimes feel that our deeper understanding of things involves a returning to them a second, third, or further time; and the length and rhythm of modular courses makes that difficult.

6 As well as a knock-on effect on postgraduate study and professional training, a broadened first degree would have a 'knock-back' effect

on secondary schooling. If it became the norm to study three subjects to first degree level, then the gradient of specialisation would allow more than this at A level, perhaps twice that many, though obviously not to current A level standards; and consequently there would be less need to drop subjects further down the curriculum, allowing a more effective core curriculum. There seems to me to be a fairly clear relationship between 'time to PhD' and breadth in the curriculum; and the fact that the United Kingdom produces some of the youngest PhDs in the world (if they finish on time) entails specialisation from the age of 12/13 onwards.

6 Education for Adults

Introduction

There is no single point, in a modern industrialised society, at which a person suddenly and unambiguously becomes an adult. In the United Kingdom it is a process which is often thought to begin at the age of 16 with the termination of compulsory pupil status, and to be complete by the age of 21, with the attainment of full adult rights, roles, and responsibilities. In between, there are many important markers, such as the right to vote, drink, or marry without one's parents' consent; and of course the social and psychological processes of maturation may vary greatly from one individual to another. In educational terms, the definition of 'adult' tends to come later rather than earlier, primarily because there is already distinct provision for 16–19-year-olds (described in Chapter 4) and for some 18–21-year-olds in higher education (described in Chapter 5). Adult education therefore is often thought to begin where these end, and is sometimes referred to as 'post-initial' for that reason. Some institutions even use the age 25 to distinguish between ordinary and 'mature' students; whereas others are more concerned with the number of years spent outside the educational system. By contrast, some regulations specify only post-compulsory (16) or post-secondary (18) status. It is clear that definitions of 'adult' in adult education, are not and cannot be clear.

This is true also of the 'education' in adult education. It is much more difficult to specify or classify the range of provision and activity in this sector of education than in any other: indeed, it is hard to call it a sector at all. Some forms of adult study and learning go beyond not only formal education, but beyond formality, and become virtually indistinguishable from the everyday learning that characterises, and indeed makes possible, our lives. Nevertheless, it is useful to think of education for adults under four broad headings:

(a) Educational institutions which exist primarily to teach adults, such as local authority adult education services, university extra-mural departments, the Open University, adult education residential colleges, and the Workers' Educational Association (WEA);

(b) Educational institutions which teach adults along with younger students, such as polytechnics, colleges of higher and further education, and universities;

(c) Non-educational institutions or organisations which teach adults as a secondary function or by-product of their main activity, such as companies, armed and civil services, churches, trade unions, voluntary associations, and clubs;

(d) Non-institutionalised, independent adult learning, carried out by individuals using whatever resources are to hand: friends, shopkeepers, the mass media, bookshops, libraries, museums, and so forth.

The scope of 'education' in adult education is thus very wide and rather ill-defined, particularly in the cases of (c) and (d). However, the problems of scope and definition are not due only to the elusiveness of the terms 'adult' and 'education'.[1] Adult education, as a phrase, has had a particular meaning in the United Kingdom for many decades, connoting courses of a non-vocational, liberal, or recreational nature which do not lead to any paper award. The reasons for this restrictive connotation are complex and cannot be gone into here, but one consequence of the restriction has been the almost theological distinctions that are made by those in the field between adult education (in its older, restricted sense), adult education (in its newer, inclusive sense), the education of adults (all-encompassing), continuing education (typically but not always vocational-professional), lifelong education, recurrent education, and *education permanente*.[2] To many of those who work in adult education, these labels are important, because they signify particular emphases in a field which has always been normatively strong even though structurally and financially weak, as much a movement as a service. Consequently, one finds the labels of departments, agencies, and institutions continually changing, somewhat to the bewilderment of those outside the faith.

Whereas the older meaning of adult education confined it to two or three of the headings in Figure 2 (liberal, recreational, basic) the newer meaning – any form of education or training that adults engage in – excludes nothing in the diagram. Some adult education is academic or professional, and there is continuing in-service education for teachers. In recent years, there has been a growth of interest in continuing vocational education and training. Some forms of adult education have always been concerned with roles, social change and awareness, and personal development. Much local authority adult education is recreational, and the work of the WEA and university extra-mural departments is intended to be of a liberal nature. Basic education for adults is now an established service in the United Kingdom, and of course much more important in developing countries. If the old conception of adult education was rather restricting, the new, all-inclusive sense is liberating in its scope. But it has an important consequence in curriculum terms. Where one could in the past associate adult education with certain of the headings in Figure 2, and where one can still associate 16–19 provision and higher education with other headings, one cannot now associate the education of adults with anything in particular: in curriculum terms, it has become coextensive with education itself. Thus attempts to define adult education in terms of the curriculum – that is, in terms of what is taught – seem doomed to failure. Does this mean that adult education is simply education for people who happen to be adults? Obviously there are forms of adult education – for example, role education of some kinds – which are peculiar to adults. But is the rest any different in curriculum terms from what is taught to younger people? Is it essentially the same content, inflected towards older, voluntary, and probably part-time students? If so, adult education cannot be defined in terms of unique purpose or content. The counter-argument, that adult education, although increasingly catholic and eclectic, does have a unique identity and underlying unity, has been made in three ways: in terms of its students (as adults); in terms of its orientation (towards groups as well as individuals); and in terms of its mode of operation (not only formal, but non-formal and informal). These three kinds of arguments will now be examined.

Adults and adulthood

There is nothing inherent in the concept of education which links it to childhood and adolescence. Nevertheless, the fact that most education is still so linked has led some adult educators to define the nature of their enterprise in terms of the atypical nature of their students – namely, the fact that they are adults. This leads to a view of adult education which is student-centred not in the simple sense

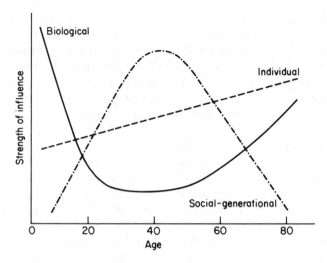

Figure 3   The conceptualisation of adulthood (adapted from P. B. Baltes, *et al.*, 1980 'Life-span Developmental Psychology', *Annual Review of Psychology*, Academic Press)

of using methods which allow the student a good deal of control over curricula and teaching, but in the profound sense that the whole activity of education turns on the student, rather than on, say, organised knowledge, or formal certification.

This implies some idea of what an adult is. Much of the early work on adult learning stressed age and ageing as the primary characteristic of adulthood, and for this reason tended to see adults' educational potential very much in terms of decrement and decline.[3] In recent years, however, the emphasis has shifted away from age as a determinant of adulthood, to age as an aspect of adulthood, and this allows other kinds of factors to be admitted. One recent and useful model has been suggested by Baltes (1980), who argues that there are three main kinds of influence on adulthood: biological ageing; social experience as a member of a particular generation or group; and individual life-events. Moreover, Baltes suggests that the influence of these three factors varies along the lifespan (see Figure 3). Biological factors are very important in childhood and old age, but recede into the background during most of adult life, except in the case of serious illness. Generational factors, weak at first in the confines of the family, become more and more important as the adult reaches maturity and becomes engaged in society through work, leisure, and other social involvements. Thereafter, the influence of this factor may decline gradually, and then perhaps sharply in old age, when many people withdraw or disengage from society. It is much more difficult to assess the importance of individual life-events in adulthood (events such as getting a job, marriage, having children, becoming unemployed, getting divorced, deaths in the family), but Baltes suggests that the cumulative effect of these is to make individuals more different from one another as time goes by, and hence he argues that their importance increases with age.

It should be stressed that what is being said here is an interpretation of a model which the author himself presents as tentative. However, Baltes's approach seems to provide a useful framework for thinking about what adulthood is. This is a prerequisite for any theories of adult education which refer primarily to the nature of the student. The model also suggests that, with the exception of old age, the most important aspects of adulthood are social-generational and individual-experiential, rather than biological (though that is not to discount interactions between all three factors). If adult education turns primarily on the nature of its students, therefore, one would expect a strong emphasis on individual and collective experiences, on roles, significant life-events, self-concepts, and relations with others. Such an emphasis does indeed appear in the four ways of thinking about adult students that are described briefly below: in terms of adult learning, adult thinking, adulthood and adult development.

The first of these is concerned primarily with teaching and learning, but has important implications for the curriculum. The word 'pedagogy' refers, strictly speaking, not to teaching but to the teaching of children. Although Knowles (1978) did not invent the word 'andragogy' (the teaching of adults), he has given it wider currency than any other writer on adult education in the English-speaking world. While Knowles does not suggest that there is a clear-cut distinction between children and adults as learners, he does argue that teaching based on andragogical assumptions is appropriate to people in their late teens and beyond. The simple antithesis between pedagogy and andragogy has caught the imagination of many who work in adult education, perhaps because it offers a means of defending a rather embattled professional identity. It is worth pointing out, however, that Knowles is somewhat ambiguous about identifying andragogy solely with adult education; in some cases he presents it as a more enlightened approach to teaching younger age-groups as well.

Knowles makes five key assumptions. The first is that 'as a person grows and matures his self-concept moves from one of total dependency (as is the reality of the infant) to one of increasing self-directedness' (Knowles, 1978, p. 55). Thus, Knowles argues, when conventional teaching imposes the traditional dependent or teacher-led role on the adult student, she reacts with resentment or resistance. It is as if her adulthood is being questioned or challenged at a fundamental level.

The second basic assumption has to do with the perception of experience. The child regards experience as something that happens to him, whereas for the adult increasingly his experience constitutes what or who he is. He owns or identifies with it, whereas to the child it is an aspect of an often incomprehensible or uncontrollable world. Thus in andragogy there should be less emphasis on teaching as the transmission of knowledge, attitudes, and skills, and more emphasis on 'experiential techniques which tap the experience of the learners and involve them in analyzing their experience' (Knowles, 1978, p. 56).

Thirdly, adults are more likely to be ready or motivated to learn if they perceive a learning need, and such needs are typically related to the developmental tasks, phases, or roles of adult life. The shorthand term for this orientation to learning is 'relevance', and Knowles goes on to argue that this implies two things about the curriculum: that it should aim at immediate rather than deferred application and meaning; and that it should be problem-centred rather than subject-centred. Children, he suggests, have been conditioned to accept a subject-centred approach, with the promise that each stage will allow them to progress to the next stage in the system, and eventually to make a career. The adult, by contrast,

comes into an educational activity largely because he is experiencing some inadequacy in coping with current life problems. He wants to apply tomorrow what he learns today, so his time perspective is one of immediacy of application. Therefore, he enters into education with a problem-centred orientation to learning. (Knowles, 1978, page 58)

From these basic assumptions, Knowles draws out a number of implications for the adult curriculum and adult teaching. The planning and evaluation of courses should be carried out jointly between teachers and students, in a climate of mutual respect and collaboration. There should be less emphasis on authority, formality, and competition. The curriculum should be structured around problems, not subjects, and sequenced not according to the logic of the subject-matter but the psycho-logic of the students. Experiential or inquiry techniques of teaching and learning should predominate. Knowles identifies pedagogy as a *content* model of teaching, and andragogy as a *process* model.

Allowing for transatlantic differences of terminology and style, Knowles's views encapsulate what many adult educators in the United Kingdom would generally regard as good practice, common sense, and accumulated wisdom in the teaching of adults. The ethos of adult education classes is often informal, collaborative, and student-centred. The syllabus looms less large than in most other sectors of education (comparisons are sometimes rightly drawn with primary education) and the teaching methods (often involving a good deal of discussion and project work) typically draw on the students' experience wherever possible. Some adult education organisations (such as the WEA) and many teachers of adults try to make 'mutuality' a reality not only in the teaching, but planning and organisation of courses. Knowles's model is valuable in two ways: first, it alerts people, and in particular teachers in other sectors of education, to the fact that teaching adults may be different, and therefore to the need to adapt or rethink their styles, and it provides pointers, in general terms, to the possible nature of that difference. The criticisms of Knowles's model come at a more theoretical level. They are, first, that andragogy is only apparently different; secondly, that the difference has to do not with age, but with educational aims; and thirdly, that the model does not recognise the inherently contingent nature of teaching and learning.

The first criticism – that andragogy is a superficial or deceptive phenomenon – arises out of both micro and macro studies of education. At the micro level, where classroom interaction and dialogue are observed and analysed in detail, it may turn out that the control of events, despite an apparent mutuality, still lies firmly in the teacher's hands. The change is simply that the procedures and tactics used have become covert and informal rather than overt and formal. Cues or signals from the teacher may steer 'open' discussion in the direction in which he wants it to go: there may be the appearance of 'student-centred learning', or 'discovery', or 'dialogue' but a fine-toothed analysis will show where the real power lies. Perhaps teachers, like other groups who have power, do not relinquish it easily, and substitute subtle means of maintaining it when the more blatant means are ruled out. In fairness to teachers, it is worth stressing the potentiality of all classroom situations for breakdown. Even when this is not likely to result in rampaging children, there is at the back of many adult educators' minds a barely conscious nightmare: that things will 'get out of hand' or 'fall apart' or that the thing will simply 'dry up'. Teaching is an exposed activity, with some of the characteristics of performance on a stage. It is only when that subconscious fear of things going dreadfully wrong is replaced by a confidence that the class (the students and teacher) can co-operatively provide momentum and recover from breakdown, that the teacher becomes genuinely as distinct from superficially willing to hand over some power. Paradoxically, unless she does hand it over at some stage, she will never know if the class can sustain itself, and hence never be able to shift the burden and the control. So, at some point, a leap of faith is required; a leap which becomes easier to make if the teacher has been taught, or has acquired, ways of retrieving situations which have gone wrong.

Macro studies of education also cast doubt on the reality of andragogy. Teachers and students do not exist in isolation; they are always acting in a context of institutions, roles, regulations, and norms. In so far as these militate against 'mutuality', student-centred teaching, or problem-centred studies, it will be difficult for the teacher to practise andragogy in Knowles's sense. In non-examined, non-vocational courses, where attendance is purely voluntary, it may be easier to engage in mutually agreed, experien-tial, problem-centred teaching and learning; but wherever examina-tions and syllabuses impinge, or there is an element of pressure on students to attend, the teacher will tend again to become the custodian of the curriculum.

A second and very different criticism of Knowles is that his distinction between pedagogy and andragogy is in fact a distinction between different types of educational aims, which is only inciden-tally or accidentally to do with the age of the students (Hartree, 1984; Jarvis, 1984). Indeed, Knowles partly intimates this when he suggests that a bit more andragogy might be a good thing in the schools too. According to this view, Knowles is simply one in a long line of 'progressive' educational theorists (a line including Rous-seau, Pestalozzi, and Dewey) who have argued for student-centred as against subject-centred teaching, the importance of experience in learning, relaxed rather than formal procedures, and a democratic rather than authoritarian ethos. Thus his views are open to the standard criticisms of 'progressive' education: that it may work for motivated and able students, but not others; that it fails to distinguish between legitimate and illegitimate authority; and so on.

The third criticism arises from the inherently contingent nature of teaching. The teacher, whether of adults, or of children, has to consider not only who he is teaching (the students), but what he is teaching (the content), and where he is teaching (the setting)

(Squires, 1982a). Each of these three dimensions of teaching can be broken down for further analysis: the 'who' into group characteristics, individual characteristics, and the teacher's characteristics; the 'what' into subject-matter, level, and aims that go beyond or 'through' these; and the 'where' into the physical, institutional, and cultural contexts. Questions as to 'why' one is teaching may be seen as deriving from the who, what, and where, or treated as another dimension of the situation.

At the practical level, this leads to a contingent model of teaching. The answer to the question: how shall I teach? is typically: it depends. It depends on the students, content, and setting. There are perhaps a few general rules or principles which apply to all teaching, across the board, but even these have to be modified or interpreted in the light of the analysis of the situation. On the face of it, this contingent model does not tell one much about how to teach: but once the process of analysis is begun, it can lead to a detailed awareness of the various factors one has to take into account. There is no point in teachers being highly skilled at analysing objectives and content if they are insensitive to students or oblivious to the place they teach in; and likewise with the other two dimensions.

As a model of curriculum and teaching, Knowles's andragogy does not take adequate account of the various dimensions and contingencies of the education of adults (Goodnow, 1982). What he says is true or appropriate in some circumstances, but not in others. Adults *may* be subject-centred, just as children *may* be problem-centred. (There is a problem with the word 'problem': it is often used rather narrowly to refer only to 'real-life' as against 'theoretical' problems.) Adults do not always want to 'apply' what they learn, immediately or later. In some settings, authority and formality *may* be appropriate. In some subjects – ones which are abstract or remote from sense experience, such as mathematics and the natural sciences – 'experience' may be of little relevance, whereas, say, in literature or social studies it may provide much grist for the mill. The adult's attitude to his or her experience is also important (Usher, 1985).

A rather different approach from that of Knowles is that of Riegel, who is concerned not so much with how adults learn as how they think, although clearly 'learning' and 'thinking' overlap. Riegel's starting-point is Piaget's theory of mental operations which distinguishes between four stages/levels of development: sensory motor intelligence; pre-operational intelligence; concrete operations; and formal operations. Riegel goes on to add a fifth stage/

level; that of dialectical operations. He argues both that this is the highest mode of operation, and that it is characteristic of adults, whereas formal operational intelligence is of use mainly in the more arid aspects of formal education:

> ... it has never been shown convincingly that the highest level of operation (i.e. formal operational intelligence) characterizes the thinking of mature adults. Only under the most exceptional circumstances of logical argumentations and scholastic disputes would a person engage in such a form of thinking ... Piaget's theory describes thought in its alienation from its creative, dialectical basis. It represents a prototype reflecting the goals of our higher educational system that, in turn are reflecting the nonartistic and noncreative aspects in the intellectual history of Western man. (Riegel, 1979, pages 49–50)

Adult thinking, by contrast, embraces contradictions not as a failure, or a sign of incomplete development, but as a characteristic feature of the mature consciousness.

> The mature person achieves a new apprehension of contradictions. Contradictions are no longer regarded as deficiencies that have to be eliminated by rational thinking at all cost but in a confirmative manner as the basic source for all activities. In particular, they form the basis for any innovative and creative work. Adulthood and maturity represent the period in life during which individuals knowingly reappraise the role of formal, that is non-contradictory thought, and during which they may succeed again (as the young children have unknowingly succeeded in their primitive dialectics) in accepting contradictions in their thoughts and actions (scientific dialectics). (Riegel, 1979, page 130).

Riegal is an interesting, if eclectic and sometimes polemical writer. His theory involves two critiques: first, of the disjunction between theory and practice, as exemplified for him in formal operations and to some extent academic education; and, second, of the idea of human development as an evolutionary, gradualist affair. In support of his first critique, he cites Hegel; in support of the second, Kuhn, among others; in the first case, he stresses the importance of dialectical thought; and in the second the importance of crises. Dialectical psychology, according to Riegel, is committed to the study of action and change. Where the influence of Dewey can be discerned in Knowles's approach, in Riegel's case it is Hegel and Marx, and the more general European (rather than American) critique of alienation or alienated thought. This is a complex critique, and here one can do no more than hint at some of the main problems with Riegel's approach.

The first point has to do with what is meant by 'dialectical operations'. Some writers interpret this very much in theory/ practice terms: 'In the process of dialectical thinking, abstract thought, i.e. ideas and concepts, are reunited with concrete reality and experience' (Nottingham Andragogy Group, 1983, p. 6). The problem with this is that it implies that 'concrete reality and experience' are in some way independent of or free from abstraction: an example of a more general tendency in some writing on the theory/practice issue to treat terms like 'experience', 'concrete', 'action', 'context', and 'use' as if they were obvious and unproblematic. The counter-argument is that even these apparently practical matters are shot through with theory and abstraction; that there are no facts without concepts; that practice embodies ideas, whether one realises it or not; that there is nothing which is not interpretation. Indeed the whole effort of phenomenology to 'discover' the structures which constitute what we call the world, or real life, or everyday existence, has shown how difficult it is to find anything which might be called direct or primordial experience. It is one thing to say that dialectical operations are concerned with contradictions in thought, but it does not necessarily follow that such contradictions arise only out of a separation and reunion of 'abstract thought' and 'concrete reality'.

A second problem lies in Riegel's assertion that dialectical operations are somehow higher or more advanced than other kinds of thinking. If this is not simply to be a *parti pris* inherited from Hegel and Marx, one has to ask why or how they are higher? Part of the answer seems to be that they are less 'alienated', but this raises the question: alienated from what? The unstated assumption is that there is a 'natural' mode of thought or state of existence from which we have either grown away, or been forced away, and that it is the job of the dialectic to return us to our natural home. But one may ask whether this is not a kind of romantic nostalgia for a primordial existence in which nature and community were somehow organic; in the end, a suppressed desire for an order pre-dating modern consciousness.

Thirdly, Riegel asserts that dialectical operations are not simply a higher, but a later stage in thinking, associated typically (though not necessarily) with adulthood. This view can be criticised on the basis of a contingency model. It may well be that adult thinking in certain circumstances is concerned (often fruitfully) with contradictions, or at least with problems that are other than obviously 'logical' or 'systematic'. But in other circumstances it may not; and a contingent model of mental operations would suggest that adults can often deploy a range or repertoire of approaches or modes of thinking, and vary them as appropriate. Indeed, some of the research on cognitive styles suggests as much: that people are not always locked on to a particular style, but can to some extent choose how to think or approach problems (Kogan, 1976; Messick, 1978; Squires, 1981). There is a need for more empirical work on this aspect of adult's cognitive styles.

If the 'difference' of adults lies not so much in how they learn or think, perhaps it lies in the state or status of being an adult, in the adulthood of adults? After all, even in everyday conversation we do not use the word 'adult', or its associated terms, lightly. We tell people to 'grow up', 'act their age', not to be 'childish' or 'immature'. Even humorous phrases like 'for children of all ages' tell us something about our expectations of adults and adulthood, expectations which are moral and social as well as psychological. In sociological terms, this is most likely to be expressed in terms of role; adults have many congruent and incongruent roles which involve expected patterns of behaviour, and when these patterns are transgressed or absent, the conception of adult is itself modified. Such roles may be quite closely related to age, in that we expect young adults, middle-aged adults, and older adults to do or not do certain things. Age-roles cross-cut with social and gender roles, and in any case seem to have become more fluid in recent decades; but there is still perhaps a slight sense of shock when one sees a retired person driving a sports car, or a middle-aged couple at a disco. Adult students bring their roles with them into the classroom – how could they not? – and although what they study there may not be a direct extension of those roles (indeed, it may be an escape), role is a significant element in any adult teaching situation: not only the roles of the students, but the role of the teacher or trainer in relation to those roles.

The argument that the adulthood of adults constitutes an important and even defining aspect of adult education can also be stated in more philosophical terms. Paterson, for example, links age with certain assumptions about moral and emotional maturity:

> ... there is nothing arbitrary or paradoxical in our judgement that a person's age, his objective relationship to time, of itself engenders objective presumptions of moral and emotional maturity. If a child's transition to adulthood is always more than a bare movement through

time, this is because the mere passage of time, the very process of growing older, in itself creates new validities and altered expectations. Whereas we rightly expect a man of forty to display qualities of prudence, self-control, and perseverence, it would be quite unfair to expect a boy of ten to possess these qualities in anything like the same measure. We are entitled to expect people above a certain age to show tact and awareness in personal relations, and to respond with understanding to the needs of others. We are entitled to expect them to assume a measure of responsibility in several different spheres. We are entitled to expect them to be in possession of an adequate body of experience, ready to use it, and capable of modifying and extending it. There is, in short, a wide but recognizable spectrum of moral qualities and personal capacities, habits of outlook and modes of conduct, which we consider to be distinctive of 'maturity' because we consider that the passage of time, and therefore the attainment of a certain age, is peculiarly relevant to the degree and manner in which a person may be expected to exhibit them. . . . It is, then, because we may justifiably presume in someone of a certain age a sufficient measure of these attributes and competencies distinctive of maturity that we correctly ascribe to him the various rights and responsibilities which constitute the status of 'adulthood'. (Paterson, 1979, pages 12–13).

Paterson goes on in his book to work out the educational implications of terms such as 'adulthood', 'maturity', 'awareness', 'reasonableness', and 'rights'. In short, he derives a theory of adult education from the nature or characteristics of adulthood; just as one might do similarly with the concept of 'childhood' or 'adolescence'.

There are two main objections to this kind of argument. First, it is somewhat circular. Adult education, as Paterson points out, is distinguished by reference to its students or clients, unlike for example, higher education which is distinguished by its level, technical education which is distinguished by its content, or liberal education which is distinguished by its purpose. The argument proceeds from the assumption that adulthood is important, but it is not self-evident that it is the adulthood of adults which is the most significant thing about them: it could be their gender, social background, personality, ability, motivation, and so on. Nor is it self-evident that the student is the most important element in teaching, that the content or setting should be seen in terms of the student, rather than the other way round. This point can perhaps be seen more clearly by taking two similar examples, one serious and one trivial. If one took women's education or the education of red-haired people as one's starting-point, one could construct arguments for planning curricula and teaching in terms of these; in either case, the adulthood of the students would become a minor consideration. Clearly, the adulthood of adults is not a trivial consideration in curricula or teaching; but that is not to say that the whole enterprise of educating adults should be conceptualised and organised around it.

The second objection to Paterson's argument is that it is too static: that it conceives of adulthood as a state rather than a developmental process. That state is marked by the attainment of certain qualities or characteristics (maturity, self-control, and so on). There is little sense that that state may itself change and develop, either because of age, or of changes related or unrelated to age. In other words, there is no dynamic element in the concept, no emphasis on human growth or potential.

This kind of criticism is not wholly justified, since it is quite arguable that there are degrees of awareness, responsibility, and maturity – the kinds of qualities which Paterson believes the adult should display. Nevertheless, it is clear that in recent decades there has grown up a school of thought about adults and adult education which is quite different from the traditional philosophical approach of Paterson and others like him (Lawson, 1975). This school of thought comes under the broad heading of lifespan developmental psychology, and it stresses not so much the state of adulthood as the process of adult development. Its main sources and influence have been in the United States, though it has had some impact in the United Kingdom as well. Cross (1982) provides a useful overview of the field, but one of the most detailed expositions of the various facets of the notion of development – cognitive, moral, ego, and so on – is to be found in the book edited by Chickering (1981), who argues that it provides a new rationale not simply for adult education but higher education.

At their simplest, models of adult development draw attention to the fact that adult life is not some kind of plateau, but full of ups and downs and changes: changes in jobs, changes in family circums-tances and personal relationships, role changes, changes in attitudes and beliefs, and to some extent physical changes. Such models dispute the fairly widespread assumption that adults, having attained maturity, simply settle down into a predictable routine, and cease to learn or develop in any way, until biological ageing obtrudes and forces them into decline. At this level, the writing on adult development is a very useful corrective to the simplistic, even unthinking attitudes towards adult life, and in particular middle age, which have for long permeated our educational thinking.

Beyond this, things become more problematic. Cross draws an important distinction between thinking about life-phases and life-stages. Life-phases refer to the chronologically identified periods in the lifespan which are age-related (though within wide margins) and which Shakespeare, to mention only an early example, described in his Seven Ages of Man speech. Conventionally, it is common for people to distinguish between early adulthood (Young Turks, and so on), the prime of life, middle age, retirement, and old age.

It is also fairly widely recognised that the age of transition from one phase to another may vary considerably from one individual to another ('You're as young as you feel . . .') and also as between groups: women and men, different social classes, different cultures. In some country districts, a man of thirty may still be called a lad by older men, whereas in a modern city environment, that would be unthinkable. Developmental psychologists attempt to describe each of these phases in terms of its characteristic conditions and tasks: for example, finding a job, choosing a partner, rearing children, coping with ageing relatives, or fighting ill-health. While many of these headings are apt and recognisable, they may also seem a little simplistic and linear, failing to take account of both the unique trajectory of individual lives, and the deeper kinds of changes that take place.

It is the attempt to model those deeper changes, however, that is most problematic. In Cross's terms, this is the writing about life-stages, rather than life-phases, and the basic idea here is that adult life is a matter not only of change, but of development, or regression: of more or less, better or worse, with the emphasis usually on the potential for the positive. Some of the writing in this vein has been about specific facets of development: Perry's (1970) work on cognitive development, and Kohlberg's (1973) theories of moral development are obvious examples. Some of it is about development in a more general sense, what one might call the development of the person or the self, and here the work of Erickson (1968) and Loevinger (1976) is widely referred to. It is worth noting that the latter, more general models of development owe a good deal to earlier work in psychotherapy (Jung, for example) and indeed to philosophies and theologies which have explored the notion of individual or spiritual growth.

There is not room here to discuss life-stage theories properly. As was pointed out earlier in the book, they beg a lot of questions. They can be criticised for abstracting individuals from their social and economic context, of being individualistic in a pejorative sense:

there is little sense in much of the writing of the social constraints under which most people live, or little evidence for concern with the development of the community or society. They appear naively optimistic about the horror of old age as described by, say, Proust or Yeats, and seem remote from the more ironic or pessimistic strands in European culture. The chief problem, however, is that they attempt to identify a path of development which is not based on any coherent or consensual view of human existence. It was one thing for Buddhists or Christians to map out a spiritual path (however tortuous) in the days when those religions supplied the general world-view in their particular cultures. In a modern, pluralistic, and in some ways more sceptical culture, that task is infinitely more difficult. This kind of objection applies not only to the general writing about human development of someone like Erickson; it can be raised in connection with Perry's more limited work on cognitive and ethical development. Perry, broadly speaking, maps out a progression from initial dualism, through relativism, to commitment within relativism, and the implication is that the last is better than the first. It is by no means self-evident, however, that relativism is an advance on dualism (what if the world *is* a battle between good and evil?) or that commitment is in all cases preferable to detachment (a view that Buddhists would at least want to question).

Life-phase, and even more, life-stage theories of adult development thus appear to raise some serious problems, of both a descriptive and normative kind. On the other hand, they stimulate some very interesting questions about the nature of personal and social education for adults. These headings are never entirely absent from any curriculum at any stage, but adult development theories give them a particular prominence. They point to an aspect of education where perhaps it begins to turn into something else; they blur the conventionally sharp distinction between knowledge and self-knowledge.[4]

The four conceptions of adult students described briefly here – in terms of adult learning, adult thinking, adulthood, and adult development – all have possible implications for the curriculum. Of the four, it is the third (adulthood) which seems most compatible with traditional liberal and academic forms of education; the other three in various ways seem to point towards more personal and social concerns. But the assumption in all cases is that education is still largely of the individual and for the individual: an orientation which is not shared by some who teach adults.

Individuals and groups

It is one of the paradoxes of compulsory education that although its aims are individualistic, its means are collective. Examinations test individual achievement, not the achievement of a group. Norm-referenced examinations in particular set one child in competition with another. The stated aims of the schools are often expressed in terms of 'individual development' or 'personal development', yet most work in schools is done in groups, in classes ranging from under ten in a sixth form to more than thirty in some lower forms. Indeed, the 'declining' sixth form is given as one of the problems that necessitates the bringing together of school sixth forms in sixth-form or tertiary colleges.

This paradox has been modified somewhat in recent years. True, the public school tradition has always emphasised the collective aims and values appropriate to a future ruling elite. The whole structure of 'houses' and 'teams' in public schools encourages a collective identity as well as an individual one. The competitive ethos of the classroom is to some extent counterbalanced by the emphasis on 'teamwork' on the field or the water. Military cadet training also tries to balance 'leadership' with '*esprit de corps*'. But the competitive grammar schools did not typically lay the same emphasis on collectivity, partly because of their non-residential nature, and partly because they laid great stress on individual, upwardly mobile, scholastic achievement. And, as Hargreaves (1982) has pointed out, the modern comprehensive often seems to downplay or even reject any corporate or collective identity, producing in his eyes a general sense of anomie and rootlessness, what he describes at one point as the Luton Airport effect. This is mitigated in some comprehensive schools by collective artistic activity (orchestras, drama groups) and social work projects (helping the aged, and so on), and in others by a continuing tradition of identity, rooted in the school and its locality.

On the other hand, teaching has become slightly less collectivised. Most work still goes on in the traditional class and classroom, but there has been increased use of small group work (three or four students working together on a project or topic) and of independent study using prepared materials. The quantum jump in educational technology represented by the micro-chip will probably mean that independent study, long heralded as the way forward in teaching, will in fact increase in importance; though one must be sceptical as to how quickly or widely any new methods will be adopted at any level if they impinge on traditional teaching patterns and roles.

In higher education, individual ends are also pursued by collective means, though here the pattern is rather different from the schools. Teaching alternates between extreme collectivity (mass lectures) and extreme individuality (library-based studies or tutorials), though a middle ground of small group/seminar work has become much firmer in recent years. Scientists have always worked in small groups in their laboratories. But the aims or ends of higher education are still typically stated in individual terms: the development of this person's intellectual capacities, that person's competency to do a job, or the other person's general maturity. Indeed, one can argue that in the United Kingdom particularly, the emphasis on treating students as individuals is especially strong (Squires, 1980). This can mean various things: an awareness of individual differences, implied by individualised teaching and favourable staff: student ratios; a concern for the student as a person, embodied in tutoring/counselling/pastoral/support provision; or an attempt to develop the student's autonomy, as evidenced in the apparently *laissez-faire* attitude to work, and regulations, and the aversion to 'spoon-feeding'. British academics on the whole pride themselves on not only the quality of research and teaching in their institutions, but on the quality of care, and look askance at the disorganised impersonality of Continental universities and the organised impersonality of the larger American ones. No doubt the care is often deficient, and doors which are always supposed to be open, are not, or if they are, the lecturer is not there. But 'treating students as individuals' is part of the formal rhetoric and the informal vernacular of British higher education. There is also a residual collectivist ethos. This derives from the collegial Oxbridge tradition, and the various attempts to reproduce it in a few civic universities and several of the 'new' universities. But the importance of the Oxbridge colleges as teaching or research units had already declined sharply *vis à vis* their universities by the time the collegial model was resuscitated in the 1960s.[5]

It has been necessary to look briefly at the themes of individuality and collectivity in some of the other parts of the education system to put such notions into a proper perspective in adult education. For in adult education – or, rather, in certain forms of it – there is a distinct and different tradition of concern not only for the individual student, but for students as or in a group. This manifests itself in various ways. There is the tradition of adults coming together as a group, deciding what they want to learn, and finding someone who can teach them. This may range from an existing group which invites a visiting speaker, to a study group which hires a tutor to do a whole course. There is the tradition of negotiation between tutor and group as to what shall be covered or accomplished in a particular class – a kind of consensual specification of objectives. There is also a tradition of groups of adults coming together and teaching themselves, combining and exchanging whatever expertise they already have. There is the tradition that even the amateur learner or person who thinks he knows nothing has something to contribute to the group's learning. There is the emphasis in some forms of adult education on group projects (a collective production such as a survey or book) or on group action (actually doing something about housing/local amenities/co-operative production/ political conditions).

In all these cases, the typical individualism of educational purposes is modified by a concern with people as or in a group (De Sanctis, 1984). Of course, things are not necessarily as democratic or collective as they seem. The will of the group may be the will of a few activists; tutors may provide what they want to provide rather than what is needed; negotiation may be a ritual rather than a reality. The action or development that arises out of the group work may be pre-planned or short-lived. What is important here, however, is the ideology of collectivity in adult education, and its contrast with what prevails in the rest of the system.

This ideology is expressed in, and takes, several forms. The mildest of these is suggested by the word 'association'. Associations are groups of adults freely coming together to pursue a common interest or purpose. Many of those interests and purposes will not be specifically 'educational', though systematic learning always goes in a nonformal or informal way. Some associations are explicitly educational: for example, the WEA. Some will aim to influence people and institutions outside themselves. Many will have a mixture of aims and motivations, including providing a meeting-place for people, giving them a pleasant time, improving or reforming society, educating members, monitoring situations of interest to them, and so forth. One becomes a member of an association deliberately: simply living in a particular place or doing a particular job is not enough (there are, of course, professional associations which compel membership). Conversely, one can deliberately and freely leave at any point. The adult educator tends to see himself, in theory anyway, in a service role *vis à vis* the association; as someone who acts as a resource for the members.

Adult education may also be sometimes oriented towards 'the community' (Fletcher and Thompson, 1980; Brookfield, 1983). For example, a recent Open University reader on education for adults has a section entitled 'community learning'. As Michael Newman (1983) points out in one paper in that section, 'community' can mean many different things: the working class; the quiescent poor; the disadvantaged; the 'whole community'; the 'acceptable community'; and society. Nevertheless, there is a common thread running through most 'community education' and 'community development', and that is its concern for people in groups, rather than simply as individuals. In Third World countries, this often means the village or rural community; in industrialised countries, it tends to be the poorer areas of urban communities. Communities, unlike associations, are not something that one deliberately joins or leaves. One is a member, like it or not. Of course, the term 'community' may also suggest a strong interaction between people living or working together, which may not exist. Thus it is possible to say, somewhat paradoxically, that there is 'very little sense of community in this community'. Adult educators tend to believe in the 'community' in the first sense, and see themselves in a catalytic role *vis à vis* its members, as a facilitator, *animateur*, or person who enables the community to articulate its consciousness and raise it (Freire, 1983).

Whereas the term 'community' suggests people living together or working together, the word 'movement' suggests people progressing in a particular direction. Adult education has in the past been linked with various movements. The political purposes of much adult education latent in the word 'association', implicit in the term 'community', become explicit in the word 'movement'. Education is seen as a resource for action: action engaged in by groups. One is reminded of the slogan of one such movement (the Irish Land League): agitate, educate, organise; which might well stand for all of them. Movements, by their very nature, require not only formal adherence but real commitment. Whereas associations can and do tolerate 'sleeping' members, movements cannot. There will be great importance attached to role models (charismatic leaders) past and present. While the term 'movement' nowadays tends to connote political purposes, it should be remembered that in the past many such movements were primarily religious, and only saw themselves incidentally as social or political. The role of the adult educator in the movement is neither a service nor a catalytic one, but as a committed functionary, contributing his particular expertise and know-how to the common cause.

There is another, and very different, form of collectivity in adult education. That is where people have to be trained or educated in groups because they operate or function as a group. To train them individually would miss much of the point of the exercise, which is to improve communication, co-ordination and teamwork within the group. There are obvious examples of this in sports and military training. A football team has to be trained as a team, though individual skill training has its place as well. And in the armed services, training exercises may involve a whole ship's company or battalion or squadron. Individuals are expected to have acquired their skills before the whole thing is 'put together'. Group training or education is also found in professional, commercial, and industrial contexts. Much of the non-formal or informal continuing education of, say, a primary health care, or social work, team will be concerned with how that group operates as a group: with questions of liaison, control, interaction, and feedback. Staff meetings in educational institutions are also partly taken up with such matters: and sometimes a residential weekend is devoted to analysing how and where the institution or department is going. Continuing education for managers may also involve group sessions: anything from a routine meeting in which such issues are discussed, to more specific day- or weekend-schools. And there has been some use of group training approaches with production workers. Through all these examples runs the realisation that work is typically not carried on in an isolated, individualistic way, but involves communication and co-ordination with others.

The collectivist aims or methods of adult education come under fire from various directions, and for various reasons. Professional educators sometimes regard the activities of associations and community groups as amateurish. The professional historian or archaeologist may have mixed feelings about the quality of work of the local history society, or the amateur archaeological association. The professional social worker or counsellor will often be wary about the use of voluntary workers in these fields. True, the traditions and ethos of adult education in the United Kingdom make most adult educators view such activities in a favourable light, as something to be welcomed and built on and perhaps refined. But there is often a vague question mark hanging in the air about the 'standards' of adult education work.

Educators may also worry about the activities of associations, community groups and movements in respect of indoctrination. The local country-dancing club or bee-keeper's association is unlikely to be a source of concern in this respect. But what about the local housing action committee, or rate-payer's association? What about political parties, religious or 'cult' groups, feminist groups, animal rights groups, environmental pressure groups? How far do these educate or indoctrinate their members? How far does the ultimate aim of doing or changing something lead people to sub-ordinate analysis to commitment, individual doubts to collective will? Indoctrination tends to be associated with certain types of educational content (religious, political, social) and with doctrines which challenge rather than reinforce existing norms. (Thus we tend to accuse the Young Socialists of indoctrination, rather than the Boy Scouts.) But it is more accurate to see it as a process, applicable to any kind of content, which lacks or rejects certain of the characteristics which are associated with the word 'education': the making explicit of assumptions and values, the exposure to conflicting ideas and arguments, the tolerance of doubt and indeci-sion, the encouragement of rationality rather than belief, and the limiting of pressure on the student to conform.

A good deal of education probably fails to satisfy these conditions, and in any case they are open to criticism themselves. Do they not encourage a kind of amoral detachment? Do they not imply an overemphasis on cognition at the expense of affect? Do they not 'teach' that thought is separate from action? Do they not foster a pseudo-neutrality? There is room here only to register these points rather than discuss them in detail. But what can be said is that the charge of indoctrination is laid at collective adult education in particular, for two reasons: first, the potential for strong peer-group pressure on the student, inducing him to think or act in a particular way; and secondly, the relative weakness of the professional educa-tor's influence on the group, assuming that such influence is 'educational' rather than 'doctrinaire'. (It is worth pointing out, in passing, that the strongest peer-group pressures in the education system probably exist in the 'total institutions' of children's boarding-schools.) From the point of view of the educator as defined in the last paragraph, there are certainly dangers to education in bringing religion or politics into education; but perhaps there is a greater danger, to the society, in withholding education from religion and politics.

Criticisms of the collectivity of some forms of adult education also come from outside the educational system. From the political left comes the charge that many associations and community groups are reformist and diversionary, leading people to engage in marginal battles when they should be engaged in the main struggle. Strict Leninists regard large-scale, untidy movements as largely a waste of time; political change, they argue, necessitates a relatively small, highly organised and disciplined party. Criticism from the political right is of two kinds. There is the economic argument that associations, groups, and movements can become special interest groups in the society, which 'collude' with one another to protect their members' interests, and obstruct the beneficial operation of the free market. This criticism is directed mainly at the large, national, professional, or pressure groups which represent the interests of their members and seek to influence both government policy and economic activity. Examples might be taken from the fields of transport (public and private) and health care. The second right-wing criticism goes beyond economics, to a more general attack on collectivism in all its forms as an inevitable degradation of individual values and freedom. At its simplest, this is often expressed as a 'lowest common denominator' effect (that is, when people come together they bring out the worst in each other) or, for example, a general distaste for decision-by-committee or impersonal bureaucracy. At its most complex, it forms part of a general critique of collectivism (Hayek, 1944).

There is a third kind of criticism made of collectivity in adult education which is 'centralist' rather than 'centrist'. This springs from the belief that all education provision should be made by a benevolent, centralised state, as a service to the community. There is hence a corresponding suspicion of 'voluntarism' in all its forms. A mixture of motives seems to lie behind this criticism. There may be the genuine belief that the state has the resources and expertise to do things properly, whereas voluntary agencies do not. The state may also be seen as the guardian of equality, or even-handedness, ensuring comparable standards and provision across all regional and social disparities. There may also be a subconscious reluctance to devolve power and influence to groups who are likely to take on a certain political life of their own. But probably the main reason for what might be called 'benevolent centralism' is the sheer growth of state provision of education over the long term, and the expectation that the trend will continue. Whatever government policies are in this regard (and the current UK government is trying to reverse the trend), there seems to be a long, rolling wave of expectation in both the profession and among many of the public, that where an educational need arises, the state will provide.

Despite these criticisms of and reservations about collective forms of adult education it seems likely that an emphasis on groups will continue to be an important strand in adult education thinking. As Keddie (1980) has pointed out, there may be more rhetoric than reality to this; and there is some evidence that collective aims and activities may be less common on the ground than some of the writing about adult education would suggest (Titmus and Hely, 1976). None the less, the emphasis on groups as well as, or in contrast to, individuals, seems to distinguish adult education from most other forms of compulsory and post-compulsory education. As with 'adult development' it perhaps marks a point where education begins to turn into something else – in this case, politics rather than therapy. But the collectivist strand gives a particular resonance and complexity to the concept of social education in relation to adults, a point which will be taken up again in the final section of this chapter. Before that, the third claim to unity and uniqueness must be examined. This is in terms of the mode of operation of the curriculum, and the spectrum that runs from the formal through the non-formal to the informal.

The formal, non-formal, and informal

Adult education has been, and has had to be, much concerned with the failures of compulsory education: failures both in the sense of the students who are dubbed, or dub themselves, failures; and in the more abstract sense of the shortcomings or defects of the school system. A good deal of adult education is, and always has been, compensatory rather than continuing: it does not build on what went before: rather, it starts the job anew. And sometimes it has to demolish some bad construction work before it can begin again.

The reasons why students or educational systems fail are complex, and have been the object of a great deal of research into both student characteristics (ability, motivation, social background, learning styles, and so on) and system characteristics (among them, teacher training, teaching methods, curricula, institutions, assessment, and guidance). Failure itself has been conceptualised in terms such as under-achievement, wastage, and also the more elusive measures of attitudes to education. Adults, and the educators of adults, may attribute 'failure' in varying degrees to the student himself or to the system. Adults themselves often seem to internalise 'failure' and attribute it at least partly to themselves, whereas 'irrelevance' they will typically attribute to the system. It is one thing to be bored, but another to be 'no good'. Adult educators tend to blame the system, partly because they have a generally optimistic attitude towards 'potential', and partly because they can cite many instances where a second chance has reversed the initial verdict.

Of course, these students are only the ones who come back to education; and most 'failures' do not.

There is another way in which adult educators have to be concerned not so much with the failures as the limitations of formal schooling, and that is where organised school education, as a system, fails to engage the commitment or meet the needs of whole communities. This is most dramatically the case in some developing countries, where the schools cater for only a small proportion of the population, or may provide something which does not seem to meet the general needs. The school system in such cases provides a narrow, steep, and rather academic ladder to urban desk jobs or elite occupations in the modern sector of the economy. It seems to do little for agriculture, for the 'petty trader', or for the health, welfare, and development of the local community. Education – formal education – seemingly does not reach the great majority of the population, or if it does, is perceived as a selective mechanism, not as a source of knowledge and skills. This kind of 'failure' is less dramatic and less obvious in industrialised countries, but in these, too, questions can be raised. What does the formal education system do for the unskilled factory worker? For the unemployed? For the self-employed? For the neighbourhood? For people's problems with health or money or work or housing or personal relations?

Both the individual failures among students and the more generalised failure of the education system have led many educators who are concerned with adults to look for alternative ways of engaging adults in education: ways which would not simply repeat the 'mistakes' of schooling. Over time, these alternatives – and they are numerous and various – have come to be known generically as 'non-formal' education. It must be stated right away that 'non-formal' is not a precise term, although definitions of it exist.[6] It is relative to 'formal', and there are many ways in which education can be considered formalised: uniforms, regulations, designated buildings, professional labels, teaching methods, time-frames, knowledge categories, syllabuses, authority structures, examinations, qualifications, styles of talk and interaction, standardised environments (desks, classrooms, blackboards), and even smells. When one goes back into a school building as an adult after a long absence, there is a sudden rush of recognition, a hundred sensory cues which constitute 'school'. It is these, rather than what one learned, which come back suddenly; and it is these, and the memory of these, which in many people's minds constitute the experience of education.

Non-formal education can vary or do away with any or many of these characteristics. The teacher may not be a 'proper' teacher; she may be called a facilitator, or group leader, or resource person, or animateur – anything but a teacher. Or there may be no one specifically in charge at all. There may be no textbooks, no red ink on written work, no set syllabus, no examination. The class, if it is called that at all, may be held in someone's front room, or a library, or, in a country with a warmer climate, under a tree. There may not even be a *group* of students, but rather a network of mutually assisting individuals or a one-to-one helper–learner relationship. There may be no 'teaching' but rather 'discussion' and 'talk' and 'interaction'. One may not know who the 'teacher' is for a while. Chalk may be deliberately banished. Indeed, the whole thing may be so unlike school that people may not even realise that education is going on. Non-formal education is found not only in social and recreational education for adults: many of the methods and procedures used in continuing professional and vocational education are strikingly non-formal as well (Houle, 1980). Some novel and interesting techniques, such as 'audit', have been developed, in addition to the use of more conventional means such as journals, conferences, short seminars, and distance study packages.

The strenuous efforts of teachers of adults to become something which they are not has its comic side. But there is a serious point, in that the 'packaging' or 'presentation' or 'delivery' of education often seems to loom larger in people's experience than the thing itself. The development of non-formal education has shown that much of what is seen as essential to 'education' is incidental to it. One could, for example, run the secondary schools like adult education services: put on a wide variety of courses in a number of venues, allow students to choose which ones they want, and whether they want a qualification or not, and whether they attend at all or not, and see what 'goes'. One could install teachers in offices, advertise their knowledge and skills, and let people come to them if and when they need them. No doubt there are good arguments against doing these things, but the growth of non-formal education has opened up a wide range of questions about what is normal or necessary in formal education.

These questions have been sharpened by the rapid growth in some countries of what a recent Carnegie Commission report has called 'Corporate Classrooms'; namely, organised education outside the formal education system, in corporations, professional bodies, government departments both central and local, and all sorts and sizes of business and industry (Eurich, 1985). When these activities are added to the non-vocational, non-formal activities of voluntary organisations, and the educational and educative potential of distance learning, using radio, television, computers, or learning packages, it may be that, whereas formal education for adults is still the most visible form of education, it is no longer the *normal* form. This may come as something of a shock to those who work in the formal system. If it does, it is a reflection on the monopoly that formal education has at the compulsory and consecutive stages, that education or learning outside the system should be considered marginal or abnormal.

Non-formal education also draws intellectual sustenance from a much wider critique of, and disillusion with, institutions. Western man seems to have an ambivalent relationship with his institutions, at times seeing them as the highest expression of his humanity (a codification and concretising of his rationality) and at other times regarding them as impediments to a natural, free, spontaneous existence. In the 1960s and 1970s the negative view often prevailed in educational writing. For a moralist like Illich (1973) unconvivial institutions prevented us living the good life, which he defined in terms of autonomy and heteronymy. Other writers, such as Reimer (1971), Henry (1963), and Goodman (1971) attacked institutions from slightly different bases. Marxist critics regarded schools as capitalist institutions, merely reproducing and reinforcing the wider institutionalised inequities of wealth and power (Bowles and Gintis, 1976). The institutionalisation of knowledge and its control – the control of possibilities – gave another and more subtle dimension to the critique.

The dual, or complex, nature of the critique of institutions and, *inter alia*, of formal education, has meant that non-formal education too has been interpreted in several ways. For some, it is a rediscovery of natural education, man's in-built propensity to enquire into, discover, exchange, and pass on knowledge. For others, it is a pragmatic solution to the problems of 'delivery', a response to the failure of formalism. For others again, it is a way of bypassing, counteracting, or subverting the influence of undesirable, formal institutions.

Although non-formal education has been associated primarily with the education of adults, the term (and the practices) are now being explored in other areas of education, and in particular in relation to the 'risk groups' in the 16–19 age bracket. It is felt that in so far as such school leavers need education, it should be as different as possible from the schools they have just left and often spurned. It will be interesting to see how far these ideas permeate other sectors of the system as well, or whether they will always tend to be associated with a kind of educational residue – those whom the formal system failed, or who failed it. If non-formal education is associated with such a residual or recuperative function only, then it will inevitably be seen as a marginal and low-status form of the activity by those who work in education. Indeed, it seems to reflect a modern form of educational streaming in some cases already.

Non-formality or informality in learning can, however, be seen in a different and more individual light. (The distinction between non-formal and informal is being treated here as a matter of degree.) Some years ago, the Canadian researcher Tough (1971) put a very simple question to a number of adults: have you spent at least seven hours over the last few months trying to learn, understand, or master something to the point where you could teach another person a bit about it? Many of Tough's adults at first said they hadn't, but on reflection and with prompting, began to realise that they had. These 'learning projects', as Tough dubbed them, were interesting in several ways. First, they were quite numerous. Secondly, they were relatively evenly distributed across social and educational categories, more so than formal education achievement and participation. Thirdly, they often involved little or no contact with formal educational provision. And lastly, they varied enormously, from fairly 'intellectual' activities, through essentially interpersonal ones, to practical skills and tasks. Learning projects can involve anything from learning how to cope with a baby, to planning a foreign holiday, to mastering a new piece of equipment at work, to installing double glazing.

Tough's work has been reported in detail in several publications, and there will be no attempt to summarise it here, except to point out that the later work takes on the wider, more diffuse theme of 'intentional changes' in people's lives (Tough, 1982), rather than the earlier and more sharply delimited 'learning projects' (Tough, 1979). In one sense, that delimitation was always artificial: a rather arbitrary set of criteria imposed on natural or everyday adult learning. The newer laxity recognises that informal learning comes in many stages and forms, and at many different levels of intensity. However, it was precisely the rigid nature of Tough's original criteria (seven hours' study over several months to the point of being able to teach someone) which served to quantify what people had always believed went on: that is, everyday learning. The originality of Tough's work lay not so much in directing attention to informal learning, but in finding a way of showing that it is not purely random and inconsequential: that it is significant, according to certain criteria of time, mass, and outcome.

Reaction to Tough's work can be of two, sometimes coexisting, kinds. First, there is the recognition that he has profoundly altered the map, or perhaps more aptly, the chart of adult learning: for if Tough is correct, what is usually called adult education (enrolment in formal provision) is only the tip of an iceberg. For every adult who enrols on a course, or even takes a book from a library, there are many more who are engaged in unrecorded, informal learning endeavours which are substantial or cumulative enough for one to speak of them having greater 'knowledge' or 'skill' or 'understanding' by the end of them. This realisation is both sobering and heartening for those who teach adults: sobering because it means that what one thought was the whole thing is only a small part of it; and heartening because it means that, despite the formal evidence, education, or at least informal learning, really is continuing for the vast majority of the population.

The other reaction to Tough's research is: so what if most adults are doing their own learning, and have been for generations, unbeknownst to teachers and lecturers; what difference does it make to teachers and lecturers? It seems either that formal educators cannot assist in what is being done without them anyway, or that, if they did, more of the informal learning would become formalised. Tough's work appears to have identified and quantified an essentially separate, autonomous activity which has few or no implications for the formal education system.

Tough does, in fact, address this issue. He suggests that professional teachers and lecturers can and should develop a more positive attitude towards informal or non-formal learning in general, and provide assistance for it in specific cases. In general, for example, he argues that there should be less emphasis on educational credit, a clear distinction drawn between teaching and evaluating, and more emphasis on student-centred methods and curricula. He suggests that people do need assistance with planning their learning, and obtaining the relevant knowledge, answers, and resources (Tough, 1979). In sum, Tough joins the by now long line of educators and psychologists who have suggested that, to some degree and in certain ways, people can 'learn how to learn': that their natural or normal aptitude for learning can in some way be enhanced by directing attention to the *process* of learning, rather than to what is being (or not being) learned.[7]

If the emphasis on informal and non-formal education for adults does nothing else, it will still have achieved a great deal if it directs attention to student learning and learning to learn. As with learning to teach, learning to learn has several aspects or elements. There is a concrete aspect of skills: the techniques and tricks that study guides often contain. It is important for students to take notes effectively, to know about alternative ways of structuring an essay, to be able to organise and classify information, to know how to tackle a long reading list; and there are useful skills, although not always recipes, connected with each of these activities. For example, when people are told to 'get organised' they typically think of making a list: but lists are not the only, or always the best, way of organising information. An open 'network' or 'pattern' of notes may be more useful in some cases, or a hierarchical tree-structure, or a two-dimensional graph or typology. Similarly, there is more than one way of reading a book. At school, one tends to learn that one should start at page one, and work sequentially through to the end: anything else is considered vaguely immoral. But there are cases where it might be better to spend half an hour browsing through the book first, or even going directly to a summary or the index. Most of the study habits and skills that students have are not 'natural' but learned. Even reading – the linear, word-by-word tracking action of the eyes – is not 'natural'. The first, and most concrete step in learning to learn is to become aware of what one does already. Study skills are both useful in themselves and as sources of confidence.

But learning to learn cannot simply be a matter of discrete skills, because learning is not. There are strategies, approaches, styles, inclinations, and conceptions involved. Many of these operate below the threshold of awareness. People may not realise that the reason they are always turning work in late is that they have a bit of the perfectionist in them; or that their fixed belief that they are 'no good' at maths dates from a particular maths teacher at school; or that their need to 'see where they're going' may indicate a preference for holistic strategies in solving problems. Attitudes towards 'trying' and 'giving up' may also be deeply ingrained. The person who typically throws up his arms (metaphorically) after the first failed attempt to remember something shows a different attitude from the person who tries out other ways, and even attempts an educated guess. (How many times were we told at school: don't guess!) The way that one studies and learns depends on how one sees oneself as a student, and how one sees the subject, the class, the teacher, and the institution. All of these aspects of learning can be brought to light gradually, over a period of time, and as a result the learner will be more aware of the contingencies which operate in his particular situation.

A detailed discussion of learning-to-learn would take us too far from the curriculum, too close to teaching-and-learning, for the purposes of this book. As with learning-to-teach, there are many questions to be asked about the best way to organise and facilitate learning-to-learn. However, two basic points can be made. First, it is not enough to think of learning-to-learn as a by-product of learning something: the priorities of the second (time, coverage, standards) will always take precedence over the 'meta-objective' of reflection on the learning process. Learning-to-learn needs to be a planned part of the curriculum, and if it is not always to be a remedial exercise for adults (as it typically is at the moment) this means that it has to go into the school curriculum. Secondly, in so far as all teachers and trainers accept learning-to-learn as a meta-aim, transcending the particular aims and objectives of any course, it may also provide something that unifies all the enormously diverse and disparate forms of post-school education, indeed of the whole of education.

The emphasis on non-formal and informal learning may also affect the formal curriculum in a second and very different way, through the accreditation of experiential learning. It has always been recognised that people learn a great deal from their experience, whether at work, or in the family or community, or in some of the specialised roles they play. What is relatively new, however, is the suggestion that they should get formal recognition of and credit for this. This credit is not for the experience, but for what has been learned from it, where it corresponds to something that might have been learned as part of the formal curriculum. The main work on the accreditation of experiential learning has been done in the United States under the auspices of what is now the Council for Adult and Experiential Learning (CAEL).[8] Some interest has been shown in it in the United Kingdom, particularly by the CNAA. Getting people to describe or demonstrate what they have learned experientially, and assessing that learning in educational terms, is a complex and fairly time-consuming business, and there is no room here to discuss the conceptual or practical problems. The point to be made here is that over the longer term the accreditation of non-formal or informal learning could affect the formal curriculum not simply by giving students exemptions or advanced standing on some courses, but in terms of how one conceives of organised knowledge, and in particular the relationship between theory and practice.

Implications

The analysis in this chapter suggests that in the education of adults the process of curriculum disintegration which begins with the break-up of the compact model of general education reaches its logical, specific conclusion. The curriculum in adult education is more diverse in terms of aims, content, and form than anything that precedes it. The answer to the question: what is taught to adults? is everything. Nothing in Figure 2 can be excluded. What is more, the form and context of teaching are more varied than they are in school, 16–19 education, or higher education. The scope of the adult curriculum is so wide that it tests the limits of education itself, by turning into politics, therapy, entertainment, or work. The form of adult education at its most informal is indistinguishable from everyday experiential learning. It is little wonder that adult educators have difficulties in defining the boundaries of their work.

If the education of adults is boundless in its scope, and diverse in its operation, is there anything that unifies it? Is there any common thread? Clearly, the curriculum cannot be restricted to any of the headings in Figure 2. The historical restriction of the term 'adult education' to liberal, non-vocational courses was unfortunate, because it hindered the development of continuing vocational and professional education, and tended to marginalise the concept of adult education.[9] Empirical research shows that certain curricular patterns exist in some forms of adult education, though whether these represent current aggregated demand, or covert patterns of supply, is open to question (Mee and Wiltshire, 1978; Parrott and Flude, 1983).[10] Various writers, such as Griffin (1983), have argued that socialism can provide a unifying purpose for the curriculum, but such arguments proceed primarily from ideological bases beyond education, rather than from anything peculiar to adult education; it can equally be argued that adult education is important to the functioning of a market economy.[11] There is some basis for suggesting that a common thread may lie in the way adults learn, and need to be taught, though as pointed out earlier in this chapter, Knowles's 'andragogical' arguments seem to be overstated, and do not apply in all circumstances. There are some kinds of courses which are peculiar to adults (some forms of role education) or characteristic of adult education (recreational courses), but these only account for a small proportion of the total adult educational activity and can hardly be said to provide a unifying principle.

One is forced to the conclusion that education for adults *is* inherently diverse, and that there are few if any common elements in all the different kinds of teaching and learning that exist. This is only a problem in so far as institutions and professionals need to be able to define what they do, and the solution would seem to lie in much narrower definitions. Individuals or institutions which define their purpose in terms of (say) adult basic education, or continuing professional development, or higher education for adults, or community development, can know fairly well what they are about. Within each of these fields, and others of similar scope, there will be common problems and approaches. But it is unrealistic to expect that two people engaged in teaching adults in widely differing circumstances will have much in common, simply because their students are adults. After all, one does not talk about 'child education' but rather distinguishes between teaching five, ten or fifteen year olds. If it is difficult to generalise about an eleven or twelve year span, how much more it must be with a forty or sixty year one. Adult education, as a concept, grew up for the essentially negative reason that education until very recently has connoted childhood. The point has now been made that education, like health, is a lifelong matter, and therefore the need to use adult education as a distinguishing label disappears.

And yet there must be a residual doubt. Is there nothing in the preceding analysis that suggests peculiar or unique features in what adults are taught or teach themselves? Is the difference simply that it is all much more diverse and heterogeneous than what went before? If there is a particular flavour or emphasis in the adult curriculum it is likely to lie in the greater importance of social and personal considerations in what is taught and how.

This is partly a matter of the form of the curriculum. Continuing education for adults may sometimes take a full-time, consecutive form, as when mature students embark on full-time degree courses, or graduates do intensive one-year conversion courses, but in the main continuing education takes an intermittent form, alternating with the other activities of adult existence – work, family life, leisure interests, community responsibilities. The natural form for adult education to take is therefore modular, not necessarily in the relatively long, assessed modules that were discussed in relation to 16–19 education in Chapter 4, but typically in short bursts, of a day, weekend, or few weeks, or on a part-time basis over a period of months. This kind of format interleaves adult education with everything else that is going on in the adult's life, and thus makes it more likely that what is being studied will be located in the adult's social and personal context. Adults are not usually professional students, with the degree of role closure which that allows.

But the emphasis on the social and personal also derives from the thinking about content and process reviewed in this chapter. What was said by Knowles about adult learning, by Riegel about adult thinking, and by others about adult development all point towards a greater embeddedness of 'knowledge' in existence and experience. The non-formal and informal modes of learning imply much weaker boundaries between education and everything else. The orientation of some adult education towards groups rather than individuals points to the relating of knowledge to 'context' or 'society' or 'action'. It has been argued in this chapter that of all the areas of post-school education, adult education is the least susceptible to generalisation; indeed, it can hardly be called a sector at all. But there may be a kind of underlying tendency in different sectors of education which does not necessarily manifest itself in structural unity. Thus in the 16–19 phase (perhaps even 14–19) a kind of 'vocational drift' may affect whatever structures or policies are put in place, a tendency on the part of many students to judge curricula in terms of employment. In higher education, the phrase 'academic drift' has been widely used to describe the tendency for institutions and curricula to gravitate towards an academic norm or ideal type. If there is any such tendency in adult education, it is likely to be some form of existential drift, a vague but nevertheless powerful pull towards, for want of a better word, life.

NOTES

1 The problems of defining the scope of 'adult', 'education', and 'adult education' are reflected in descriptions of the system of provision, which vary in what they include and exclude. The maps drawn by Lowe (1970) and Russell (1973) are still fairly accurate, but do not include more recent additions, for which see Legge (1982), Jennings (1985), or publications of the Advisory Council for Adult and Continuing Education, in particular *From Policies to Practice* (1982a) and *Adults: Their Educational Experience and Needs* (1982b), as well as the literature on mature access to higher education referred to in the previous chapter. On continuing professional education, there is nothing as comprehensive as the American volume by Houle (1980), but see the interesting collection edited by Titmus (1985). There is no complete account of developments in continuing education in general (hardly surprising given the range of the field), but Evans (1983) describes some innovative examples; and the work by Belbin (1972), though limited and now dated, is still relevant. There have been many attempts over the years to conceptualise what is meant by adult education, but the recent models proposed by Boyd *et al.* (1980) and Tight (1985) are interesting, though not, to my mind, convincing.

2   The older restricted definition was a consequence of the way in
    which some key, early reports on adult education interpreted its
    scope, and of the terms of reference given to the 'responsible
    bodies' and later the local authority services. A detailed account is
    given by Kelly (1970), who distinguishes between adult education
    (restricted sense) and the education of adults (broad sense), a
    distinction pursued by Lowe (1970). Even though the earlier
    definition was limiting, it at least ensured that adult educators
    knew what they had in common, whereas it is no longer clear what
    the common thread is in all the multitude of educational and
    training activities involving adults: a problem which tends to
    preoccupy at least the early stages of any conference or book on the
    subject. The newer labels are to some extent associated with
    particular agencies which helped to popularise them: recurrent
    education with OECD, lifelong education with UNESCO, *educa-
    tion permanente* with the Council of Europe. It will become clear in
    this chapter that I tend towards an all-inclusive definition (any
    educational or training activity engaged in by adults) which
    subdivides into a number of much more specific fields such as
    adult basic education, continuing professional development, high-
    er education for adults, and so on. The distinction between adult
    and continuing seems to me to be merely a re-translation of the
    non-vocational/vocational one, with all the problems that implies.
3   For useful overviews of the research on adult learning see Knox
    (1977), Cross (1982), and Allman (1983). The generally more
    positive view now taken of adults' learning capacities is due to
    several factors: a realisation that earlier studies were confounding
    ageing and generational effects; a rethinking of the measures used,
    which has led both to the distinction between fluid and crystallised
    intelligence and to a search for capabilities which may be charac-
    teristic of adults rather than children (complex decision-making,
    self-awareness); the recognition that test conditions may not be a
    good guide to normal behaviour; and a growing belief that positive
    interventions may improve adults' physical and mental perform-
    ance at least over the short term. There is now a fairly good
    consensus that most adults can learn what they could have learned
    as young people, with the exception of fast, complex skills, and
    before old age takes a marked physical toll.
4   Mezirow (1983) has written interestingly on what he calls 'perspec-
    tive transformation', drawing on Habermas's (1974) concept of
    emancipatory knowledge: both phrases suggest to me a blurring of
    the conventional distinction between what one knows and what
    one is. That distinction is buttressed by the firmly impersonal
    conventions of much of education – in particular, academic and
    technical education; but it is worth noting that knowledge may
    mean a great deal to academics and technicians in a personal sense.
    One of the most difficult things for most academics to deal with is

not disagreement, but indifference: to confront the student to whom it means nothing. That indicates that knowledge is meaningful for the academic in two senses: the internal logic or coherence of the field or discipline; and the existential significance of the knowledge.

5 I suspect that collegial institutions are now to be found mainly at the fringes of the educational system – for example, in the smaller agriculture and art colleges. The trend in recent years has been towards larger, polyvalent institutions, and not many monotechnic colleges are left. That trend was and is justified in terms of student choice, cultural diversity, and economies of scale. I believe that the advantages of the small, homogeneous institution, in terms of the interpenetration of the social and the educational, have been rather ignored; a consequence perhaps of abstracting curriculum from context.

6 The distinctions between informal, non-formal, and formal education are usually traced back to the work of Coombs (1973) on education in the Third World, but since then the terms have become common currency in industrialised countries as well; see Fordham (1979), for example. Broadly speaking, formal education refers to education conducted by the mainline educational system, both compulsory and post-compulsory; non-formal education is education carried out by institutions or agencies whose primary purpose is not education; and informal education refers to the systematic and cumulative aspects of everyday experiential learning. The distinctions are useful, but like all useful distinctions have tended to become rather blunter with use. Also, the relative failures of formal education have tended to throw a burden of expectation (and fashion) upon non-formal education which it may not be able to bear: after all, if individuals and communities are able to educate themselves naturally without the need for formal institutions, many development problems should not exist: and they do. Having said that, the recognition of the non-formal and informal modes, and some support for them, should help to undermine the 'radical monopoly' which Illich believes the formal system has; and this must surely be beneficial.

7 Learning to learn (or LTL for short) seems to have developed as a field in two ways. Some psychologists (such as Harlow, 1949) have taken an interest in it, though it has always remained a marginal or maverick concern (De Bono, 1976). Quite separately, many educators, sensing a practical need, have over the years produced 'cookbooks' on study skills and techniques. More recent writing has tended to be much more sophisticated: see Smith (1978), Gibbs (1981), Squires (1982b), and Smith (1983). It has always seemed a scandal to me that so much effort should be devoted to training teachers to teach and so little to training learners to learn, and I do not believe the latter is any more difficult than the former.

8   For a general account of the accreditation of experiential learning
    and other non-traditional entrance procedures, see Squires (1983).
    For a detailed description of the work of CAEL, see Keeton
    (1976). For a UK view which relates this to opportunities for adult
    learning in general, see Evans (1985).

9   This point applies particularly to university extra-mural depart-
    ments whose terms of reference specify liberal education (see
    Ellwood, 1976). The effect of this was to limit the scope of their
    work to only part of what the parent institution did, and it has
    taken a series of recent initiatives to develop continuing profession-
    al education in the universities: something which the extra-mural
    departments should always have been doing, along with their
    liberal provision. My view is that the scope of a continuing
    education department, however labelled, should be the scope of
    the parent institution: if it has a department of philosophy, then
    courses for adults in philosophy are appropriate; if it has a
    department of electronics, the same applies. Universities provide
    both professional and academic/liberal studies at undergraduate
    level, so it is illogical to restrict their provision for adults to the
    liberal only. One would hope also that EMDs would be able to go
    beyond undergraduate provision in putting on more experimental
    courses, of an interdisciplinary, problem-centred, or otherwise
    innovative nature. For an interesting discussion of the liberal/
    professional tension, see Abrahamsson (1983).

10 It becomes difficult to use the word 'curriculum' at all in some
    forms of adult education, where there is no conventionally labelled
    body of knowledge, no teacher, no apparent continuity or accu-
    mulation of understanding, no assessment of what has been
    learned. Just as adult education tests the limits of the concept of
    education, by slipping over into other things, so it does with the
    notion of a curriculum as an organised course of study. Tough
    seems to me to have suggested the absolutely minimum definition
    of curriculum: something which one has learned which one could
    teach someone else. That may be too minimal for some curriculum
    theorists, used to working in the formal, compulsory sector. But
    the absence of an overt curriculum may be deceptive: there may be
    an internal logic, purpose, and continuity; and in this respect I find
    B. Snyder's recent notion of an 'inner curriculum' appealing.

11 This recalls the concept of educational ideologies mentioned in
    Chapter 1. The point being made here is that one can distinguish
    (though not absolutely) between general ideologies (capitalism,
    socialism, corporatism) which are applied to education along with
    all other aspects of society (production, health care, justice, and so
    on) and educational ideologies which are apparently derived from
    an analysis of the educational process (such as progressivism,
    instrumentalism and liberalism). Of course, in many respects the
    second reflect the first, and some would argue that they are entirely

derivative of them; but that does not explain why similar general ideologies can produce differing educational and curricular ideologies; some socialist writers favour a highly 'progressive' curriculum, while others (for example, Gramsci) favour a rather traditional academic one. Adult education can certainly be used as a vehicle for general ideologies; indeed, the increasingly evident limitations of compulsory education may be making some ideologues of both left and right place more emphasis on adult education as their last, best hope, thus politicising it more than in the past. What I am questioning here is the possibility of constructing an ideology of adult education derived from an analysis of adulthood, or any other aspect of the activity.

7 Conclusion

The purpose of this book has been to offer a framework for the analysis of the curriculum beyond school. Much has been written on the 'whole curriculum' in school, but beyond school writing on the curriculum tends to be localised, and confined to particular sectors or types or levels of courses. The attempt here has been to locate each of the many kinds of post-school education in a total picture, so that even if there is not a comprehensive system, one could at least have a comprehensive view.

The analysis has turned on the fundamental distinction between general and specific education. Whereas compulsory education tends to be general, post-compulsory education tends to be specific. But the three dimensions of general education – knowledge, culture, and abilities – provide, in a looser form, the three orientations of specific education. They constitute a triangle of tensions within which the main types of post-school curricula can be placed: academic, teacher, professional, vocational, social, role, personal, recreational, liberal, and in the middle basic and post-basic. These are not discrete, isolated curricular types, but rather identifiable points in a field of force.

The triangle of orientations and its headings provide a means of analysing the three major sectors of post-school education: the consecutive phase (16–19), higher education, and education for adults. The first two sectors are associated with, though not limited to, certain curricular headings, whereas the education of adults no longer connotes any particular type of curriculum. Each of the three sectors has characteristic themes and problems: the notion of transition at the 16–19 stage, the concept of discipline in higher education, the idea of non-formal education in adult education. But the way that many of these themes apply to all sectors suggests that post-school education is not as neatly demarcated in sectors and types as is sometimes assumed. The problem with post-school education is that it is difficult to conceptualise it as a whole, but just as difficult to see simply in terms of its parts; and the hope is that this book has reflected that tension accurately, without presuming to resolve it.

It was noted in the introduction that the curriculum beyond school is in some ways an impossibly wide and complex topic. What is difficult to write about is even more difficult to draw together in a conclusion, and rather than attempting to achieve some grand synthesis, this final chapter will confine itself to making three general points, to do with access, structure, and priorities, respectively.

The very specificity and complexity of post-school education, together with the fact that it is not compulsory, make the issue of access central in a way that it is not with the schools. There is no point having a sophisticated system of post-school education and training if people – individuals and organisations – do not know how to make use of it. If this book does nothing else, it will surely have demonstrated that education beyond the end of compulsory schooling is extraordinarily difficult to grasp, both organisationally and conceptually; and that is from inside the system. How much more difficult it must be for those who have little knowledge of it or contact with it. The already well-educated student, or the large company which knows what it wants in continuing education or applied research, may find what they want. But for the vast majority of individuals, companies, and other organisations, post-school education is something of a jungle, and the situation is not helped by the fact that the tribes in one part of the jungle often know little about what goes on in other parts; besides, they may have an interest in attracting explorers to them. The matching of complex needs and complex provision entails guidance, not as a gate through which all enquiries have to pass, but as a cross-institutional and national service available to all who need it (NIACE, 1986).

The second point has to do with structure, and is, in a way, a negative one. Post-school education is, and has to be, organised some way: there have to be some kinds of sector, institutional, and curricular categories and boundaries. The problem is to identify the organising principles for such categories and boundaries. In the current system, four such principles are used: (1) level, as in higher education; (2) aims/content, as in liberal or vocational or technical education; (3) age, as in 16–19 or adult education; and (4) domicile, as in local or regional colleges or services. Institutions which are said to be comprehensive or polyvalent are ones which combine two or more of these principles. For example, the polytechnics were originally intended to provide not only various types of course content, but various levels of study as well. There is some evidence that they have tended to drop lower-level courses, as part of a more general 'academic drift'; on the other hand, they have become much more comprehensive in terms of age than was originally envisaged.

The point to be made here is that although this book has been concerned with curriculum and content categories, these are not the only organising principles. While the aims/content of studies, as categorised in Figure 2, is an obvious consideration in how post-school education is structured, there is no suggestion here that it is the only or even primary one. The analysis in Chapter 6 implies that age is not perhaps as important a variable as it might seem, and that institutions and classes might be better organised in terms of what they are studying, at what level, and where. However, in some cases, a homogeneous class of 16–19-year-olds, middle-aged, or retired people might be a much more effective set-up than one which attempted to mix age groups. The issues are complex, and no simple conclusion can be offered here; but more overt discussion of the organising principles listed above (and any others) is surely desirable.

The final point has to do with priorities. No analytic framework is quite 'neutral' with respect to priorities, although it is hoped that the one presented here is sufficiently open to allow a range of diverging conclusions to be drawn from it; the intention has been to analyse rather than prescribe. However, some implications of the analysis have been drawn out at the end of each chapter, and these have gone beyond mere description to suggest certain policy options and priorities: not simply what is taught, but what should be taught, to hark back to Taylor and Richards' original two questions. The second question can illuminate the first, as well as vice versa.

Figure 2, however, suggests a rather indifferent pluralism. No priority is given to any of the ten headings, beyond the fact that the triangle is the way up that it is. There has been no suggestion that professional education is *per se* more important than social education, or that more emphasis should be placed on basic education at the expense of recreational education. Arguments of that kind would require a second and different book, concerned not so much with the analysis of post-school curricula as with curriculum policy in post-school education. In fact, and in the writing, it is impossible to separate the two entirely, but a book about the second would have to engage in a much wider analysis of philosophical, social, and ideological considerations as a foundation for the analysis of policy.

It may, however, be appropriate to end with some questions about curriculum policies and priorities, which lead away from description and analysis towards judgement: from what is, to what should be. It is useful first to distinguish between internal priorities and external ones. One of the by-products of the analysis of post-school education as a whole is some sense of the relationship between the various sectors; a sense which does not come from a more local perspective. The post-school education system is not itself neutral in respect of policies; its size, complexity, and the relative professional autonomy of those who work in it mean that it generates its own priorities, its own internal scales of values. Just as the Civil Service does not simply service government, so the educational service does not simply service society.

The first internal priority of all institutions is survival: organisations, even if they are only a few weeks old, do not willingly self-destruct. But beyond that, what internal priorities or values does post-school education embody? The diversity of provision and activity points to pluralism, but a question may be raised about the dominant position of higher education in the system. Higher education is not simply the highest level of study, it is higher in a normative sense as well. It represents in some ways the ideal type of curriculum, the form that other curricula lead towards or aspire to. The point is obvious in terms of secondary-school examinations, with their 'academic' emphasis, but there is a discernible influence on other forms of post-school education, in terms of 'academic drift', the high status of disciplines and theory, the incorporation of continuing education into higher education structures, and the belief that research is the logical and ideal outcome of all studies. The conceptual pluralism of Figure 2, in which no one type of curriculum is any more important than another, contrasts in reality with what can only be described as a hegemony of the academic-professional.

This hegemony has been challenged and modified in recent years in various ways. Determined attempts have been made to construct secondary school curricula and examinations which do not simply reflect the needs of the minority of children who will eventually go on to higher education. The current policy emphasis on vocational education and training, and in particular the stress on work experience and induction into the work culture, can be seen as a counter-balance to theory and abstraction. Some forms of adult education have always been determinedly non-academic and even anti-academic, in their emphasis on outreach, action, practice, and personal development. But the issue is still whether it is possible to have a plurality of curriculum aims and values in a system which is essentially vertical.

If the internal priorities of the system have tended towards the academic, what of the external priorities imposed from outside? Here, comment becomes particularly hazardous, because whereas there has been a certain consistency in the internal values of the education system (in terms of the orientation towards organised knowledge), external priorities change with changes in the political and social climate. Nothing in educational research dates quite so fast as the writing on educational policy. Nevertheless, it may be a useful if transient exercise to comment on the current external policy emphasis on the economic and employment relevance of post-school education, an emphasis apparent in all the three main sectors of post-school education – 16–19, higher education, and adult or continuing education. Economic and employment relevance is very much the policy flavour of the decade in most OECD countries, just as access and equality were in previous decades. The long-term relative economic decline of the United Kingdom compared to other industrialised countries has, however, given the policy a particular edge in this country. The rapid rise of the MSC in non-advanced vocational education and training, the restructuring of higher education, and the advent of PEVE and PICKUP in continuing education are all manifestations of a general policy emphasis, which affects the schools as well.

The first question that can be raised is whether the connection between post-school education and the economy should be seen primarily in terms of identifiable skill shortages, or in broader economic culture terms. The existence or prospect of skill shortages or bottlenecks has always been an emotive issue in economic policy, leading to calls for the education system to gear itself more closely to the needs of the economy. But the analysis in Chapter 3 suggests that manpower planning of this kind is very difficult to carrry out effectively, and in fact the evidence that skills shortages have actually impeded economic growth in any direct way over the last few decades is rather sparse (Lindley, 1981). Of course all labour forces, even in centrally planned economies, experience pockets of skills shortages at various levels, because the mechanisms of allocation, either by planning or through the market, are imperfect (Fulton, 1982). And it can be argued that when economies are undergoing major, structural changes, such shortages are likely to become more serious, as they may in, for example, the information technology field in the United Kingdom in the next decade. But this is still a long way from saying that skill shortages are typically a general impediment to economic growth in industrialised countries.

The qualification 'in any direct way' in the last paragraph is an important one, however, because it has been argued recently (Hollenstein, 1982; Worswick, 1985) that the general level of qualifications in the workforce, and the degree of competence which that indicates, is a factor which helps to explain the differing economic performances of say, Britain and Germany. A mild degree of 'over-training' may improve productivity in various ways: operatives can do basic repairs on their machines, thus avoiding downtime; middle-level technicians can exploit the margin for improvement that exists in most procedures and processes; high-level manpower can innovate in substantial and sometimes radical ways.

There can be no doubt that at the lower and intermediate levels, the United Kingdom has undertrained for many decades compared to some other industrialised countries (NEDO, 1984). Current government policy in establishing training opportunities for everyone in the 16–19 age-group thus reverses a long-term neglect, even though, as was explained in Chapter 4, one may be critical of the way the policy is being implemented, particularly in England and Wales. But the comparisons frequently made with Germany in this respect raise questions about the relationship between education/training systems and the economic culture. The economic successes of Germany, the United States and Japan have been achieved with very *dissimilar* education/training systems, a fact which makes it difficult to argue that there is any simple correlation between the structure of education and training, and economic performance. As the NEDO report does, however, make clear, what these three countries all have is a strongly consensual economic culture, although the nature of the consensus is different in each case.

Economic culture arguments are even less easy to substantiate than skill shortage ones. But there is a prima facie case for thinking that the United Kingdom's economic decline may be due to deep-seated cultural factors, rather than contingent economic ones, so long and persistent has it been, and apparently impervious to changes in governments and government policies. And some of the economic culture arguments implicate the education and training system in that decline. Ministers in the current government have accused education of failing to promote an 'enterprise culture'. One suspects that there is a good deal of truth in this, not because teachers are anti-capitalist (though some certainly are) but simply because, as public sector professionals who earn rather than make money, they do not have much contact or sympathy with the world of the entrepreneur. The same might be said, *inter alia*, of those who work in the health service, local government, or the armed forces, but since education is meant (to some degree) to service the economy, the charge is more serious there. There is little hard evidence on the question, partly because such values, if they are transmitted, are likely to be so through the hidden rather than overt curriculum.

Wiener's (1981) contention that English culture contains a strong anti-industrial bias (which is not quite the same as an anti-enterprise one) provides a second version of the economic culture thesis. Again, he implicates education, and in particular higher education in this, citing the influence of Oxbridge and the low status of engineering as evidence. While Wiener's argument seems overstated (see Sanderson, 1972, for an account of university–industry links), it does seem to account for a good deal that is otherwise difficult to explain. The hegemony of the academic leads to the preference for pure science over applied technology; the anti-industrial ethos of much of the humanities draws on the powerful traditions of pastoral. 'Mechanistic' is a pejorative word in many fields, education included. One suddenly understands the peculiar passion that infuses the singing of Blake's 'Jerusalem'.

What of the credit side? In what ways does education support a positive, adaptable economic culture? In so far as one of the problems of that culture has been the contrast between high-trust political relations and low-trust economic relations (Halsey, 1978), one might think that the democratising effects of mass education would gradually soften the economic confrontation between classes, a matter of regret for some. In so far as education has provided an avenue for upward social mobility, even if only of individuals, it may have eased or diverted the class conflict which has been so evident for so long on the shop floor. But education may support the economic culture in a more oblique and long-term way, in counteracting the tendency among organisations (as well as individuals and cultures) to relapse into implicit and unreflective modes of thought and behaviour. As organisations (and individuals and cultures) attain a kind of maturity, and find a way of operating in the world that is reasonably successful, there is less need for them to *explicate*: to spell out their situation, air their problems and decisions, analyse the choices open to them. Consequently, they may become increasingly tacit in the way they operate, lose the capacity to analyse alternatives, and hence the capacity to adapt to a changing environment. The married couple who stop talking, the small textile firm that sees no need to look for new markets, the culture that lives on its rituals, all exemplify a kind of sclerosis which education with its built-in emphasis on explication and reflexivity may help to arrest or cure.

All modern economic cultures need to renew themselves all the time, but it may be that the need is even greater in the United Kingdom than in other countries. It has the oldest industrial culture in the world, much older than that of the United States or Japan. It has never undergone the catastrophic changes of revolution or defeat in war which may have forced other countries such as France and Germany to reassess their economic and social orders; at the same time, it has had to adapt to profound long-term shifts, such as the loss of empire, which have gradually altered the objective circumstances of its economic situation without at any one point signalling a dramatic change. It may therefore be that the burden of renewal falls on education and training to a peculiar degree in the United Kingdom, as compared to other countries, in a society which in many ways seems to value the tacit or implicit: a subtle, deeply embedded culture with an evident distaste for 'philosophising' or 'analysing' at many levels. Whether the education and training system can in fact open up that culture again and enable it to confront and analyse itself is anyone's guess, but it is expecting a great deal of it, especially when the current level of financial and moral support for education from government is low.

All this presupposes that economic and vocational relevance should be a curriculum priority, and that the argument is simply about the relative importance of overt curriculum aims and hidden curriculum messages: skills shortages and manpower supply relate to the overt curriculum, whereas the complex of attitudes that comprise the economic culture is more likely to be shaped or transmitted by the 'content of the process'. But should economic relevance be the priority that current policy affirms? The answer to that question depends on one's wider political and social values, not just one's view of education. But a distinction can be drawn between tactical adjustments and conceptual shifts. There are, in my view, compelling reasons for believing that unless the United Kingdom improves its economic performance over the next decade, the social consequences will be little short of disastrous. That economic task seems to me one to which education should be firmly geared, even at the temporary expense of values and activities which I and many others cherish.

This does not imply a narrowed definition of education. A limited view of the curriculum implies a limited view of life. The economy is only one facet of the culture; and the culture, it has been argued, is only one of the three basic orientations of the curriculum. The fact that economic discourse dominates so much of current educational, and indeed public, policy is tolerable as long as it is seen for what it is: a short-term response to a particular problem. But whatever the internal defects of the models of the curriculum presented here in Chapters 2 and 3, they should make it much more difficult to mistake that part for the whole.

Bibliography

ABRAHAMSSON, K. (1983) *Between Liberal Education and Professional Training*. Stockholm: National Board of Universities and Colleges, mimeo.

ADVISORY COUNCIL FOR ADULT AND CONTINUING EDUCATION (1979) *A Strategy for the Basic Education of Adults*. Leicester: ACACE.

ADVISORY COUNCIL FOR ADULT AND CONTINUING EDUCATION (1982a) *Continuing Education: from Policies to Practice*. Leicester: ACACE.

ADVISORY COUNCIL FOR ADULT AND CONTINUING EDUCATION (1982b) *Adults: Their Educational Experience and Needs*. Leicester: ACACE.

ADVISORY COUNCIL FOR ADULT AND CONTINUING EDUCATION (1983) *Political Education for Adults*. Leicester: ACACE.

ALLMAN, P. (1983) 'The Nature and Process of Adult Development', in TIGHT, M. (ed.) *Adult Learning and Education*. London: Croom Helm.

ANDERSON, D. (1982) 'The Teacher as Classroom Researcher: a Modest Method for a New Opportunity', in PAYNE, G. and CUFF, E. (eds) (1982) *Doing Teaching*. London: Batsford.

APPLE, M. (1979) *Ideology and Curriculum*. London: Routledge and Kegan Paul.

APPLE, M. (1981) 'Social Structure, Ideology and Curriculum', in LAWN, M. and BARTON, L. (eds), *Rethinking Curriculum Studies*. London: Croom Helm.

ARCHER, M. (1984) *The Social Origins of Educational Systems* (University edn). London: Sage.

ARGYRIS, C. (1982) *Reasoning, Learning and Action*. San Francisco: Jossey-Bass.

ATKINSON, G. B. J. (1983) *The Economics of Education*. London: Hodder and Stoughton.

BALTES, P. B., *et al.* (1980) 'Life-Span Developmental Psychology', *Annual Review of Psychology*, Academic Press, 31, 65–110.

BANDURA, A. (1971) *Social Learning Theory*. New York: General Learning Press.

BANTOCK, G. (1980) *Dilemmas of the Curriculum*. Oxford: Martin Robertson.

BARNETT, R. A. (1981) 'Integration in Curriculum Design in Higher Education', *Journal of Further and Higher Education*, 5(3), 33–45.

BARON, J. (1978) 'Intelligence and General Strategies,' in UNDERWOOD, G. (ed.) *Strategies of Information Processing*. London: Academic Press.

BARON, J. (1985) *Rationality and Intelligence*. Cambridge: Cambridge University Press.

BARROW, R. (1976) *Common Sense and the Curriculum*. London: Allen and Unwin.

BECHER, T. (1981) 'Towards a Definition of Disciplinary Cultures', *Studies in Higher Education*, 6(2), 109–22.

BECHER, T. (1984) 'The Cultural View', in CLARK, B. R. (ed.) *Perspectives on Higher Education*. Berkeley: University of California Press.

BECKER, G. (1964) *Human Capital*. New York: National Bureau of Economic Research.

BELBIN, E. and BELBIN, R. M. (1972) *Problems in Adult Retraining*. London: Heinemann.

BELL, R. (1971) 'The Growth of the Modern University', in HOOPER, R. (ed.) (1971) *The Curriculum: Context, Design and Development*. Edinburgh: Oliver and Boyd.

BENNER, H. (1982) *Demarcation of Occupational Groups/Occupational Fields with regard to Vocational Training at Skilled Level in the European Community*. Berlin: European Centre for the Development of Vocational Training (CEDEFOP).

BERG, I. (1973) *Education and Jobs: the Great Training Robbery*. Harmondsworth: Penguin.

BERGER, P. and LUCKMANN, T. (1971) *The Social Construction of Reality*. Harmondsworth: Penguin.

BERNSTEIN, B. (1971) 'On the Classification and Framing of Educational Knowledge', in YOUNG, M. F. D. (ed.) *Knowledge and Control*. London: Collier-Macmillan.

BLACKSTONE, T. (1981) 'The Entrenched Generalists', *New Universities Quarterly*, 35(3), 280–92.

BLAUG, M. (1970) *An Introduction to the Economics of Education*. Harmondsworth: Penguin.

BLAUG, M. (1983) *Where are We Now in the Economics of Education?* London: University of London Institute of Education.

BLOOM, B., *et al.* (1956) *Taxonomy of Educational Objectives, Handbook 1: Cognitive Domain*. London: Longman.

BOBBITT, F. (1918) *The Curriculum*. Boston: Houghton Mifflin (reissued, 1971).

BOUCHER, L. (1983) 'Reform of the Swedish Post-Compulsory Schools', *Compare*, 13(2), 129–43.

BOURDIEU, P. and PASSERON, J-C. (1977) *Reproduction in Education, Society and Culture*. London: Sage.

BOWLES, S. and GINTIS, H. (1976) *Schooling in Capitalist America*.

London: Routledge and Kegan Paul.

BOYD, R. D., et al. (1980) *Redefining the Discipline of Adult Education*. San Francisco: Jossey-Bass.

BOYER, E. L. (1983) *High School*. New York: Harper and Row.

BRATCHELL, D. F. (1968) *The Aims and Organisation of Further Education*. London: Pergamon.

BRENT, A. (1978) *Philosophical Foundations for the Curriculum*. London: Allen and Unwin.

BROADY, M. (1978/9) 'Down with Academic Standards', *New Universities Quarterly*, 33(1), 3–19.

BROOKFIELD, S. (1983) *Adult Learners, Adult Education and the Community*. Milton Keynes: Open University Press.

BROUDY, H., et al. (1964) *Democracy and Excellence in American Secondary Education*. Chicago: Rand McNally.

BRUNER, J. S. (1960) *The Process of Education*. Cambridge, Mass.: Harvard University Press.

BRUNER, J. S. (1968) *Toward a Theory of Instruction*. New York: Norton.

BRYANT, I. (1983) *The Educational Needs of Long-term Unemployed Adults*. University of Glasgow: Dept. of Adult Education.

BURNS, R. B. (1982) *Self-Concept Development and Education*. London: Holt, Rinehart and Winston.

BUTLER, L. (ed.) (1984a) *Educational Guidance for Adults: a New Service*. Leeds: The Open University.

BUTLER, L., et al. (1984b) *Case Studies in Educational Guidance for Adults*. Leicester: National Institute of Adult Continuing Education/Advisory Council for Adult and Continuing Education.

CANTOR, L. M. and ROBERTS, I. F. (1972) *Further Education in England and Wales* (2nd edn). London: Routledge and Kegan Paul.

CANTOR, L. M. and ROBERTS, I. F. (1979) *Further Education Today*. London: Routledge and Kegan Paul.

CAREERS RESEARCH AND ADVISORY CENTRE (1975) *Interdisciplinary Courses: Degree Course Guide* (with an introduction by G. Squires). Cambridge: CRAC.

CARNEGIE COMMISSION (1979) *Giving Youth a Better Chance*. San Francisco: Jossey-Bass.

CARNEGIE FOUNDATION FOR THE ADVANCEMENT OF TEACHING (1977) *Missions of the College Curriculum*. San Francisco: Jossey-Bass.

CARR, W. (1982) 'Treating the Symptoms, Neglecting the Cause: Diagnosing the Problems of Theory and Practice', *Journal of Further and Higher Education*, 6(2), 19–29.

CATTELL, R. (1971) *Abilities: Their Structure, Growth and Action*. Boston: Houghton Mifflin.

CHICKERING, A. W., et al. (1981) *The Modern American College*. San Francisco: Jossey-Bass.

CHOPPIN, B., et al. (1973) *The Prediction of Academic Success*. Windsor: National Foundation for Educational Research.

CITY AND GUILDS OF LONDON INSTITUTE (1983) *List of Publications and*

Candidate's Guide. London: CGLI.

CLAXTON, G. (ed.) (1980) *Cognitive Psychology: New Directions.* London: Routledge and Kegan Paul.

COLEMAN, J. S. (ed.) (1974) *Youth: Transition to Adulthood.* Chicago: University of Chicago.

COMMISSION OF THE EUROPEAN COMMUNITY (1984) *Technological Change and Social Adjustment (Com (84)).* Brussels: EEC.

COOK, T. G. (ed.) (1973) *Education and the Professions.* London: Methuen.

COOMBS, P. H., et al. (1973) *New Paths to Learning.* New York: International Council for Educational Development.

CORNBLETH, C. (1984) 'Beyond Hidden Curriculum', *Journal of Curriculum Studies,* 16(1), 29–36.

COUNCIL FOR NATIONAL ACADEMIC AWARDS (1986) *Handbook of CNAA's Policy and Regulations.* London: CNAA.

CREMIN, L. A. (1971) 'Curriculum-making in the United States', *Teachers College Record,* 73, 707–12.

CRITTENDEN, B. (1982) *Cultural Pluralism and the Common Curriculum.* Melbourne: Melbourne University Press.

CROMBIE, A. D. and HARRIES-JENKINS, G. (1983) *The Demise of the Liberal Tradition.* Leeds: University of Leeds Dept. of Adult and Continuing Education.

CROSS, K. P. (1976) *Accent on Learning.* San Francisco: Jossey-Bass.

CROSS, K. P. (1982) *Adults as Learners.* San Francisco: Jossey-Bass.

CUFF, E. C. and PAYNE, G. C. F. (eds) (1985) *Crisis in the Curriculum.* London: Croom Helm.

DALE, R. (ed.) (1985) *Education, Training and Employment.* Oxford: Pergamon.

DAVIE, G. (1961) *The Democratic Intellect.* Edinburgh: Edinburgh University Press.

DE BONO, E. (1976) *Teaching Thinking.* London: Temple Smith.

DE SANCTIS, F. M. (1984) 'Problems of Defining the Public in the Context of Lifelong Education', *International Journal of Lifelong Education,* 3(4), 265–78.

DEFORGE, Y. (1979) 'Basic Training and Polyvalent Training', in COUNCIL OF EUROPE, *Occupational Basic Training.* Strasbourg: Council for Cultural Co-operation.

DENT, H. C. (1977) *The Training of Teachers in England and Wales 1800–1975.* London: Hodder and Stoughton.

DEPARTMENT OF EDUCATION AND SCIENCE (1980) *Post-Experience Vocational Provision for those in Employment.* London: DES.

DEPARTMENT OF EDUCATION AND SCIENCE (1985) *The Development of Higher Education into the 1990s.* (Cmnd. 9524) London: HMSO.

DEWEY, J. (1938) *Experience and Education.* New York: Macmillan.

DORE, R. (1976) *The Diploma Disease.* London: Allen and Unwin.

EDUCATION ACT (1944). London: HMSO.

EDWARDS, A. D. and FURLONG, V. J. (1978) *The Language of Teaching.*

London: Heinemann.

EDWARDS, A. (1983) 'The Re-construction of Post-Compulsory Education and Training in England and Wales', *European Journal of Education*, 18(1), 7–20.

EISER, J. R. (1978) 'Interpersonal Attributions', in HAJFEL, H. and FRASER, C. (eds), *Introducing Social Psychology*. Harmondsworth: Penguin.

EISNER, E. W. (1967) 'Educational Objectives: Help or Hindrance?', *School Review*, 75, 250–60.

EISNER, E. W. (1982) *Cognition and Curriculum*. New York: Longman.

ELLWOOD, C. (1976) *Adult Learning Today*. London: Sage.

ERAUT, M. (1985) 'Knowledge Creation and Knowledge Use in Professional Contexts', *Studies in Higher Education*, 10(2), 117–33.

ERICKSON, E. (1968) *Identity: Youth and Crisis*. London: Faber and Faber.

EURICH, N. P. (1985) *Corporate Classrooms*. Princeton: Carnegie Foundation for the Advancement of Teaching.

EVANS, K. (1983) 'Innovations in Continuing Education and Training in the U.K.' Guildford: University of Surrey, mimeo.

EVANS, N. (1985) *Post-Education Society*. London: Croom Helm.

EVANS, R. N. (1971) *Foundations of Vocational Education*. Columbus, Ohio: Charles E. Merrill.

EYSENCK, M. (1984) *A Handbook of Cognitive Psychology*. London: Lawrence Erlbaum.

FIDGEON, F. (1979) 'The Broad-Base Education and Training Concept in the United Kingdom', in COUNCIL OF EUROPE, *Occupational Basic Training*. Strasbourg: Council for Cultural Co-operation.

FINNISTON, Sir M. (Chairman) (1980) *Engineering Our Future*. (Cmnd. 7794). London: HMSO.

FITTS, P. M. and POSNER, M. I. (1973) *Human Performance*. London: Prentice-Hall.

FLETCHER, C. and THOMPSON, N. (1980) *Issues in Community Education*. Lewes: Falmer Press.

FLOWER, F. and KUSSELL, R. (1982) *The Industrial Tutor in the Federal Republic of Germany*. Blagdon: Further Education Staff College.

FODOR, J. A. (1983) *The Modularity of Mind*. Cambridge, Mass.: MIT Press.

FORDHAM, P. (1979) 'The Interaction of Formal and Non-formal Education', *Studies in Adult Education*, 11(1), 1–11.

FREDERICKSEN, N., et al. (1984) 'The Place of Social Intelligence in a Taxonomy of Cognitive Abilities', *Intelligence*, 8, 315–37.

FREIRE, P. 'Education and Conscientização', in TIGHT, M. (ed.) (1983) *Adult Learning and Education*. London: Croom Helm.

FULTON, O. (ed.) (1981) *Access To Higher Education*. Guildford: Society for Research into Higher Education.

FULTON, O., et al. (1982) *Higher Education and Manpower Planning*. Geneva: International Labour Organisation.

FURTHER EDUCATION UNIT (1982a) *Basic Skills*. London: FEU.
FURTHER EDUCATION UNIT (1982b) *Progressing from Vocational Preparation – the Issues*. London: FEU.
FURTHER EDUCATION UNIT (1982c) *Progressing from Vocational Preparation: towards a Solution*. London: FEU.
FURTHER EDUCATION STAFF COLLEGE (1983) *The 'New' FE*. Blagdon: FESC.
FURTHER EDUCATION STAFF COLLEGE (1984) *YTS: a Critical Review of Policy and Practice*. Blagdon: FESC.
GAFF, J. G. (1983) *General Education Today*. San Francisco: Jossey-Bass.
GAGNE, R. (1969) *The Conditions of Learning*. London: Holt, Rinehart and Winston.
GARDNER, H. (1983) *Frames of Mind*. London: Heinemann.
GARFINKEL, H. (1967) *Studies in Ethnomethodology*. Englewood Cliffs N. J.: Prentice-Hall.
GHISELLI, E. E. (1966) *The Validity of Occupational Aptitude Tests*. New York: John Wiley.
GIBBS, G. (1981) *Teaching Students to Learn*. Milton Keynes: Open University Press.
GLEESON, D. and MARDLE, C. (1980) *Further Education or Training?* London: Routledge and Kegan Paul.
GLEESON, D. (ed.) (1983) *Youth Training and the Search for Work*. London: Routledge and Kegan Paul.
GOACHER, B. (1984) *Selection Post-16: the Role of Examination Results*. (Schools Council Examinations Bulletin 45.) London: Methuen.
GOLBY, M., GREENWALD, J. and WEST, R. (eds) (1975) *Curriculum Design*. London: Croom Helm.
GOLBY, M. (1981) 'Practice and Theory', in LAWN, M. and BARTON, L. (eds) (1981) *Rethinking Curriculum Studies*. London: Croom Helm.
GOODINGS, R., et al. (1982) *Changing Priorities in Teacher Education*. London: Croom Helm.
GOODLAD, S. (ed.) (1984) *Education for the Professions*. Guildford: Society for Research into Higher Education and NFER-Nelson.
GOODMAN, P. (1971) *Compulsory Miseducation*. Harmondsworth: Penguin.
GOODNOW, W. E. (1982) 'The Contingency Theory of Education', *International Journal of Lifelong Education*, 1(4), 341–52.
GORZ, A. (ed.) (1972) *The Division of Labour*. Hassocks: Harvester Press.
GRIFFIN, C. (1983) *Curriculum Theory in Adult and Lifelong Education*. London: Croom Helm.
GRIFFITHS, R. (1982/3) 'Generalist and Specialist: a Non-Issue', *Universities Quarterly*, 37(1), 25–30.
GRIGNON, C. (1971) *L'Ordre des Choses*. Paris: Minuit.
GUSTAFSSON, J-E. (1984) 'A Unifying Model for the Structure of Intellectual Abilities', *Intelligence*, 8, 179–203.

HABERMAS, J. (1974) *Theory and Practice* (trans. J. Viertel). London: Heinemann.

HAJNAL, J. (1972) *The Student Trap*. Harmondsworth: Penguin.

HALSEY, A. H. and TROW, M. (1971) *The British Academics*. London: Faber.

HALSEY, A. H. (1978) *Change in British Society*. London: Oxford University Press.

HAMILTON, D. (1976) *Curriculum Evaluation*. London: Open Books.

HAMILTON, D. (1981) 'An Introduction to Curriculum, Teaching and Learning', in SSRC, *Curriculum Research: Agenda for the Eighties* (Proceedings of an Invitational Seminar.) Birmingham: University of Birmingham, mimeo.

HAMMERSLEY, M. and HARGREAVES, A. (eds) (1983) *Curriculum Practice: Some Sociological Case-studies*. London: Falmer Press.

HARGREAVES, D. (1982) *The Challenge for the Comprehensive School*. London: Routledge and Kegan Paul.

HARLOW, H. F. (1949) 'The Formation of Learning Sets', *Psychological Review*, 56, 51–65.

HARRISON, D. (1984) in *Professional Preparation in Higher Education* (DES/UHA Anglo-Swedish Conference Papers), mimeo.

HARTREE, A. (1984) 'Malcolm Knowles' Theory of Andragogy: a Critique', *International Journal of Lifelong Education*, 3(3), 203–10.

HASLEGRAVE, H. L. (Chairman) (1969) *Report of the Committee on Technician Courses and Examinations*. London: National Advisory Council for Industry and Commerce.

HAYEK, F. A. (1944) *The Road To Serfdom*. London: George Routledge.

HAYES, C., *et al.* (1983) *Training for Skill Ownership*. Brighton: Institute of Manpower Studies.

HAYES, C., *et al.* (1985) *Study on the Use of Occupational Families in Youth Training Schemes*. Brighton: Institute of Manpower Studies.

HEARNDEN, A. (1976) *Education, Culture and Politics in West Germany*. Oxford: Pergamon.

HENRY, J. (1963) *Culture Against Man*. Harmondsworth: Penguin.

HERRICK, V. E. and TYLER, R. (eds) (1950) *Toward Improved Curriculum Theory*. Chicago: University of Chicago Press.

HIRST, P. H. (1969) 'The Logic of the Curriculum', *Journal of Curriculum Studies*, 1(2), 142–58.

HIRST, P. H. (1974) *Knowledge and the Curriculum*. London: Routledge and Kegan Paul.

HIRST, P. H. (ed.) (1983) *Educational Theory and Its Foundation Disciplines*. London: Routledge and Kegan Paul.

HOLLENSTEIN, H. (1982) *Economic Performance and the Vocational Qualifications of the Swiss Labour Force Compared with Britain and Germany*. London: National Institute for Economic and Social Research.

HOLLOWAY, B. J. (1972) 'Higher Education and Employment: a View from the Interface', in JEVONS, F. and TURNER, H. D. (eds) *What Kinds of Graduates do we Need?* Oxford: Oxford University Press.

HOLT, M. (1980) *The Tertiary Sector*. London: Hodder and Stoughton.

HORE, T. and WEST, L. H. T. (eds) (1980) *Mature Age Students in Australian Higher Education*. Clayton, Victoria: Monash University.

HORTON, T. and RAGGATT, P. (eds) (1982) *Challenge and Change in the Curriculum*. London: Hodder and Stoughton.

HOULE, C. O. (1980) *Continuing Learning in the Professions*. San Francisco: Jossey-Bass.

HYMAN, H. H., *et al.* (1975) *The Enduring Effects of Education*. Chicago: University of Chicago.

HYMAN, H. H. and WRIGHT, C. R. (1979) *Education's Lasting Influence on Values*. Chicago: University of Chicago.

ILLICH, I. (1973) *Tools for Conviviality*. London: Calder and Boyars.

ILIFFE, A. H. (1968) 'The Foundation Year at the University of Keele', *Sociological Review Monograph No 12*.

JACKSON, J. (1970) *Professions and Professionalization*. Cambridge: Cambridge University Press.

JACKSON, J. A. (ed.) (1972) *Role*. Cambridge: Cambridge University Press.

LORD JAMES OF RUSHOLME (Chairman) (1972) *Report of a Committee of Enquiry into Teacher Education and Training*. London: HMSO.

JARVIS, P. (1983) *Professional Education*. London: Croom Helm.

JARVIS, P. (1984) 'Andragogy – a Sign of the Times', *Studies in Adult Education*, 16, 32–8.

JASPERS, K. (1960) *The Idea of the University*. London: Peter Owen.

JENKINS, D. (1976) *Six Alternative Models of Curriculum Evaluation* (Unit 20, E203 *Curriculum Design and Development*). Milton Keynes: Open University Press.

JENKINS, D. and SHIPMAN, M. D. (1976) *Curriculum: an Introduction*. London: Open Books.

JENNINGS, B. (1985) *The Education of Adults in Britain*. Hull: University of Hull Department of Adult and Continuing Education.

JOCHIMSEN, R. (1978) 'Aims and Objectives of German Vocational and Professional Education in the Present European Context', *Comparative Education*, 14(3), 199–210.

JOHNSON, R. (1984) *Occupational Training Families*. London: Further Education Unit.

JOINT BOARD FOR PRE-VOCATIONAL EDUCATION (1985) *The Certificate of Pre-Vocational Education*. London: JBPVE/CGLI/BTEC.

KAISER, M. and WERNER, H. (1979) 'The Concept of Occupational Families in Relation to Occupational Training', in COUNCIL OF EUROPE, *Occupational Basic Training*. Strasbourg: Council for Cultural Co-operation.

KALLEN, D. (1983) 'Youth, Education and Employment – a European Overview', in WATSON, K. (ed.) *Youth, Education and Employment –*

International Perspectives. London: Croom Helm.

KEDDIE, N. (1980) 'Adult Education: an Ideology of Individualism', in THOMPSON, J. (ed.) *Adult Education for a Change*. London: Hutchinson.

KEETON, M., *et al.* (1976) *Experiential Learning*. San Francisco: Jossey-Bass.

KELLY, A. V. (1977) *The Curriculum: Theory and Practice*. London: Harper and Row.

KELLY, T. (1970) *A History of Adult Education in Great Britain*. Liverpool: University of Liverpool.

KING, E. J., MOOR, C. H. and MUNDY, J. A. (1975) *Post-Compulsory Education: the Way Ahead*. London: Sage.

KLINE, P. (1975) *Psychology of Vocational Guidance*. London: Batsford.

KNOWLES, M. (1978) *The Adult Learner: a Neglected Species* (2nd edn.). Houston: Gulf.

KNOX, A. B. (1977) *Adult Development and Learning*. San Francisco: Jossey-Bass.

KOGAN, M. and BOYS, C. J. (1984) 'Expectations of Higher Education'. Uxbridge: Brunel University Department of Government, mimeo.

KOGAN, N. (1976) *Cognitive Styles in Infancy and Early Childhood*. New York: Wiley.

KOHLBERG, L. (1973) 'Continuities in Childhood and Adult Moral Development Revisited', in BALTES, P. and SCHAIE, K. W. (eds) *Life-Span Developmental Psychology: Personality and Socialization*. New York: Academic Press.

KOLB, D. A. (1984) *Experiential Learning*. Englewood Cliffs, N.J.: Prentice-Hall.

KRATHWOHL, D. R., *et al.* (1964) *Taxonomy of Educational Objectives, Handbook 2: Affective Domain*. London: Longman.

KUHN, T. S. (1962) *The Structure of Scientific Revolutions*. Chicago: University of Chicago.

LAKATOS, I. and MUSGRAVE, A. (eds) (1970) *Criticism and the Growth of Knowledge*. Cambridge: Cambridge University Press.

LANE, M. (1975) *Design for Degrees*. London: Macmillan.

LAUGLO, J. (1983) 'Concepts of "General Education" and "Vocational Education" Curricula for Post-Compulsory Schooling in Western Industrialised Countries: When Shall the Twain Meet?', *Comparative Education*, 19(3), 285–304.

LAUWERYS, J. (1967) 'Opening Address' in LAUWERYS, J. (ed.) *General Education in a Changing World*. The Hague: Martinus Nijhoff.

LAWN, M. and BARTON, L. (eds) (1981) *Rethinking Curriculum Studies*. London: Croom Helm.

LAWSON, K. H. (1975) *Philosophical Concepts and Values in Adult Education*. Nottingham: University of Nottingham.

LAWTON, D. (1983a) *Curriculum Studies and Educational Planning*. London: Hodder and Stoughton.

LAWTON, D. (1983b) *Culture and the Curriculum* (Unit 3, E204, *Purpose and Planning in the Curriculum*). Milton Keynes: Open University Press.

LEGGE, D. (1982) *The Education of Adults in Britain*. Milton Keynes: Open University.

LEVIN, L. and LIND, I. (eds) (1985) *Interdisciplinarity Revisited*. Paris: OECD.

LEVINE, A. (1978) *Handbook on Undergraduate Curriculum*. San Francisco: Jossey-Bass.

LINDLEY, R. (ed.) (1981) *Higher Education and the Labour Market*. Guildford: Society for Research into Higher Education.

LOBKOWICZ, N. (1967) *Theory and Practice*. Notre Dame, Ind.: University of Notre Dame Press.

LOCKE, M. and BLOOMFIELD, J. (1982) *Mapping and Reviewing the Pattern of 16–19 Education*. London: Schools Council.

LOEVINGER, J. (1976) *Ego Development: Conceptions and Theories*. San Francisco: Jossey-Bass.

LOWE, J. (1970) *Adult Education in England and Wales*. London: Michael Joseph.

LUTZ, B. (1981) 'Education and Employment: Contrasting Evidence from France and the Federal Republic of Germany', *European Journal of Education*, 16(1), 73–86.

MACDONALD-ROSS, M. (1975) 'Behavioural Objectives: a Critical Review', in GOLBY, M. *et al*. (eds) *Curriculum Design*. London: Croom Helm.

MACE, J. (1984) 'The Economics of Education: a Revisionist's View', *Higher Education Review*, 16(3), 39–56.

MACFARLANE, N. (Chairman) (1980) *Education for 16–19 Year Olds*. London: Department of Education and Science.

MCCLELLAND, D. C. (1973) 'Testing for Competence rather than for "Intelligence"', *American Psychologist*, 28, 1–14.

MCGUIRE, J. and PRIESTLEY, P. (1981) *Life after School: a Social Skills Curriculum*. Oxford: Pergamon.

MCKEACHIE, W. (1975) 'Instructional Psychology', *Annual Review of Psychology*, 29, 161–93.

MANSELL, T., *et al*. (1976) *The Container Revolution: a Study of Unit and Modular Schemes*. London: The Nuffield Foundation.

MANPOWER SERVICES COMMISSION (1981a) *A New Training Initiative*. London: MSC.

MANPOWER SERVICES COMMISSION (1981b) *A New Training Initiative: an agenda for action*. London: MSC.

MANPOWER SERVICES COMMISSION (1982) *Youth Task Group Report*. London: MSC.

MARSDEN, W. E. (1979) 'Historical Approaches to Curriculum Study', in MARSDEN, W. E. (ed.) *Post-War Curriculum Development: an Historical Appraisal*. Leicester: History of Education Society.

MARTON, F. *et al*. (eds) (1984) *The Experience of Learning*. Edinburgh: Scottish Academic Press.

MASLOW, A. H. (1954) *Motivation and Personality*. New York: Harper.
MASLOW, A. (1973) *The Farther Reaches of Human Nature*. Harmondsworth: Penguin.
MEE, G. and WILTSHIRE, H. (1978) *Structure and Performance in Adult Education*. London: Longman.
MEIGHAN, R. (1981) *A Sociology of Educating*. London: Holt, Rinehart and Winston.
MESSICK, S., et al. (1978) *Individuality in Learning*. San Francisco: Jossey-Bass.
MEZIROW, J. (1983) 'A Critical Theory of Adult Learning and Education', in TIGHT, M. (ed.) *Adult Learning and Education* London: Croom Helm.
MITTER, W. (1984) 'Education for All', *International Yearbook of Education*, 36, 101–14. Paris: UNESCO.
NATALE, S. (1972) *An Experiment in Empathy*. Slough: National Foundation for Educational Research.
NATIONAL INSTITUTE OF ADULT CONTINUING EDUCATION (1986) *The Challenge of Change: Developing Educational Guidence for Adults*. Leicester: NIACE.
NATIONAL INSTITUTE OF ADULT EDUCATION (1955) *Liberal Education in a Technical Age*. London: Max Parrish.
NEAVE, G. (ed.) (1978a) *Research Perspectives on the Transition from School to Work*. Amsterdam: Swets and Zeitlinger.
NEAVE, G. (1978b) 'Polytechnics: a Policy Drift?', *Studies in Higher Education*, 3(1), 105–11.
NEAVE, G. (1979a) 'The Professionalization of Higher Education', *Higher Education Review*, 12(1), 69–76.
NEAVE, G. (1979b) 'Academic Drift: Some Views from Europe', *Studies in Higher Education*, 4(2), 143–59.
NATIONAL ECONOMIC DEVELOPMENT OFFICE/MANPOWER SERVICES COMMISSION (1984) *Competence and Competition*. London: NEDO.
NEWMAN, M. (1983) 'Community', in TIGHT, M. (ed.) *Adult Learning and Education*. London: Croom Helm.
NOTTINGHAM ANDRAGOGY GROUP (1983) *Towards a Developmental Theory of Andragogy*. Nottingham: University of Nottingham Dept. of Adult Education.
NUNN, P. C. (1979) 'The Application in the United Kingdom of the Concept of Basic Training', in COUNCIL OF EUROPE, *Occupational Basic Training*. Strasbourg: Council for Cultural Co-operation.
OLDHAM, G. (ed.) (1982) *The Future of Research*. Guildford: Society for Research into Higher Education.
ORGANISATION FOR ECONOMIC CO-OPERATION AND DEVELOPMENT (1972) *Interdisciplinarity*. Paris: OECD.
ORGANISATION FOR ECONOMIC CO-OPERATION AND DEVELOPMENT (1973) *Short-cycle Higher Education*. Paris: OECD.
ORGANISATION FOR ECONOMIC CO-OPERATION AND DEVELOPMENT (1976) *Beyond Compulsory Schooling*. Paris: OECD.

ORGANISATION FOR ECONOMIC CO-OPERATION AND DEVELOPMENT (1977) *Selection and Certification in Education and Employment*. Paris: OECD.

ORGANISATION FOR ECONOMIC CO-OPERATION AND DEVELOPMENT (1979) *Policies for Apprenticeship*. Paris: OECD.

ORGANISATION FOR ECONOMIC CO-OPERATION AND DEVELOPMENT (1981) *Educational Reforms in Sweden*. Paris: OECD.

ORGANISATION FOR ECONOMIC CO-OPERATION AND DEVELOPMENT (1983a) *Policies for Higher Education in the 1980s*. Paris: OECD.

ORGANISATION FOR ECONOMIC CO-OPERATION AND DEVELOPMENT (1983b) *The Future of Vocational Education and Training*. Paris: OECD.

ORGANISATION FOR ECONOMIC CO-OPERATION AND DEVELOPMENT (1983c) *Education and Work*. Paris: OECD.

ORGANISATION FOR ECONOMIC CO-OPERATION AND DEVELOPMENT (1985) *Education and Training after Basic Schooling*. Paris: OECD.

ORTEGA Y GASSET, J. (1946) *Mission of the University*. London: Kegan Paul, Trench, Trubner and Co.

PARROTT, A. and FLUDE, R. (1983) 'A Curriculum Fit for Adults?' *Adult Education*, 56(2), 117–21.

PATERSON, R. W. K. (1979) *Values, Education and the Adult*. London: Routledge and Kegan Paul.

PATTY, W. L. (1938) *A Study of Mechanism in Education*. New York: Columbia University Teachers College.

PAYNE, G. and CUFF, E. (eds) (1982) *Doing Teaching*. London: Batsford.

PEDDIWELL, J. A. (1939) *The Saber-Tooth Curriculum*. New York: McGraw-Hill.

PERCY, K. and RAMSDEN, S. (1980) *Independent Study: Two Examples from English Higher Education*. Guildford: Society for Research into Higher Education.

PERKIN, H. (1973) 'The Professionalization of University Teaching', in COOK, T. G. (ed.) *Education and the Professions*. London: Methuen.

PERRY, W. G. (1970) *Forms of Intellectual and Ethical Development in the College Years*. New York: Holt, Rinehart and Winston.

PETERS, A. J. (1967) *British Further Education*. Oxford: Pergamon.

PHENIX. P. H. (1964) *Realms of Meaning*. New York: McGraw-Hill.

PINAR, W. and GRUMET, M. (1981) 'Theory and Practice and the Reconceptualisation of Curriculum Studies', in LAWN, M. and BARTON, L. (eds) *Rethinking Curriculum Studies*. London: Croom Helm.

POPHAM, W. (1978) *Criterion-referenced Measurement*. Englewood Cliffs, N.J.: Prentice-Hall.

PORTAL, C. (1983) 'Empathy as an Aim for Curriculum: Lessons from History', *Journal of Curriculum Studies*, 15(3), 303–10.

POWELL, J. P. (1966) *Universities and University Education: a Select Bibliography*. Slough: National Foundation for Education Research; (1971) Vol II, 1965–70.

POWELL, J. P. (1985) 'The Residues of Learning: Auto-biographical

Accounts by Graduates of the Impact of Higher Education', *Higher Education*, 14(2), 127–47.

PRATLEY, B. (1985) *Signposts '85: a review of 16–19 education*. London: Further Education Unit.

PRING, R. (1984) *Personal and Social Education in the Curriculum*. London: Hodder and Stoughton.

PROST, A. (ed.) (1983) *Les Lycées et leurs Etudes an seuil du XXIᵉ Siècle*. Paris: Ministère de L'Education Nationale.

PSACHAROPOULOS, G. (1982) 'The Economics of Higher Education in Developing Countries', *Comparative Education Review*, 26(2), 139–59.

PUGH, G. (1983) 'Parent Education: the Role of Adult Education', *Adult Education*, 55(4), 357–63.

RAFFE, D. (1983) 'Education and Unemployment; Does YOP make a Difference (and will the Youth Training Scheme)?' in GLEESON, D. (ed.) *Youth Training and the Search for Work*. London: Routledge and Kegan Paul.

REID, W. (1978) *Thinking about the Curriculum*. London: Routledge and Kegan Paul.

REIMER, E. (1971) *School is Dead*. New York: Doubleday.

REVANS, R. W. (1982) *The Origins and Growth of Action Learning*. Bromley: Chatwell-Pratt.

REYNOLDS, J. and SKILBECK, M. (1976) *Culture and the Classroom*. London: Open Books.

RICHARDS, C. (1984) *Curriculum Studies: an Introductory Annotated Bibliography*. (2nd edn.) London: Falmer Press.

RIEGEL, K. F. (1979) *Foundations of Dialectical Psychology*. New York: Academic Press.

LORD ROBBINS. (Chr.) (1963) *Higher Education (Report of the Committee under the chairmanship of Lord Robbins)*. London: HMSO.

LORD ROBBINS. (1971) in *Financial Times*, 12 June.

LORD ROBBINS. (1980) *Higher Education Revisited*. London: Macmillan.

RODERICK, G. and STEPHENS, M. (1978) *Education and Industry in the Nineteenth Century*. London: Longman.

ROEBUCK, M. (1985) *The 16+ Action Plan in Scotland*. Blagdon: Further Education Staff College.

ROGERS, C. (1961) *On Becoming a Person*. Boston: Houghton Mifflin.

ROGERS, C. (1969) *Freedom to Learn*. Columbus, Ohio: Merrill.

ROIZEN, J. and JEPSON, M. (1985) *Degrees for Jobs*. Guildford: Society for Research into Higher Education/NFER-Nelson.

ROTHBLATT, S. (1976) *Tradition and Change in English Liberal Education*. London: Faber and Faber.

RUDD, E. (1975) *The Highest Education*. London: Routledge and Kegan Paul.

RUSSELL, B. (1946) *History of Western Philosophy*. London: George Allen and Unwin.

RUSSELL, SIR LIONEL (Chairman) (1973) *Adult Education: a Plan for*

Development. (Report of the Committee of Enquiry) London: HMSO.

RUSSELL, R. (ed.) (1982) *Learning about the World of Work in the Federal German Republic.* Blagdon: Further Education Staff College.

RUSSELL, R. and NEALE, M. (1983) *Experiments with the First Year of Apprenticeship in the Federal Republic of Germany.* Blagdon: Further Education Staff College.

SANDERSON, M. (1972) *The Universities and British Industry 1850–1970.* London: Routledge and Kegan Paul.

SAWDON, A., *et al.* (1979–81) *Study of the Transition from School to Working Life.* London: Youth Aid.

SCHEIN, E. H. (1972) *Professional Education: Some New Directions.* New York: McGraw-Hill.

SCHUTZ, A. and LUCKMANN, T. (1974) *The Structures of the Lifeworld* (trans. Zaner and Engelhardt), London: Heinemann.

SCHWAB, J. (1969) 'The Practical: a Language for the Curriculum', *School Review,* 78(1) 11–23.

SCOTTISH EDUCATION DEPARTMENT (1983) *16–18s in Scotland: an action plan.* Edinburgh: SED.

SCRIMSHAW, P. (1983) *Educational Ideologies* (Unit 2, E 204 *Purpose and Planning in the Curriculum*). Milton Keynes: Open University Press.

SIMON, H. A. (1969) *The Sciences of the Artificial.* Cambridge, Mass.: MIT.

SIMON, H. A. (1979a) 'Information Processing Models of Cognition', *Annual Review of Psychology,* 30, 363–96.

SIMON, H. A. (1979b) *Models of Thought.* New Haven, Conn.: Yale University Press.

SIMPSON, R. (1983) *How the PhD Came to Britain.* Guildford: Society for Research into Higher Education.

SMITH, B. O., STANLEY, W. O. and SHORES, J. H. (1950) *Fundamentals of Curriculum Development.* New York: World Book Co.

SMITH, M. (1978) 'Teaching to Learn', *Studies in Higher Education,* 3(2), 221–5.

SMITH, R. M. (1983) *Learning How to Learn.* Milton Keynes: Open University Press.

SMITHERS, A. (1976) *Sandwich Courses.* Slough: National Foundation for Educational Research.

SNYDER, B. (1971) *The Hidden Curriculum.* New York: Knopf.

SOCIAL SCIENCE RESEARCH COUNCIL (1981) *Curriculum Research: Agenda for the Eighties* (Proceedings of an Invitational Seminar, chairman P. Taylor.) Birmingham: University of Birmingham, mimeo.

SOCIETY FOR RESEARCH INTO HIGHER EDUCATION (1977) *Interdisciplinarity.* Guildford: SRHE.

SQUIRES, G. *et al.* (1975) *Interdisciplinarity.* London: The Nuffield Foundation.

SQUIRES, G., et al. (1976a) *Breadth and Depth*. London: The Nuffield Foundation.

SQUIRES, G. (1976b) 'The Resuscitation of General Education', *Studies in Higher Education*, 1(1), 83–9.

SQUIRES, G. (1979) 'Innovations in British Higher Education and their Implications for Adult Education', in Organisation for Economic Co-operation and Development *Learning Opportunities for Adults Vol. II*. Paris: OECD.

SQUIRES, G. (1980) 'Individuality in Higher Education', *Studies in Higher Education*, 5(2), 217–26.

SQUIRES, G. (1981a) *Cognitive Styles and Adult Learning*. University of Nottingham: Dept of Adult Education.

SQUIRES, G. (1981b) 'Mature Entry' in FULTON, O. (ed.) *Access to Higher Education*. Guildford: Society for Research into Higher Education.

SQUIRES, G. (1982a) *The Analysis of Teaching*. Hull: University of Hull Dept of Adult Education.

SQUIRES, G. (1982b) *Learning to Learn*. Hull: University of Hull Dept of Adult Education.

SQUIRES, G. (1983) 'New Groups in Higher Education', in Organisation for Economic Co-operation and Development *Policies for Higher Education in the 1980s*. Paris: OECD.

SQUIRES, G. (1985) 'Organisation and Content of Studies', in Organisation for Economic Co-operation and Development *Education and Training After Basic Schooling*. Paris: OECD.

SQUIRES, G. (1986) *Modularisation*. Manchester: Consortium for Advanced Continuing Education and Training of the Universities of Manchester and Salford, UMIST and Manchester Polytechnic.

STARTUP, R. (1979) *The University Teacher and His World*. Farnborough: Saxon House.

STENHOUSE, L. (1975) *An Introduction to Curriculum Research and Development*. London: Heinemann.

STERNBERG, R. J. (ed.) (1982) *Handbook of Human Intelligence*. Cambridge: Cambridge University Press.

STERNBERG, R. J. (1985a) *Beyond IQ: a Triarchic Theory of Human Intelligence*. Cambridge: Cambridge University Press.

STERNBERG, R. (1985b) *The Triarchic Theory of Human Intelligence* (paper presented to a SRHE/BPS Conference on *Cognitive Processes in Student Learning*, at the University of Lancaster), mimeo.

STRIKE, K. and EGAN, K. (eds) (1978) *Ethics and Educational Policy*. London: Routledge and Kegan Paul.

TABA, H. (1962) *Curriculum Development: Theory and Practice*. New York: Harcourt, Brace and World.

TAYLOR, C. W. (1968) 'Cultivating New Talents: a Way to Reach the Educationally Deprived', *Journal of Creative Behaviour*, 2(2), 83–90.

TAYLOR, M. (1981) *Education and Work in the Federal Republic of Germany*. London: Anglo-German Foundation.

TAYLOR, P. H. and RICHARDS, C. M. (1985) *An Introduction to Curriculum Studies*. (2nd edn) Windsor: NFER-Nelson.

THORNDIKE, E. L. (1913) *Educational Psychology* Vol. II: *The Psychology of Learning*. New York: Columbia University Press.

THORNDIKE, E. L. (1924) 'Mental Discipline in High School Studies', *Journal of Educational Psychology*, (1, 2), 1–22, 83–98.

TIBBLE, J. W. (1966) *The Study of Education*. London: Routledge and Kegan Paul.

TIGHT, M. (1985) 'Modelling the Education of Adults', *Studies in the Education of Adults*, 17(1), 3–18.

TITMUS, C. (ed.) (1985) *Widening the Field: Continuing Education in Higher Education*. Guildford: Society for Research into Higher Education and NFER/Nelson.

TITMUS, C. and HELY, C. G. (1976) 'Collective and Individual Dimensions in the Adult Education of Working People', *Studies in Adult Education*, 8(1), 15–28.

TOUGH, A. (1971) *The Adult's Learning Projects*. Toronto: Ontario Institute for Studies in Education.

TOUGH, A. (1979) 'Fostering Self-Planned Learning', in *Learning Opportunities for Adults*, Vol. II. Paris: OECD.

TOUGH, A. (1982) *Intentional Changes*. Chicago: Follett.

TOUGH, A. (1983) 'Self-Planned Learning and Major Personal Change', in TIGHT, M. (ed.) *Adult Learning and Education*. London: Croom Helm.

TOYNE, P. (1983) 'The Education Counselling and Credit Transfer Information Service', in SQUIRES, G. (ed.) *Innovation through Recession*. Guildford: Society for Research into Higher Education.

TRIPP, D. and WATT, A. J. (1984) 'Core Curriculum and Why We Don't Need One', *Journal of Curriculum Studies*, 16(2), 131–41.

TROW, M. (1975) 'The Public and Private Lives of Higher Education', *Daedalus*, 104(1), 113–27.

TROW, M. (1976) 'The American Academic Department', *Studies in Higher Education*, 1(1), 11–22.

TUNSTALL, J. (1974) *The Open University Opens*. London: Routledge and Kegan Paul.

TURNER, C. and RAWLINGS, P. (1982) *Vocational Education and Training in Sweden*. Blagdon: Further Education Staff College.

TURNER, J. D. and RUSHTON, J. (eds) (1976) *Education for the Professions*. Manchester: Manchester University Press.

TYLER, R. (1949) *Basic Principles of Curriculum and Instruction*. Chicago: University of Chicago Press.

USHER, R. S. (1985) 'Beyond the Anecdotal – Adult Learning and the Use of Experience', *Studies in the Education of Adults*, 17(1), 59–74.

VEBLEN, T. (1957) *The Higher Learning in America*. New York: Saga-more.

WARREN, H. B. (1982) 'Recent Themes in General Education', *Journal of General Education*, 34(3), 271–91.

WATTS, A. G. (1983) *Education, Unemployment and the Future of Work*. Milton Keynes: Open University Press.

WELSH, J. (1979) *The First Year of Postgraduate Research Study*. Guildford: Society for Research into Higher Education.

WEST, M. and NEWTON, P. (1983) *The Transition from School to Work*. London: Croom Helm.

WIENER, M. (1981) *English Culture and the Decline of the Industrial Spirit, 1850–1980*. Cambridge: Cambridge University Press.

WILLIS, P. (1977) *Learning to Labour*. London: Saxon House.

WILLIS, P. (n.d.) *Transition from School to Work: Bibliography (Work Series: SP No. 27)*. University of Birmingham: Centre for Contemporary Cultural Studies, mimeo.

WILTSHIRE, H. (1983) 'The Role of the University Adult Education Department', *Studies in Adult Education*, 15, 3–10.

WORSWICK, G. D. N. (ed.) (1985) *Education and Economic Performance*. Aldershot: Gower.

YOUNG, M. F. D. (ed.) (1971) *Knowledge and Control*. London: Collier-Macmillan.

Index